BOLD GALILEAN

The Power of Rome Encounters Christ

CHRISTIAN EPICS

BOLD GALILEAN

The Power of Rome Encounters Christ

LeGette Blythe

EDITED AND INTRODUCED BY JAMES S. BELL, JR.

MOODY PRESS

CHICAGO

To my daughter Caitlin Joy,
whose innocence in infancy
is my pure delight.
The Galilean said, "The kingdom
of God belongs to such as these."

LeGette Blythe (1900–) has been a prolific writer of fiction, especially biblical fiction. His novels include *Alexandriana, Man on Fire* (now with Moody Press as *Soul on Fire*), *A Tear for Judas, The Crown Tree, Call Down the Storm, Hear Me, Pilate!* and *Mountain Doctor*.

James S. Bell, Jr. (B.A., College of the Holy Cross; M.A., University College, Dublin) has added a refreshing touch to *Bold Galilean* by retelling the story in today's language while remaining true to the author's purpose and style. An experienced editor, he has revised and updated many books, including *Ben Hur, Simon of Cyrene, Soul on Fire,* and *Devotional Prayers*. He has worked as director of religious publishing at Doubleday and as executive director at Bridge Publishing. Several years ago he came to Moody Press as the editorial director, and resides in West Chicago with his family.

Introduction

For a book concerned with events taking place nearly two thousand years ago, this dialogue between the two main characters sounds strangely relevant and timely:

> "Centurion," he said, "the world's in a bad way. Everywhere nations—Rome, Greece, Egypt, everywhere you look—are striving for power, building armies that overrun defenseless people, seeking alliances under the guise of strengthening their defenses. We are nominally at peace, we Romans, generally speaking. We may be at our supreme power, I don't know.... But we aren't strong, centurion. We are rotten at the center. Morally, we are decadent. Our philosophy is wrong. It won't work. It will lead, I don't know when, but I know it will in time, to disaster."
>
> His expression changed again, softened. "This rabbi's plan, though, if I understand it, will work. Our concept leads invariably to war and ruin. But his idea if carried out would bring all nations and individuals to a peaceful way of life. If the individual man would just maintain a right feeling toward other men and toward this—this divinity the rabbi seemed always to be in communion with, according to what I have always heard of him, Gaius, why wouldn't that solve all this trouble between the races and peoples everywhere?"
>
> "I think it would, Marcus. But still, what do you think of him?"
>
> "I—I don't know. He's a mystery to me. But he seems to have had a command upon some tremendous power—"

Earlier in the Christian Epic series, in the novel *Simon of Cyrene*, we viewed the person of Christ in the eye of a typical pious Jew. His preconceptions and expectations initially prevent him from recognizing Jesus as the Messiah. In *Bold Galilean*, LeGette Blythe portrays first-century Palestine from the mind-set of the ruling Romans. They are convinced that might is right, and that material possessions and the pleasures of the flesh will satisfy the deepest yearnings of the human spirit.

Yet in every culture there are those individuals who seek the higher good, going beyond the needs of the individual and even the nation. Such a man is Gaius, the centurion from Capernaum. He respects the ethics of Jewish law and their transcendent view of the one God Jehovah and even helps them with their local synagogue. His friend Marcus, on the other hand, sees money as equivalent to happiness. His father is an influential Roman senator, and Marcus has a thriving Phoenician business in textiles and glass. He has no time to ponder questions of love of neighbor or who God may be. He feels secure in this life to partake of the best it can offer and that is all that matters.

Together they discuss the wonder-working teacher from Nazareth and His impact upon His own people as well as potentially on Rome. Neither realizes that each, based upon his own need, will encounter this "bold Galilean" and face a reality that extends far beyond their Roman point of reference or even the contemporary Jewish culture they seek to understand.

Gaius, in fact, is revealed as the God-fearing centurion we are familiar with in the Scriptures who tells Jesus, in relation to his deathly ill servant, that he is not worthy for the master to enter his dwelling yet is confident of His healing power. Jesus marvels at the faith of this Gentile. Marcus crosses paths with the Savior in a far more extraordinary way, however, and must go through a harrowing journey in order to take His claims seriously.

In the midst of his quest for success, Marcus discovers true love in the person of a woman who turns out to be Mary of Magdala. Yet he cannot bring himself to reveal to her the dark secret of her past that only he knows.

The reader will especially appreciate Blythe's ability to re-create scenes from the life of Christ and infuse them with their full dramatic potential. We see the bloodthirsty cunning of Herodias coupled with the pathetic, bloated figure of Herod himself. Pathos and hope combine as a weeping Jesus confronts the ugly tragedy of death with His friend Lazarus. Extrabiblical accounts such as a raid on a Roman party by Bar Abbas and his band of brigands illustrate the seething sedition beneath the surface of this turbulent society.

Woven throughout the story are the crystal clear pure words of the rabbi from Galilee. Words that bring healing and life; and yet for some, like the rich young ruler, confrontation and sadness. This is, after all, not primarily the story of Roman or Jewish characters, with all their strengths and weaknesses. Rather it is a "tale of the Christ," as Lew Wallace described *Ben Hur*. Blythe adeptly and sensitively portrays his dual nature in one person. The Word of God, creator of all that is, reveals His power and transcendence —in a word, we see the Father in this story. Yet we also behold a muscular, tanned carpenter who has a love for the wildflowers and hills of His native Galilee. He needs to lean on His friends' support in His hour of trial and weeps over His friend Lazarus' demise.

Those eyewitnesses who viewed the unjust agony of the crucifixion could not help but ask, "He saved others, why can't He save Himself?" After being invaded by such a presence, their future hopes lost meaning. Yet in the early hours of Sunday morning a new message dawned in which characters who followed Him could play a part. They, and we also, can live happily ever after. For this reason alone, *Bold Galilean* is worth reading.

JAMES S. BELL, JR.

9

Cast of Characters

Gaius Sempronius, centurion stationed in Capernaum

Marcus Calpurnius Lupinus, wealthy merchant and son of a Roman senator

Sejanus, Roman prefect, representing the emperor

Pontius Pilate, procurator of Judea and Peraea Galba

Lucius Mallius, a Roman tribune

Herod Antipas, tetrarch from Galilee

Herodias, wife of Herod Antipas and former wife of Herod Philip, the brother of Antipas

Salome, daughter of Herodias

Tullus, overseer to Marcus

Simon Peter, disciple of Jesus Christ

James and John, the sons of Zebedee and disciples of Jesus Christ

Naamah, also known as Mary of Magdala, lover of Marcus

Judas of Kiriot, betrayer of Jesus Christ

Simon the Leper, a Pharisee

Bar Abbas, Jewish robber and a revolutionist who roamed Galilee

Joseph Caiaphas, Jewish high priest

Annas, father-in-law to Caiaphas

Rabbi Nicodemus, Pharisee and follower of Christ

John the Baptist, prophet and forerunner of Jesus Christ

Andreas, servant boy to Gaius

Jesus Christ, the rabbi from Nazareth in Galilee

Mary, Martha, and Lazarus, friends of Jesus living in Bethany

Nathanael, Thomas, Levi, and others, fellow disciples of Christ

1

A thousand pardons, sir! I'm—I'm sorry. I might have knocked you off the wharf." Darting out from behind the long row of merchandise baled for shipment and piled high, the speaker had collided with a man coming leisurely along the narrow walkway at the water's edge. "I wasn't looking. I had my neck craned for a glimpse of the *Cleopatra*."

"No harm done." Centurion Gaius Sempronius straightened his military cloak. "I was looking out across the harbor myself to see if I could see the ship I was expecting—" Abruptly he broke off. "Marcus! What in the world brings you to Tyre?"

"By the immortals! Gaius!" The expression on the young man's tanned face was skeptical. "What are you doing here yourself? Still in the army, I see." He clapped his hand on his friend's shoulder. "The last time I saw you—" he hesitated "—Gaius, it must have been that night down in the Subura near that house in which they claim Julius Caesar was born. You remember, that night after the races at the Circus Maximus, where I'd lost all my money!"

"You're right. That was the place—four years ago, too, but I recall it well. There was a red-haired Helvetian—"

Marcus laughed. "You should remember her. She was a shapely wench, and she had a ring in your nose. I remember it all, even if I had drunk much wine."

"I needed strengthening of the spirit that night. It was my last one at home for a long time. The next day, you recall, I left Rome on the expedition."

"My spirits were low, too. I had dropped a tidy sum of the senator's money. But we forgot our troubles that night, eh, Gaius?"

Gaius laughed, "But say, Marcus,"—he was surveying the tall Roman from his cropped head to his sandaled feet—"I can hardly believe you're here in Tyre. How does it happen?"

"I'm living here. Have been out here this time for almost a

year. By now I'm practically a Phoenician. But why are you out here?"

"I had hoped that when I got back to Rome from this expedition we could raise enough money to buy my entrance into the equestrian class and in that way get me a good promotion. I was sure it could be arranged—with Sejanus, perhaps. But"—he shrugged his shoulders—"it wasn't arranged, and I was sent out to Palestine."

"I had no idea you were out here. Where are you stationed?"

"Capernaum. It's in the province of Galilee, over on the little Sea of Galilee, in fact."

"I know the place. I go through there occasionally on my way to Tiberias. How long have you been there?"

"It will be two years this spring, Marcus. In Rome they must have forgotten me. Yes, I'm virtually an exile." There was a trace of bitterness in his words.

"Sometimes, you know, it's better when Rome forgets."

"Sometimes, perhaps. But tell me,"—he sat down on a bale and motioned to Marcus to sit beside him—"how does it happen that Marcus Calpurnius Lupinus, the playboy of Rome, has abandoned his father's villa at Baiae and deserted his beautiful women to take up residence in ancient but certainly less interesting Tyre?"

Marcus laughed. Then quickly he was serious. "I was sent out here, too. And Sejanus had a hand in it. The old rascal is never averse to having his palms weighted with gold, as you said, and my father, who knows well how to drive a good bargain, even though he's a senator and presumably retired from such activities, knew just what to do to obtain trading concessions in this part of the world. And Sejanus knew what to call it. 'Promotion of Roman trade, development and expansion of the empire.' My father owned some manufacturing in Phoenicia—dyeworks and weaving plants here at Tyre and glassworks at Sidon, along with sand properties on the Belus River south of here."

"It's straight west of Capernaum. Best sand for glass in the world."

"That's what they say. Well, Sejanus provided certain, well, subsidies, in the way of adjusted prices for ships, new machinery and equipment, and slaves taken in recent conquests, and this

12

aid, along with the skillful management of his son, of course"—
Marcus smiled—"has brought rather sizable dividends to the senator. And Sejanus likewise is receiving something more than thanks."

"Yes, Sejanus will look after himself, and well. It's a shame
that the emperor let him get the upper hand. Between Sejanus and
old Livia, Tiberius has never had an opportunity to demonstrate
his ability, if he has any. I wouldn't know, though, what goes on in
Rome. I'm an exile." Gaius's tone changed, abruptly. "So you're a
businessman? Fancy that. Operating weaving establishments and
glassworks. How does it happen that the son of a Roman senator
is engaged directly in commerce?"

Marcus grinned. "I played too strenuously—and my father finally lost his patience. He had bought these enterprises out here,
as I said, and"—he shrugged his shoulders—"I suggested that he
let me try my hand at running them." He was serious. "The playboy of Rome is no more, Gaius. I've settled down to business. It's
a different life, but I like it. And I'm doing well, too. Give me time
and one of these days I'll be buying out the senator."

"But you're the only child; you'll get all his estate anyway.
Why the hurry?"

"I want to make money now, Gaius. I'm not willing to wait. I
want more than he'll likely be able to give me, and I want to make
it myself. There's a thrill in making it, watching it pile up. And
money's power, Gaius. Give me money, and I'll buy anything I
want."

"Well, perhaps almost anything."

"By the immortals, Gaius, *anything*."

Gaius was smiling. "Love?"

"Give me enough money, centurion, and I'll buy any woman
in Rome or Athens or Alexandria. Give me enough money, and I'd
buy the emperor's wife, if he had a wife."

"That wouldn't have required much money, eh?"

"I guess Julia was more wife than Tiberius wanted, at that.
But love! What is love? The poets write prettily of it, and the
singers roll their eyes and harmonize about it. But what is it?" He
shrugged his shoulders. "Love, ha! A pretty ornament. One of the
purple-hued goblets I make at Sidon. A gorgeous coat of woolens
woven on my looms here at Tyre. Yes, or a beautiful woman, spir-

ited, a warm-blooded wench. Nothing more. Love endures while the blood is heated, my friend. Love is a robe to be worn while it is warm and beautiful, and thrown aside when it has become threadbare."

Gaius smiled. "Such a speech should not be wasted outside the Forum."

"But you questioned whether love, too, could be bought. I say it can. Love is feminine, soft, desirable at times. But love is weak. Money, on the other hand, is masculine, it is strength, it means power, and power means everything. Give me the power that money brings, Gaius, and you take your love, yes, and languish in it."

Gaius stood up. "Maybe so," he said. "I'm not sure of it. Perhaps we aren't even talking about the same thing. The way I see it, love may be stronger, certainly the more enduring. I've changed my ideas about things somewhat since I've been out here. But, Marcus, were you expecting someone on the *Cleopatra*? A friend coming out?"

"Yes," Marcus replied. "I came to meet the *Cleopatra* and friends. The best sort of friends a man can have, too. I hope the *Cleo*'s stinking hold is full of such friends!" His laugh was mirthless.

"Slaves? For your plants?"

Marcus nodded. "Yes, from some of the recent conquests. For the looms and the spinning frames, and for the glassworks up at Sidon. I can use all I can get, because I am expanding the plants and trying to increase production." He pointed to the rows of bales. "These are our products. A part of the shipment is going aboard the *Cleopatra* for Alexandria. We are trying to increase our trade to Egypt. Some are consigned to Athens, and some to Rome. Our products are being widely sold. But Gaius, why did you come down to the docks?"

"I came down to meet the new tribune. He's being sent out to take over the command of our forces at Caesarea. He is supposed to be aboard the *Cleopatra*. I had orders to meet him here and report to him on the situation in Galilee. Then when he gets to Caesarea he should be in better position to work with Pontius Pilate."

14

"The gods preserve him," Marcus observed. "He'll need all the help he can get in order to stand in the good graces of that politician. Gaius, you should have been given that post. I should think it would be more attractive than the one at Capernaum. Caesarea's a more cosmopolitan place—more life and excitement, and fewer Jews."

"I am not one of the favorites of the prefect; as I said, I didn't have enough gold with which to tickle his palm."

"But the Jews have. Raid a synagogue. Take their sacred golden vessels. Sejanus would not inquire into your methods of getting the gold, so long as you divided liberally with him. I understand that Pilate doesn't hesitate to levy heavily on the Jews and even to confiscate their religious funds. I suppose he divides with Sejanus, eh?"

"Probably so. But the Jews at Capernaum are not wealthy, and it would be of small profit to raid their synagogue, even if I were of a mind to do it, which I am not. The fact is—" Gaius paused, smiling "—it may amuse you, Marcus, but I helped them build a new synagogue."

"You, a centurion of the Roman army, helped the Jews build a synagogue! So help me Hercules, Gaius, you must be a reincarnation of that other Sempronius, the younger of the Gracchi. Ha! A liberal of the liberals, a friend of the downtrodden, a partisan of the people, and now even a friend of the Jews!"

But quickly he became serious. "That is smart politics, though, Gaius. It cannot help but serve to raise you in their esteem. And it will make them the more easily managed. It may even save clouting a few hard Jewish skulls."

"You're still a cynic, Marcus. Cannot a man, even a Roman soldier, do something out of the kindness of his heart for someone else, even a Jew?"

"It isn't the practice. As for me, all I want from a Jew is to sell him goods and get his money. And that is a difficult job. But about this new tribune." Marcus had changed his tone. "By any chance do I know this fellow?"

"I suspect not," Gaius answered. "I know him only casually. He's an aggressive fellow, as I understand, who never lets an opportunity slip to advance himself. His name is Galba—Lucius Mallius Galba, I believe."

"I've never heard of him. But you'd better warn him not to attempt to advance himself ahead of Pilate. The procurator of Judea and Peraea would resent the slightest indication that anybody might even be considering the possibility of displacing him. He has the ear of Sejanus, no doubt, and it wouldn't be well for this Lucius—" He stopped abruptly and pointed with a lean forefinger out across the breakwater that all but enclosed this north harbor of Tyre. "Look. Away over there to the left. I believe that's the *Cleopatra*. Isn't she a powerful vessel? And as graceful as a swan skimming the water."

Gaius cupped a hand over his eyes. "That looks like the boat I came out here on, Marcus. If I am not mistaken, she's the *Hispania*, one of the fastest three-tiered ships in our naval service."

"Until a year ago she was called the *Hispania*. But now she's the *Cleopatra*. My father owns her now. And he renamed her."

"Your father? But the *Hispania* is one of our best naval vessels, Marcus. She's no cargo vessel."

Marcus laughed. "Sejanus thought that she could be put to better use to the empire by employing her in the expansion of trade, particularly if—"

"If Sejanus shared in the revenue from her voyages."

"It is remarkable how quickly you arrive at an understanding of how the emperor's mind works through the mind of his faithful Sejanus."

"But wasn't it bold, and even dangerous, for your father to be seen conniving to this extent with Sejanus?"

"He did not deal directly with Sejanus, of course. Everything was handled through those clever creatures of the prefect, Pinarius Natta and Sextius Pacorianus. It was even made to appear that my father paid dearly for a vessel no longer needed by our naval service."

Gaius smiled. "Very clever, indeed. So that accounts for the vessel's new name?"

"Yes. My great-grandfather served under Marcus Antonius, and the tradition of naming everything for the general or someone associated with him continues strong with my father." His eyes

16

were still upon the graceful three-tiered ship beyond the break-water as she swept steadily nearer. "But she is well named, isn't she? Look how she flaunts her beauty. She's a queen, all right. And with her we can beat our competitors to the markets at Alexandria and Athens or anywhere else. A smart move, getting a ship like this to carry our goods, eh, centurion?" He stood up, straightened his toga. "I hope she's bringing me a cargo of healthy slaves. I need them. These enterprises in Phoenicia use them up quickly."

Gaius, too, was watching the approaching ship, its great square sail slipping slowly downward, its three banks of oars on each side rising and falling rhythmically, as it raced toward the harbor opening on a course almost parallel with the long break-water. As the vessel came opposite this opening, the sail now down, he saw the oars pause suddenly on the side nearer him, hold an instant, then drop straight into the water, rise and fall again swiftly; the ship began gracefully to swing around to starboard as the spray from the bow careened to port and fell into a sweeping arc back into the sea.

"That fellow is skillful," Marcus observed. "He has the rowers well trained and under perfect control. They are expert at feathering the oars, and feathering is important. Come, centurion. In a moment she'll be tying up. I'd like to see how they handle her at the dock. Let's get down there. And—" he added as an afterthought "—there's the new tribune, of course."

They started walking along the wharf. "By the way, Gaius, I want you and the tribune to stay with me while the ship unloads and is reloaded for Caesarea and Alexandria. That may take two days." He pointed backward over his left shoulder. "I live up there on the crest of the bluff, across the causeway in the old part of the city. And now if that fellow Tullus—he's my principal overseer—by all the gods, if Tullus has failed to get here—There he is down there; I might have known he would be. He's a prize, Gaius. I wouldn't take anything for that fellow; he can operate the business almost without me. Ha! Sejanus located him for me. Tullus is down there to see to unloading the slaves and getting them assigned to their tasks."

2

The new tribune was aboard the *Cleopatra*, and so were the slaves for the Phoenician industries of Senator Calpurnius. Marcus joined Gaius in welcoming Tribune Lucius Mallius Galba, and after he had made a quick appraisal of the slaves as they shuffled on cramped legs from their crowded quarters, he left them in the care of Tullus and started with his two guests for his house high on the bluff above the harbor.

Now it was late afternoon. They had bathed and put on fresh clothing, and since the tribune and the centurion had long been traveling and doubtless were hungry, Marcus had instructed his servants to prepare an early evening meal. The servants had brought the table and couches from their usual room to the pleasant open court, which Marcus had built behind the atrium so that he might sit and enjoy the view over the rooftops to the great harbor of Tyre. In the cooling shade of the courtyard's portico they began leisurely eating.

It was the tribune's first voyage as far east of Rome as Tyre, he told them, and he was wondering how he would relish the new assignment. "I suspect that Caesarea is not one of the most attractive posts in the Empire," he observed somewhat regretfully.

"Oh, I believe you will not find Caesarea too dull," Marcus hastened to assure him. "Here at Tyre the population is somewhat cosmopolitan. There are Jews, of course—there are Jews everywhere—but they are not dominant. There are Syrians and Greeks, and a number of Romans, too, and we have a colony of Egyptians, and even Ethiopians. And Caesarea, you will find, is much like Tyre, since it is an increasingly important port city. Now at Capernaum where Gaius is stationed, it is different. Capernaum is a city of Jews." He glanced toward Gaius, smiling. "Yet you find it pleasant there, eh, centurion, so pleasant in fact"—he faced the tribune again—"that you helped the Jews build themselves a new synagogue, didn't you?"

"With treasury funds, centurion?" There was the trace of a frown on the tribune's face.

"No, tribune," Gaius replied evenly, "with personal funds."

"Had they been treasury funds, though," Marcus hastened to observe, "it would have been money well spent for Rome. It is cheaper to chuck people under the chins, so to speak—even Jews—than to clout rebellious skulls, tribune."

"I like the Roman way better. I find it neither difficult nor distasteful to clout skulls when they get themselves in the way of Roman legionnaires. In fact, I rather relish it."

Marcus laughed. "I have the feeling, tribune, that you should get along well with Pontius Pilate. I understand that is the procurator's policy."

"I expect so. I am confident that Sejanus is satisfied with the way Pontius Pilate is governing in Judea and Perea—"

"If Sejanus were not satisfied, Pilate wouldn't long remain procurator," Marcus interrupted to assure him. "And if Sejanus is satisfied, what matters if all the rest of Rome is not?"

The tribune, who had been leaning on his elbow, sat up. "Sejanus speaks for the emperor," he said.

"Sejanus speaks for Sejanus."

"I would have you know, my friend, that I am an officer in the Roman army and as such I take orders from my superiors. And I am also a friend of the prefect."

Marcus held up his hand, and his smile was disarming. "Pray, tribune, do not be alarmed. My father is one of the favorite senators of the prefect Sejanus. They are—well, collaborators, and—"

"But your manner—"

"My father pays well for that coveted position." Marcus ignored the interruption. "The senator is adept at palm-tickling." He sat upright. "But enough of Sejanus. Tomorrow, while they are loading the *Cleopatra*, I want you two to accompany me through the dyeworks and weaving rooms, and if we can get an early start we will visit the glassworks on the coast between here and Sidon.

I'd like for you to help me sell some of our products. The tribune might speak to Pilate about them—or better still, to Pilate's wife."

"Claudia is a very discriminating woman." Tribune Lucius Mallius slowly revolved the stem of his wine glass between his thumb and forefinger. "Is this goblet one of your products?"

"Yes."

"It is a handsome piece of work. Claudia likes such things."

"I'd like to supply the procurator's palace. And by the way, Gaius, could you not help me interest Herod and his new wife in a service for the palace of Tiberias?"

"All you need to do is interest Herodias," Gaius answered. "Herod's completely under her domination."

"Herod?" Lucius wrinkled his forehead. "Yes, by the immortals, the centurion's right. I remember the fellow. A little while ago all Rome was buzzing about this Herod's stealing the other Herod's wife. This one, Herod—"

"Herod Antipas," Gaius prompted.

"Yes. He had come to Rome to visit Herod Philip, his half-brother, and he fell in love with Philip's wife. And according to the gossip, he spent a considerable time with her when Philip was away. At any rate, when he went back to Palestine, she either went with him or followed him."

Gaius laughed. "It must have caused much talk in Rome. It's a rather involved business. Herod Philip was not only her husband but also her uncle. Her father was Aristobulus, the brother of Herod Philip. Antipas is also her half-uncle. He was married to the daughter of old Aretas, a king over in Arabia, when he became involved with Herodias. Now Aretas is threatening to bring an army and punish Antipas. So you see that even though neither Capernaum nor Tiberias is a big city, we do have excitement in Galilee."

"Well, their marital affairs don't concern me," Marcus observed, "nor do I care one denarius what they do, but it seems that the conduct of the Herods would greatly disturb your Jews."

"It does," Gaius agreed. "The Jews set much store by the family, as much as we Romans do, and perhaps more. Among the devout Jews especially such behavior is unpardonable, and consequently they have been openly criticizing the Herods."

"Would they dare show their disapproval of the tetrarch's actions?" the tribune interposed to ask.

"Yes, tribune. One of their prophets, a long-haired preacher of the desert who had gained a considerable following, denounced Herod so severely that the tetrarch, goaded by Herodias, had him arrested and taken to the fortress-palace at Machaerus beyond the Dead Sea on the frontiers of Arabia, where the fellow was thrown into a dungeon."

"What had he said that made Herod angry?"

"He shook his finger under Herod's nose, told him that he was living in sin, and demanded that he give up Herodias. It made Herod angry, of course, and incensed Herodias, but Herod wouldn't have laid a finger on him, the Jews at Capernaum say, if it hadn't been for the insistence of Herodias. They say he's mortally afraid of this prophet."

"The tetrarch must be a man of little will power."

"No, tribune, I don't think Herod lacks courage, certainly not physical courage. But he is afraid of the unknown. I think that is it." Gaius picked up an olive, nibbled at the meat. "Call it superstition if you like, but Herod isn't a Jew in the strictest sense. His mother, a woman called Malthake, I believe, was a Samaritan; and he resembles his father, for old Herod, too, was at heart a ruffian. Antipas apparently has no religious convictions and adheres only to the Jewish forms sufficiently to keep his people from clamoring too loudly against him. He's not only a pagan, but a barbarian besides, and he has only a thin outer layer of civilizing graces about him."

Lucius sipped his wine slowly, licking his lips. "The tetrarch must be an interesting individual. I hope I may meet him before I finish my assignment out here. By the way, centurion, speaking of the Jews and their religion, I understand that although there are several sects, they all have but one god."

"Yes, they differ in the interpretations of their sacred writings, but all sects unite in their belief in a single deity."

"Gaius is speaking of the Jews alone, of course," Marcus interjected. "The religions here in the east, in Phoenicia, for instance, are like the fruits." He pointed to the tray of fruit from which they had been eating. "We have them to suit almost any taste. At Caesarea, tribune, you should have little difficulty finding one to your individual liking, eh, centurion?"

"Most Romans seem to have little difficulty with their religion," observed Gaius, "or lack of it," he added, smiling.

"You are joking, centurion, but you speak the truth nevertheless," Tribune Lucius Mallius said. "The trouble with our Roman system of gods is that we have so many of them that we cannot keep track of them and consequently we lose interest in all of them. Of course," he hastened to add, "I take little stock in the gods; I'm not afraid of offending any god—"

"Any god but Sejanus." Marcus was smiling, but Lucius dropped the fig he had selected from the tray, sat up straight.

"I am a soldier," he said. "I obey orders."

"No offense intended, tribune. Just my perverse way of joking. Speaking of religions, those out here are rather interesting, in an objective way, for I take no interest in any gods. But here in Phoenicia there is Astarte, the moon goddess, and there is also Moloch, the fire god. Astarte is somewhat like our Venus. She's the goddess of fruitfulness." He pointed to the piled-up figs, pomegranates, dates, grapes. "She is represented in various forms; sometimes with four wings, a pointed cap on her head, and a dove in her hand. The dove, so they say, is for chastity, though I cannot vouch for her morals, tribune. Other representations show her as a naked fat woman holding her hands folded over sagging breasts. And some even portray her as a cow. Take your choice."

"A grim sort of goddess."

"Yes, tribune." Marcus sipped his wine. "But if you think she is lacking in appeal, you should see Moloch. Repulsive looking, with none of the graces of a Roman god. He is represented as having the head of an ox on a human body whose arms are extended. When some great calamity befalls the community, they build a fire inside an ovenlike opening in the body, heat the statue until the arms are red hot, and then place a small child dressed in his finest garments upon these arms. It's a grim business, but they make a great holiday of the occasion."

"Our Roman gods at least have the virtue of being generally good-humored," the tribune observed.

"Yes, their chief virtue," Gaius added, "is that they are usually looking the other way when we mortals choose to do a little pleasant transgressing."

"But the god that you and the Jews have"—Marcus eyed the centurion, smiling—"isn't like that, eh, Gaius? I understand he's a stern, jealous, suspicious god who keeps his eyes and ears upon his subjects day and night. They cannot get away from him, even for an evening's relaxation in such a place, say, as the Subura, I hear." Reaching into the fold of his toga, he drew forth a coin, flipped it, caught it in his palm. "I have a god, too," he said, pointing to the coin. "That is the god I worship. He is really all-powerful."

"Tiberius?" Lucius set down his goblet. "Is that not a denarius?"

"Ha! That wretched old man, ranting away at his astrologers while Sejanus rules the empire. No, tribune, nor the emperor who will succeed him, nor dead Augustus. Nor Sejanus. No, my god is no man or woman who ever walked the earth, no imagined god riding the clouds or burrowing away in the bowels of the earth. My god"—he tapped the coin—"is substance, money—silver, gold, ships, merchandise, slaves." He picked up his goblet, turned it slowly on its slender stem. "It's my beautiful glass, my gorgeous textiles. These are material. You can hold them in your hand, feel them, count them, gloat your eyes upon them, yes, and sell them for money. And money is power. Give me money and I can get anything I want." He put away the denarius. "Isn't that true?"

"I cannot entirely agree," Lucius replied. "Money is powerful, but it is not the ultimate power. That is strength, power—and power in these days, and for all time, I trust, means Rome. And the power of Rome is the Roman army. Give me the army, and I'll get money and goods and ships and slaves."

"But neither of you will get happiness your way," Gaius spoke up. He was reclining on his left elbow. With his free hand he spun the goblet gently so that the whirling wine pushed up the sides to leave a purple track. "Julius Caesar had both money and power; so did Augustus. Marcus Antonius had money, the army, and Cleopatra. Tiberius had money, and he's supposed to have great power. You say Sejanus has it instead. Well, what of Sejanus? None of these had much happiness, nor does Sejanus, I am convinced."

23

Marcus sat up straight. "Well, my philosopher friend, name a Roman who is completely happy."

"I can't," said Gaius. "I don't know that I can even define happiness. I suspect that it is something that would be rather easy to acquire if we but knew its secret. I think it is something of the mind, though, and something entirely apart from one's material possessions." He selected a fig from the tray, pulled out the stem, split open the fruit. "I have an idea that great material possessions"—he turned toward the tribune—"and military power may actually be a hindrance to happiness."

"Centurion," said Marcus, frowning, "where did you get this strange philosophy, this—this heresy for a Roman? From the Jews?"

Gaius chewed on the fig. "That may have had something to do with it. Environment. But many Jews don't hold such belief. And there's heredity. You forget my name, eh, Marcus?"

"Tribune, he's one of Cornelia's modern jewels." But he was serious when he spoke to Gaius. "Did Gaius Gracchus or Tiberius Gracchus find happiness? They attained great popularity, it is true, but the multitudes whom they had befriended turned upon them and killed them."

Gaius shrugged his shoulders. "Who knows? But they were men of principle, and already cold-hearted Rome is beginning to revere their memories. The Gracchi stood for something. They were liberals. They tried to make the lives of their fellow men a little happier. Perhaps in doing that, in being that way, they found happiness, peace—whatever happiness is. I should be happy to think that I had inherited some small part of their liberality, their philosophy—whatever you choose to call their attitude toward life."

"You are a strange Roman, centurion," the tribune observed wryly. "I don't believe I have ever come upon one like you before in my assignments over the Empire. Few soldiers of Rome talk about such—such intangibles." He set down his glass. "As for me, I want something I can get my fingers upon, something I can come to grips with—a sword in my hand, a horse between my legs, screaming, angry skulls to whack down upon. Give me my legionnaires and a good stiff fight now and then, and you take the philosophy, centurion."

"And you wouldn't believe it, tribune," Marcus said, "but Gaius is one of the best swordsmen in Rome, or was a few years ago. Do you keep up your practice, centurion?"

"Yes, enough to keep in shape. And how about you?"

"I practice occasionally with Tullus. He's better than I am."

The tribune appraised Gaius with eyes that showed a new interest. "You do look fit, centurion," he said. "I cannot understand it. Perhaps it is this oriental atmosphere, this mysticism—"

"Charge it to the Jews," Marcus said, laughing. "That's the practice. If we can find no other scapegoat, we get a Jew. After all, isn't that Jewish philosophy you have been expounding?"

"As a matter of fact, the Jews aren't philosophers, in the sense that we Romans are, or the Greeks. They are a religious people. And there are many sects among them, each with its particular teaching. For instance, the Pharisees are a proud sect whose members love to parade their religion and place great emphasis upon a strict observance of all the laws and customs of their faith. They believe in immortality. On the other hand, the Sadducees, a sect that is small but has many wealthy adherents and numbers many of the priestly caste, do not believe in life after death. Then there are the Essenes, a group of ascetics living in poverty and practicing celibacy, like this wilderness preacher that Herod sent to Machaerus, who correspond somewhat to our Stoics and Pythagoreans. There are also groups within these sects, each conforming in a general way to the Jewish laws and practices but differing on details concerning their worship."

"They must get into many disputes, these Jews," the tribune suggested.

"They do," Gaius agreed. "And sometimes it flares into violence. They take their religion very seriously. It is the greatest thing in their lives, for they are an intense, emotional people, and naturally religious. Their god to them is all-powerful; he's no half-god, half-mortal, like our Roman deities. He is supreme, the one god that serves to give the Jews a unity—despite their various sects—that few other people have, if any."

"Does this Jewish god stand as high in their esteem as does the emperor in ours?"

"Far higher, tribune. No human being ever approaches in

power their god. This Yahweh, as the Jews call him, is the supreme builder and ruler of the universe. They disagree somewhat about his attributes. Some hold that he is a god of justice alone who demands exact obedience to his laws and holds the scales of justice in his hand, and weighs out reward or punishment in accordance with the manner in which man complies with his laws."

"A cold, impersonal god."

"Yes, tribune, to some. But others among the Jews contend that he is also a god of abundant mercy and love, willing and eager to forgive, and understanding and making allowances for the frailties of man. There is a young rabbi who lives at Capernaum—"

Gaius stopped, for from the atrium came the noise of angry, disputing voices. Then the doors opened, and a young Roman stepped into the courtyard.

"Why, Tullus—"

"I am sorry, sir. I was expecting to find you in the garden. And I did not know you had guests."

"But why all the noise? Who are the others out there?"

"That is why I came, sir. We have fetched three Jews who have been creating a disturbance at the docks. It was shortly after you left, sir. We were unloading the slaves, when one of them became surly and refused to obey the guard. As the guard was whipping him these three Jews came up and demanded that the guard stop chastising the slave. When he didn't, one of the Jews, a big, bearded fellow, knocked the guard down. For a time there was quite a commotion and some of the slaves might have escaped had they not been securely chained."

"But why did you bring the Jews here? Why didn't you turn them over to the authorities of the city?"

"I was going to do that, sir, but when these fellows declared they had come here from Capernaum and were friends of the centurion who commands in that city, I did not wish to become involved in any way with the Roman army, so I fetched them to you to learn what disposition you would make of the matter."

Marcus, smiling now, faced Gaius. "Some of your Jewish friends, centurion?"

For the moment Gaius ignored the question. Instead of replying, he spoke to Tullus. "The slave the guard was beating was a Jew, wasn't he?"

"Why, yes, sir, I believe he was."

Then Gaius turned to Marcus. "Yes, Marcus, I know them. They're fishermen, and good fellows. They resented the guard's beating the Jewish slave. The man who knocked the guard down is named Simon. He's a rash, hot-headed fellow who invariably speaks and acts before he thinks. The other two are the Zebedee brothers. Their father is a well-established fisherman from the Bethsaida section at the head of the Sea of Galilee, and Simon lives at Capernaum." He stood up. "They won't cause you any more trouble. If you'll excuse me, I'll go out and talk with them."

"Tell the guards to release these friends of the centurion," Marcus commanded Tullus. He smiled.

But Gaius, already opening the door that led into the atrium, ignored his friend's banter.

3

The Jews must be a stubborn, rebellious people," said the tribune, when Gaius returned. "Has not the procurator found it very difficult to deal with them?"

"The Jews rather are a proud people who have a strong feeling for each other and for their nation," Gaius answered. "The procurator has not been tactful; on many occasions he has flaunted his scorn for their religious beliefs and customs. I have had little difficulty at Capernaum. Many Jews, in fact, are gentle, easy to deal with, uninterested in politics, and obedient to authority so long as that authority does not attempt to restrict them in the exercise of their religious customs and practices." He paused, smiling. "It may seem strange to you, but those three Jews I have just been talking with are gentle fellows—until you get them aroused. In fact, they are close friends of that young rabbi at Capernaum—"

"You were going to tell us about him when those three arrived here so unceremoniously," the tribune interrupted. "Is he another rebel against the authority of Rome?"

"No, I think he has no interest in political matters. I think he is simply a religious man. I happened upon him one day down by the seashore. He was talking to a motley crowd of fishermen, water carriers, and small shopkeepers in that vicinity who had slipped away a few moments from their bargaining, and here and there in the group was a man of property. He is a persuasive speaker. No shouting, gesturing, frothing at the mouth. He talks calmly and quietly, but with tremendous power. The words seem to flow from him like the waters of a deep, strong stream. I arrived in the middle of his discourse, and although I was on a rather hurried mission, I couldn't leave until he had finished. And it wasn't until he had got into a small fishing boat—one of old Zebedee's—and started out across the lake that I realized I had been there quite a long time."

"What's he after?" Marcus asked. "Money, doubtless. All Jews want money."

"I don't think so, Marcus, although I know little of him. A few times I have had a glimpse of him on some narrow street or along a dusty road in Galilee. Usually there is a group with him and often large crowds press about him. He seems to have a strange power to draw people to him. And if he seeks their money, I have never heard of it. Already the people of Galilee and even those down in Judea and in Jerusalem are beginning to talk of him. They say he is interested only in his kingdom—"

"By the immortals!" exclaimed the tribune. "The fellow likely is advocating rebellion against the Roman authority in the hope of setting himself up as a king in this part of Syria. Does Pilate know about him?"

"That I cannot say. If Pilate doesn't know of him already, he will hear of him, I'm confident. But I don't believe this young Jew is plotting to overthrow Rome's dominion in this region. I think he is interested only in promulgating his religious doctrines, which are considerably at variance with those held by a great many of the Jews, as I understand it. For instance, I judged by his talk down at the seashore that he holds the god of the Jews to be the father not only of the Jewish nation but of all mankind, and that this god is a loving father. It seems to be a new conception of the god of the Jews."

"Then he's not a rabbi in the strictest sense, but an unorthodox fellow, a radical, wouldn't you say?"

"Yes, tribune, I suppose you might call him radical, radical in that his philosophy or religious views or whatever you wish to term his beliefs are so very simple as compared with the involved religious beliefs and practices of the Jews. He seems to emphasize the essentials of the Jewish religion rather than the formalism and trappings that seem to have attached themselves to it. And he's bound sooner or later to be challenged by the Temple leaders at Jerusalem, because he is tearing away the great structure of code and creed that these men have allowed to develop around the essentially simple religion of the ancient Jews."

"But in doing that, centurion, won't he be striking indirectly at the power and authority of Rome?" The tribune reached for a fat fig. "I understand that the leaders of the Jews work with us in keeping the people quiet and governable, although outwardly they make a pretense of opposing Rome's domination."

"Old Annas and his Temple group doubtless will contend that this man is opposing Rome in order to set Rome against him, for they will be jealous of his power with the people."

"Gaius, you must be under the fellow's spell," Marcus observed. "But, tribune, I see in him no danger to Rome. If Gaius has rightly described him, he is but a harmless visionary, a country fellow who may have got a bit too much"—he tapped his forehead—"of the desert sun. Where does he come from, centurion?"

"He's a Galilean, the son of an obscure carpenter, now dead, I understand. He's well muscled and doubtless has done much heavy work as a carpenter himself. But I know little of his history."

"I had supposed by what you have said about him that he was always rambling of such intangible things as truth, goodness, and beauty," said Marcus, smiling, "and I had set him down as a long-haired, effeminate, ascetic—"

"Oh, no, Marcus, nothing of the kind," Gaius hastened to emphasize. "He's neither ascetic, like this John who offended Antipas, nor an effeminate fellow."

"Where in Galilee does your man come from?"

"Well, I was told that he was brought up in a village on the south slope of Lebanon, which sticks up out of the Esdraelon Plain—"

"I know the country well. It's only a little way southeast of the mouth of the Belus River, where we get our sand, as I told you, and I have journeyed through there buying Galilean homespuns to study in developing my own textiles. The village couldn't be Nazareth?"

"Nazareth's the place. A small community—"

"By Jupiter and all the gods!" Marcus slapped his hand upon the table so hard that the wine sloshed in the goblets. "Tribune, have no fear of this fellow. Nazareth! A hovel of mud huts sprawled upon a hillside, ignorant peasants grubbing a miserable living out of rocky soil. Calm your fears, tribune. The priests in the Temple at Jerusalem, Pilate at Caesarea, Sejanus in Rome, old Tiberius on Capri—you're all safe! It makes little difference what is this fellow's purpose. Nazareth will not soon be destroying Rome!"

Casually Gaius reached for a ripe olive. "Julius Caesar, you will recall, came out of the Subura."

"Yes, but the Subura is still Rome, and Julius Caesar was a Roman. He was no itinerant Jew from Nazareth. Caesar's coming from the Subura was an accident of birth. He had an inborn capacity, an inner strength and drive to force his way, power—"

"There are some who say that this Jewish carpenter also has capacity, inner strength, if you wish to call it that. Some even contend that he has power to bend the forces of nature to do his will—"

"What's that, centurion?" Tribune Lucius Mallius pulled the date stone from his mouth, dropped it upon his plate. "I have heard that there are magicians in these eastern lands who can do remarkable things. Tell me more of this fellow."

"Tribune, his followers maintain that he does not perform magic. They declare that these—these manifestations, call them whatever you like, are never done for the purpose of attracting attention but only to heal—"

"A faith healer," Marcus interrupted. "I have heard of them. They heal people who have nothing wrong with them, who only imagine ailments. They're invariably persons with strong wills. They easily impress a weakling and transfer some of their own strength and confidence through suggestion to this weaker person, and he feels better and decides he had been cured."

"Tell us, centurion," said the tribune, "how does this Jew perform his—his wonders? Do you know of any incidents in which he demonstrated his abilities?"

"Yes. And I have heard that he had healed several persons of leprosy."

"I don't believe it," Marcus declared. "Leprosy—not everything that is called leprosy, but real leprosy—is incurable. I have never heard of anyone's having been cured of it. If a fellow had a headache or a pain in the stomach, I can see how your man could wave his arms, look the man straight in the eye, and utter some incantation that would either frighten or charm him into forgetting his ills, for the moment, at least. But not leprosy."

"They say he does nothing. All he requires, I understand, is

31

that the person he is healing have faith in his power to cure him."

"Strange," said the tribune. "I have never heard of a magician who operated in that manner. But tell us, can you relate some incident in which he actually healed someone?"

"I have never seen him heal anyone, but I have several acquaintances, reputable persons, who have told me that they were present when he did acts of healing. I have in mind particularly the incident involving one of the most prominent citizens of Capernaum. And he told me about it himself."

"You mean the man who was healed?" The tribune's interest was mounting.

"No, he is the father of the one who was healed. He is a member of the city's governing council. And he swears the rabbi healed his son."

"What was wrong with the boy?" Marcus asked.

"He didn't tell me. I don't think he knew, except that the boy seemed to be desperately ill."

"Yes, I thought so. And what did your Jew do? Look him in the eyes, mumble an incantation, and scare the boy into getting up from his bed?" He laughed. "Probably wasn't sick; probably just thought himself sick."

"The rabbi never saw the boy. In fact, he wasn't in Capernaum at the time."

The tribune sat down his goblet. "By Jupiter, go on, centurion."

"The boy suddenly had become ill, and in a short time appeared to be in critical condition. They were fearful that he was going to die. Then someone suggested that the rabbi from Nazareth had been healing people and that he might be willing to help. He had just returned to Galilee from Judea, and they had heard he was over in the country between Cana and Magdala.

"The father had never been interested in the rabbi, had little faith in him. But as the boy's fever mounted and he began moaning in his delirium, the father started out to search for the rabbi. He found him with some fishermen near Magdala. He went boldly up to the rabbi and beseeched him to return with him to Capernaum.

"'I was so distressed that I must have been talking frantically,' the father told me. 'No doubt the rabbi understood that I had little hope for the boy and little faith in him, but that I had come to him in desperation.'" Gaius paused, reached for a fig.

"By the gods, centurion," the tribune exclaimed, "go on with your story!"

"He said that as he told the rabbi of his boy, the rabbi listened carefully. 'You have come to me because you have heard that I am a worker of magic,' the rabbi said, when he had paused, 'but you do not believe that I have the power of my Father to heal your son.'

"The rabbi spoke kindly but with candor, he said, and his words were so true that my friend from Capernaum was completely upset and did not know how to answer the rabbi. He said that he felt that the rabbi was reading his thoughts. He was hopeless, defeated.

"'I just stood there looking at him,' he told me. 'All the time he was looking into my eyes, as if he knew everything I was thinking. I couldn't stand it, and I was on the verge of weeping. My utter helplessness, as contrasted with the impression I had of his strength, and his evident sympathy for me, overcame me.'

"The man said he cried out that he had come to the rabbi hoping that he would work some miracle, some trick of magic, anything to save the boy's life. He said he did not know what he believed; he only knew that he loved his son more than his own life. And he told me that as he looked into the rabbi's face, he grew calmer and a new feeling of confidence, faith, call it what you wish, seemed to surge through his whole body, and he cried out again, 'Oh, sir, I don't know what I believe, but I do know that you can help me if you will but return with me to Capernaum!'

"He told me that as he looked into the face of this young Jew from Nazareth this sense of confidence seemed to grow and take hold of him, and then the rabbi smiled and put his arm about his shoulder.

"'You can go now. Your son will live,' he said the rabbi promised him.

"The man told me that he was confident at that moment that the boy would get well. He said he was in no great hurry then to get back to Capernaum. And early the next day, when he neared

33

the gates of the city, one of his servants came running to meet him with the news that the boy was rapidly recovering. And when he inquired of the servant what time the fever had left the boy, he said the servant told him that it was on the day before. And, strange to say, tribune, when the man inquired further, he found that the fever had left the boy at the very hour the rabbi assured him his son would live."

"By the immortals!" exclaimed Lucius. "That was a good story." He drained his wine glass. "A good story, indeed!"

"Yes, it was a good story," said Marcus, "a dramatic coincidence, if all the facts are straight, which I doubt. But let your Jew straighten withered limbs or put back noses eaten away by leprosy, by all the gods! But fever! Don't you know that when a man has a fever, Gaius, he either dies or gets well? And a great many persons get well. And, of course, there's always a time when the fever leaves. In this case, it is very clear that after your Capernaum friend told the Jew about the fever and how long the boy had been ill, the Jew realized that it was then about the time for the fever to begin abating. Clever, of course, but nothing more."

"What if the boy had died?"

"Why then, tribune, Gaius would have no intriguing story with which to beguile you." Marcus picked a grape seed from between his lips. "There is always a practical explanation for all these mysterious tricks of the magicians and soothsayers. In this case the answer is apparent; in others it is more difficult to see how the so-called miracle has been accomplished. Your Jew simply healed a boy who would have got well anyway. The rabbi was clever enough to take advantage of his opportunity. And the warm Jewish imagination of your Capernaum friend and his tendency to be intrigued by things mystical, coupled with his distressed condition, his lack of emotional balance, all this combined to put him in a gullible frame of mind—"

"Perhaps you are right," the tribune conceded. "Yes, that must be the solution. But it's a good story, nevertheless."

"I don't think that it is explained necessarily by Marcus's rather smug deduction," Gaius observed, with a trace of feeling.

"I'm not arguing the matter," Marcus answered. "I care not a denarius whether he healed him or didn't. I was merely pointing out that a case of fever is no proper test. Let him straighten a crooked leg or foot; there are thousands of them here in Palestine. Let him restore a blind man's sight, or heal someone who is really a victim of that scourge of these eastern lands, leprosy." Turning to Lucius, he said, "Tribune, you will see much of it in these regions. One day you'll be traveling along the road when suddenly there'll be a commotion and you'll hear a veritable wailing of the damned, and then around a bend or behind the rocks you'll get a glimpse of walking death. When you hear that wailing 'Unclean! Unclean!' keep moving, but don't look too closely or you'll never be able to forget what you see. In your traveling you probably have seen a leper here and there, but perhaps not as we have them out here."

"I understand leprosy in this part of the world often disfigures a man horribly."

"Yes, it does." Marcus sipped his wine. "I remember once— it was several years ago when I had come out to Phoenicia to investigate the possibilities of establishing our business—my guide and I spent the night in a cave. We were traveling in upper Galilee buying samples of homespun, and we camped in a cave which we later learned had been used by lepers. We may have stopped at other places where lepers had stayed, too. When we found out about this one, we were somewhat alarmed, especially the guide. You see, all the natives of this region are deathly afraid of being contaminated. They won't go near a leper or a place where a leper has stayed. That's why a leper is an outcast and can never even communicate with friends or relatives."

"How long has it been since you stayed in that cave, Marcus?" Gaius's voice betrayed his alarm.

"Oh, it has been three or four years." Marcus laughed. "Don't be frightened. That cave had aired out a long time, no doubt. And I am convinced that leprosy is not as likely to be caught as the people in this region believe."

"When I see the poor devils even a long way off I begin moving," Gaius said. "There's no cure for it. It's a living death, tribune." He confronted Marcus, his expression challenging. "There's something that money can't manage. A leper's an outcast, rich or poor."

"You are right, centurion," Marcus agreed. "Leprosy is not something in the mind, and it isn't a fever. It won't cure itself, nor is there any known method of curing it. Your Jew wonder-worker, I'll wager, will never heal a leper."

4

Marcus pointed toward the line of naked slaves carrying baskets on their shoulders from the fishermen's boats in the shallow water to the low sheds of the dyeworks beyond the high tide's reach.

"Don't be alarmed, tribune," he said, "those purplish streaks on the slaves are not from the whips of overseers. It's the purple from the shellfish that get crushed in the baskets or splatters on them from the vats. It won't harm them." He paused. "I demand that my slaves get good treatment." He eyed Gaius, who silently was watching the procession of slaves climbing the slope. "If they are too harshly treated, they are unfitted for work. With too little food and too much beating, they may even die. And when a slave dies before he can be replaced that cuts down production."

"And cutting down production cuts down revenue." Gaius's smile was cynical.

"You jest, centurion, but you speak the truth," Marcus said. "Revenue is what interests me, my friend. A slave to me means so much dye running down the troughs, so many bales of wool treated, so many lengths of fine textiles manufactured. Over at Sidon it's the same way. A slave means so many goblets or pitchers or other glass products made. You and your friends, centurion, you and the philosophers, your brethren of the synagogue, your Jewish faith healers, all of you can prate of truth and goodness and beauty and all those other intangibles. That's not for me. Money is all the god I need." He shrugged his shoulders. "Let's walk over to the dyesheds. I want to show you the little fellow that is responsible for all this—" He swept his arm outward in a curve that embraced the fishing boats in the cove, the wide arc of the shoreline, the sheds, the sweating, grime-smeared slaves, and farther up the shore and well back from it the long squat sheds in which women slaves toiled by their frames and weaving looms.

"Phoenicia," he continued, as the three started toward the

dyesheds, "excels in four principal manufacturing areas, and this little shellfish is responsible for two of these industries—dyeing and textiles—really one industry. The other two products are glass and metal goods. I am engaged in the first three—all except the metal products business." He signaled to a slave trudging along under a heavily loaded basket; the fellow set it down, stood by it trembling, evidently fearful that he had done something that would bring the overseer on the run with his whip.

Marcus reached into the basket and picked up a small shellfish, held it out. "This is the murex," he explained. "This variety is the trunculus. There is another variety, not as valuable, called the buccinum lapillus. The murex is found farther from shore, in the deeper waters, while the buccinum is taken from the rocks and the shallows near the shore. It is getting rather late in the season for them and the dye from those caught from now on until the next season will be of inferior quality. Now this little animal—" He hesitated. "But maybe you aren't interested in any lecture on the dyeing industry in Phoenicia—"

"On the contrary," the tribune assured Marcus, "I am. I want to learn all I can about the business of this part of the world."

Gaius nodded. "I'd like to know more about it myself."

"I do think it's interesting." Marcus pointed to the spiraling shell of the murex. "The coloring matter is in this little sac or vein that twists through the shell. When it is extracted it is of a creamy consistency and a yellowish-white color. The sac is taken from the animal while it is still alive, because the quality of the coloring changes after death. After the matter is extracted it quickly changes to green, then to purple."

He pointed toward the ships circling the shoreline of the cove. "We catch them in baskets that are let down into the sea. The baskets are baited with mussels or frogs and have openings through which the shellfish get in but are unable to find their way out. The finest dye shellfish are found right along these shores, particularly the rocky part of the Syrian coast between the Ladder of Tyre and Haifa over near Mount Carmel." He dropped the murex into the basket, motioned to the slave to move on.

"From the ships these slaves"—he nodded in the direction of the long files of chained men trudging up the slope from the

38

shore—"bring them to the sheds, where the marrow is extracted from the murex. But the buccinum is not treated that way. Instead, we dump the animal, shell and all, into those big vats over there and the buccinum is ground into a fine pulp." He pointed toward several large low-walled round containers into which the slaves were dumping baskets of shellfish while others, trudging around the relentless circles, turned slowly in each vat a great stone that ground them down.

"The pulp is then placed in huge leaden vessels—they are over there in that shed—salt is added and it is allowed to simmer at moderate heat. They keep skimming the mixture, taking off the shells and other dross, and after some ten days the mixture is down to about one-sixteenth its original weight. When the fluid comes off, it is dark. It is inferior to the murex, as I said, but most textiles are dyed at first with murex, which produces a dull, dark purple, not greatly in favor, and, after they have dried, are dyed also with the buccinum, which is red rather than purple. The two together produce a dark rich purple, about the color of thickened blood, that held up to the light shows a rich crimson hue, a color worthy of any king, emperor, or even"—he grinned at the tribune —"Sejanus."

But Lucius did not accept his challenge, and Marcus pointed toward the squat buildings. "Let's make a quick visit to the dye-sheds and then to the weaving rooms; but they are less interesting to me than the glassworks near Sidon."

"Glassmaking is a very ancient industry, is it not?" Tribune Lucius Mallius asked. "I know very little about it."

"Yes, it goes back a long way. The beginnings are lost in antiquity, in fact. The legend of how glassmaking was discovered says that it happened near here—at the mouth of the Belus River, which you will pass in going to Caesarea. According to the story, some merchants with a cargo of natrum went ashore at that point to cook provisions. They built a fire of driftwood but could find no stones upon which to support their pots. So they went back to their ship and got several blocks of natrum, a saltpeter. They set the pots on the blocks, fanned up the fire; after a while the natrum began to fuse with the sand and a transparent liquid that hardened as the fire died down was the result. That was the first glass.

Improbable, however, since such a fire would hardly have been hot enough to fuse the sand and natrum."

"It's an interesting story, at any rate," commented the tribune.

"Phoenicia has a great abundance of fine, silicious sand, free of clay, the type excellent for glass manufacture," Marcus went on, "and our properties near the mouth of the Belus are among the best on the entire coast. But we have to import alkali from Egypt or some other quarter. If we had the alkali here we could—"

"I was looking for you, sir." The overseer stepped from the doorway just as they were reaching the nearest dyeshed, saluted. "I have the report on the slaves." He hesitated. "I didn't know that—"

"Go ahead, Tullus," said Marcus.

"Well, sir, we have the slaves assigned to their tasks, though you may wish to change some of the assignments after you see them."

"How did they stand the trip out from Rome?"

"Fairly well, sir, most of them, though they did not receive the best of treatment on the *Cleopatra*. Some are ill, though it is probably only the rigors of the voyage that upset them. They were packed in closely, and the sanitary arrangements were not the best. There are captives from several nations with which we have been at war, and evidently they were in captivity only a short while before they were put on the market. We have assigned most of the women to the looms but have kept back several of the handsomest for your inspection. It may be that you will want—" He hesitated.

The tribune smiled, but Marcus did not notice. "What do they look like, Tullus?" he asked, interrupting the overseer's report.

"There are several dark-eyed wenches from Dacia, a few from Gaul, two or three spirited half-savages from Britannia, a Greek or two, and several from Germania whose hair is like clearest honey and whose eyes are as blue as the sky. We thought you would like to save these from the looms to put to more lucrative—" He paused.

"You did well, Tullus. They'll bring more money that way."

He turned to Lucius. "These wealthy Phoenician men pay

40

well," he explained, "especially for untamed blonde wenches from the forests of Germania."

"If you are also in the business of selling women," Gaius observed, "the tetrarch Herod should make a profitable customer."

"Centurion, I understand that old pagan has never had his fill of women. Of course, I'm not in the slave business. But I'm businessman enough not to use women at the weaving looms whose faces and figures raise rich men's eyebrows. But your mentioning old Herod gives me an idea. It might pay me to send him one of the shapeliest and most spirited women in the new cargo, eh?"

"It depends upon what you consider business, I suppose. To me this entire slave traffic is detestable. I am confident that Rome eventually will be the loser because of it. Rome is fast becoming more slave than free. That to me is an unhealthy situation."

"But, centurion," Tribune Lucius Mallius interjected, "they are slaves through the fortunes of war. They were defeated by Roman arms. Had we been defeated instead, would we not have been enslaved?"

"Very likely. But that does not make the slave traffic right."

"Tribune, there's no need arguing with the centurion. I fear he has been won over to the Jews' effeminate philosophy." Marcus smiled. "But, Gaius, I still believe I would do well to give old Herod a lively young woman to help rejuvenate his old bones. I understand he keeps many but that one more is always appreciated. They say the palace at Tiberias is fairly cluttered with them."

"And at Machaerus, too, I've been told," Gaius added. "I've never been there, though Herod has invited me to accompany him the next time he goes down there for a holiday. Would you two like invitations too? I could arrange it."

"You are being sarcastic," said Marcus, "but as a matter of fact, I would like to go down there and see the old fellow when he has thrown off the conventions of society, I believe you'd express it, eh, centurion?"

"I have been told that Herod does get rid of all hampering conventions as soon as he enters the gates at Machaerus," Gaius answered. "Should you go down there, you'd doubtless see what a king looks like divested of his royal purple."

"Yes, and if I give the old fellow a pretty wench it will assure me an invitation." Marcus turned to the overseer. "Tullus, I want you to select one of the likeliest-looking women in the new lot. Choose one that is young, but not too young to have a fully developed figure, and that has a pretty face, too. Select a spirited wench, Tullus, a lusty woman who will set old Herod's eyes flaming and his thick lips drooling. Ha!" Marcus laughed. "You understand me, Tullus?"

The overseer nodded. "Yes, sir," he said, and there was the trace of a smile on his usually impassive face.

"Then see that she is carefully bathed, that her hair is groomed, and that she has proper oils and ointments. When you have done this, have her supplied with an adequate quantity of handsome garments cut from our choicest materials. And when you have completed these arrangements, provide for sending her to the tetrarch Herod as a gift from me."

Tullus bowed again. "I shall do it with promptness, sir."

The tribune Lucius Mallius laughed. "And if Herod doesn't like your choice, then what?"

"He will. Leave that to Tullus. He's a good judge of women himself, eh, Tullus?"

"I am confident, sir, that I understand what you have in mind."

"Be sure to carry out my instructions. And, now, Tullus, what about the men?"

"Generally they are in good condition, sir. Some have not entirely recovered from the fighting in which they were captured. But the wounds do not appear to be serious. Most of them can be put to work immediately, and the assignments are already being made."

"That's good, Tullus. I'll have a look at them shortly. You can go back to your work."

Tullus hesitated. "There was one boy, sir—"

"What's wrong with him?"

"We aren't certain, sir. At first we thought that he was rebellious. We gave him a rather severe lashing, but it didn't change him. I don't believe that he will be of much service to you, sir, particularly here."

"Send him to the glassworks and assign him to the furnaces."

Marcus' tone betrayed his impatience. "You see," he said to Lucius, "when we get a rebellious or defective slave we send him to the furnaces. They don't last long there, and we are reluctant to put good workers on the furnaces. The heat seems to break down their resistance."

"How old is this boy?" Gaius asked, his interest suddenly evident.

"How old is he, Tullus?"

"About fourteen, I'd say. We did not ask him his age."

"Rigorous work for a child, eh, Marcus?"

"He's a slave, is he not?" Marcus spoke curtly. "I am not responsible for his being a slave; I am not responsible for his fate. Let him look to his gods for that."

"You are a Roman citizen. You are responsible in part for what Rome does."

"And you must be forever challenging Rome, you and the Jews! Well, let this boy look to your Jewish god for deliverance. Tullus—" He confronted the overseer. "Just what does seem to be wrong with this boy? How is he affected? Is it simply fright, or obstinacy? Or is he really afflicted in some manner?"

"He is afflicted, sir. I am now convinced of it. He seems to have a palsy. He cannot handle himself; his limbs shake, and his hands tremble. I think he will be of little service."

"Where is he?"

"He is still here, sir; over there in one of the dyesheds."

"Go, fetch him."

Tullus ran toward the sheds. In a moment he returned, leading a boy by a thong that bound his wrists together. The boy shuffled along unsteadily, and his shoulders jerked; he twisted his head from side to side on the long slender column of his neck.

The child was wearing only a soiled loincloth; his feet were bare, and bony toes seemed to clutch at the sand of the seashore like the talons of a bird. On his back and across his shoulders were long reddened welts from the lashing; a bluish dark bruise showed through the pallor of his right cheek, and his right eye was half closed; stripes from the whipping crisscrossed his thin legs.

But now he stood as straight as he could, nor did he cast

down his eyes, though he could not keep his head still nor prevent the almost rhythmical jerking and twitching of his shoulders and his bony arms.

"See," said Gaius, and a scowl furrowed his forehead, "how the might of Rome prevails over her enemies."

But Marcus made no answer. Instead, he seemed to ignore the centurion's remark and turned to Tullus. "What tongue does he speak?"

"He's a Greek, sir, but he also understands the Roman."

"Where do you come from, boy?" Marcus asked the youth.

The boy seemed to twitch more violently. His fingers stabbed at the air as his hands opened and closed spasmodically, even though the thong held the wrists securely. He opened his mouth, but no sound came. He licked his lips. His eyes rolled.

"Come, boy!" said Marcus sharply. "Speak up. Where's your home? What's your name?"

"I—I come from Thracia. My name's Andreas."

"How does it happen that you are a slave?"

"The Romans—" the boy hesitated, swallowed, licked his pale lips "—they came to Philippolis. They—I—"

"Go on," said Marcus, impatiently.

"They killed my father and looted his shop, and they carried my mother and my sister away—somewhere, I don't know where —and me they sold on the slave-market block."

A dark frown clouded his pale drawn face as he looked Marcus in the eye and for the moment by the power of his scorn forced his twitching face to be still. "I—I—hate all Romans!"

Marcus laughed. "That is most unfortunate for us Romans." He seemed to be making the observation to Gaius rather than to the boy. "Eh, centurion?"

But Gaius, his face sober, said nothing, and Marcus spoke again to the boy. "How long have you been this way—palsied, I mean?"

"All my life, at times." He straightened again, held himself erect, as if by the hate that his eyes registered. "But my ill treatment by you Romans has made it worse."

"If you want to avoid getting more of what evidently you have

44

had," Marcus snapped, "you had better remember that you are a slave and learn to control your tongue."

"The boy speaks the truth, Marcus," Gaius spoke up, and there was contempt in his tone. "This slavery, particularly the sort of slavery you seem to demand, is a wretched business. You seem to feel that a slave's labor, his very life, in fact, is simply a commodity and nothing more."

"Ha, centurion!" Marcus' laugh was derisive. "You and your Jews, and this prating long-haired rabbi who has you under his spell. In fact, you have become more Jewish than Roman. Of course I view the work of a slave, his life, in fact, as a commodity. And this boy, you can see, will be of little value to me. I could send him to the glassworks, and he'd last a few months at the furnaces. But of what service would he be there even?" He paused, and a smile overspread his face.

"You know what I think I shall do? Yes, by the immortals! You are a Roman but you do not believe in our Roman ways. So I am giving this boy to you. A beautiful wench to Herod, a paralytic rebel to you." He nodded to the overseer. "Tullus, turn him over to his new owner. Free him, if you wish, centurion. Or, if you think better, keep him. Feed him and clothe him and wait upon him; be his slave."

He burst out laughing, and this time there was mirth to it. "Yes, centurion, by the great Jupiter, take him to your rabbi faith healer and let him look him in the eye and mutter his incantations, and if he has enough faith—and you enough pennies— maybe he will heal him. And if he cures this wreck of a boy, let me know; yes, by the gods, send me word of it."

"Marcus, you jest," Gaius said it calmly, evenly. "But you do not know what you say." He reached into the fold of his toga, brought forth a slender-bladed dagger. Then he stepped over to the boy and with one swift slash cut the leather thong and hurled it down the slope toward the sea. When he had put away his dagger, he massaged the deadened wrists where the thong had bound them.

5

Marcus and Gaius went with Lucius back across the causeway to the docks early the next morning to see him aboard the *Cleopatra* for the remainder of his journey to Caesarea.

"Tribune, I hope you have a pleasant voyage down the coast," said Marcus, when it was time for Lucius to go on board. "And I hope, too, that you find the procurator and his wife in most excellent spirits. The next time I go to Caesarea, I'll call upon you. In the meantime, tribune, you may be able to discover some way of impressing upon Pilate and Claudia the beauty and durable qualities of the textiles and glassware that we manufacture."

"I'll do it, centurion," the tribune replied. "First, though, I must make it my job to get the confidence of the procurator. I only know him in a casual way, and I understand that he is at times rather difficult to get along with—"

"You'll have no trouble with Pilate, tribune, if you don't do anything to make him suspect that you may be having designs upon his office. He's very proud of being procurator, and very jealous of his prerogatives."

"Marcus is right," Gaius agreed. "Pilate, I hear, is very obstinate and headstrong. Just be sure not to get in his way, tribune."

"Have no fears," Lucius hastened to assure them. "I am an army man. I can take commands as well as give them. In fact, were the place available, I don't know whether I would even want to be procurator. That office perhaps requires more patience and tact than I would be able to develop. I don't believe I would be so popular—" he smiled and glanced at Gaius "—with the Jews." Quickly he changed his tone. "No affront intended, centurion," he declared. "And I enjoyed your stories about them, especially those about that strange faith healer. I hope you can visit me soon and tell me some new stories about him. He probably will have done some even more startling tricks that you can report and—"

"Tribune," Marcus interrupted, "the *Cleopatra* is about ready to cast off. I have enjoyed seeing you and having you at my house. I hope you will soon be coming back to Tyre. When you do, I shall expect you to stay with me. You will be welcome."

"Thank you, Marcus. I have enjoyed your hospitality and the pleasant company of yourself and Centurion Gaius."

"Yes," said Gaius. "I has been a pleasant visit with Marcus, and I am happy to have met you, tribune. I trust our duties will soon bring us together again. Should you ever come up into Galilee, be certain to visit me. You will likely be coming to Tiberias on business with Herod, and Capernaum is not far away."

"If you go to see Gaius, tribune, he'll take you to the synagogue," Marcus said dryly, and Lucius and Gaius laughed.

In another moment the tribune had crossed the gangplank, the oars rose, fell swiftly to cut the water in long, even strokes, and the boat was under way. From his place at the rail, Lucius lifted his arm in salute, and the two on the dock saluted in return.

"I hope he has a pleasant journey to Caesarea," said Marcus as the boat pushed gracefully toward the opening in the breakwater that provided access to the open sea, "and that none of the cargo is spoiled. If that merchandise gets to Alexandria undamaged, it will bring me no small sum. The *Cleopatra* is crammed with valuable shipments. Should anything happen—a storm sink it, or pirates capture it, which in these days is not very likely—it would be a heavy loss. And worse, it might enable my competitors to get ahead of me in the Alexandria markets."

"Yes, Marcus, and has it ever occurred to you that a great many galley slaves would lose their lives, too?"

"Of course, Gaius. But it is not necessary to spend much time in the training of galley slaves. And the woods of Germania and Gaul are full of them. They can be had for the catching. But it takes patience and much time to teach slaves how to produce beautiful textiles and glassware. When a cargo of fine quality merchandise is lost, it means the loss of much costly materials and the work of many highly skilled slaves."

"And the mere life of a galley slave is not valuable in comparison with fine textile materials and glass products and the work of trained slaves?"

47

"No," said Marcus. "The way I figure it, money is what counts. You and your Jews and your starry-eyed rabbi can figure it any way you wish."

As they were turning to leave, the overseer came running from the direction of the customs sheds. He had in his hand a small roll of papyrus. "Master, I—I—beg pardon sir, but the lists—"

"Ah, Tullus," said Marcus, "finished already? Well, that can wait. Bring the roll to my house this afternoon, and I will check the lists. After we have eaten will be soon enough." Tullus was turning to go. "But, Tullus, hold a minute. What of the young woman I instructed you to send to the tetrarch Herod? When will she be ready for the journey?"

"She has already departed, sir. I attended to your orders immediately. She was sent early this morning, arrayed as you had instructed."

Marcus turned to Gaius. "See how punctual is my Tullus? See how he relieves me of all work?" He faced the overseer again. "Good, Tullus. I commend you. And how did the woman look?"

"Very beautiful, sir. I am confident that she will cause the old frame of Herod to pulse with renewed life."

"Fine, Tullus. But you almost cause me to regret having sent her to the tetrarch."

The serious face of the overseer relaxed into a thin smile. "I suspect, sir, that had you seen her first you would have kept her for yourself. And, now, sir, is that all you wish of me?"

"Yes, for the moment, Tullus. Bring the cargo lists this afternoon."

The overseer bowed. "Yes, sir, I shall." He started to go, hesitated a moment, turned to Gaius. "I might add, sir, that I have had your slave boy bathed, rubbed with ointments, and given proper clothing for your journey into Galilee."

"Thank you, Tullus," Gaius replied. "You are most efficient, and I appreciate your interest."

Tullus bowed again and then disappeared around the corner of a warehouse that faced upon a narrow alley leading out from the dock area.

Gaius and Marcus crossed the causeway to the mainland and returned to the house of Marcus high on the bluff. Early in the afternoon Gaius started for Capernaum. Andreas, calmer now and smiling but still struck intermittently by the seizures of his palsy, went with him. But Simon and the Zebedee brothers, the centurion discovered when he reached the eastern gate of the city, had gone on ahead.

6

The journey southeastward from Tyre through the hill country of northern Galilee had been exhausting to the ailing Andreas, and when Gaius reached Capernaum he went straight to his house without stopping at the Roman garrison. The boy was feverish.

Gaius put him to bed at once and summoned a servant to go for a physician. But the ministrations of the physician seemed to give the slave boy little relief. Gaius, who had become attached to the youth on the trip from Phoenicia, was alarmed. The boy's nervousness appeared to be increasing; he seemed to be verging upon hysteria. His hands jerked, his fingers stiffened in grotesque angles, his head turned from side to side or bobbed forward or backward, his long skinny legs drew up and twisted beneath his body as he lay upon the couch or threshed outward in quick, convulsive thrusts. He seemed to have lost all power and will to control himself.

It was on the second day after their return from Tyre that the fishermen Simon and John came to the door of Gaius's servants with a basket of fish. "These are for the centurion," Simon said to the servant who answered his knocking. "We are giving them to him; we want no money for them. The centurion has been a good friend to us even though he's a Roman. He has bought many fish from us, too; now we wish to give him these."

When the servant came and told Gaius, the centurion went back to greet Simon and the younger Zebedee. "We've had a great catch of fine bream fish, centurion," said Simon. "We have sold a great quantity throughout Capernaum, and have sent a boat laden with bream and carp down the coast to Magdala, and they may go on to Tiberias. We also sent a batch of fine perch off to Jerusalem. They'll bring a good price at the market beside the Fish Gate if they get there in good shape."

Simon handed the basket to the servant. "You have been

good to us, centurion. You helped us build a new synagogue, and you haven't disturbed us in our religious affairs. And the other day at Tyre you spoke a good word for us. We are not rich men, centurion, but what we have we like to share."

Gaius thanked them, and after the servant had emptied the basket and returned it to Simon the fishermen were turning to go when the centurion spoke. "Stay a moment. There is something that greatly troubles me. Perhaps you two can help me. You say that I have been tolerant and sympathetic in my attitude toward the religious feelings of you Jews." Gaius saw a cloud cross Simon's bronzed bearded faced, but it was gone in the same instant. He sensed that Simon was on guard.

"Be not alarmed," he said. "I contemplate no harm to you or any of the Jews. But since you two are followers of the strange young rabbi who has been teaching in Galilee, I thought that perhaps through you I might be able to see him and talk with him. You see, I have a servant boy—"

"If it is the man Jesus of Nazareth of whom you speak"— Simon's tone betrayed his caution—"I have heard him teach in the synagogue and down by the lake. But I know not where he can be found, centurion, for he is said to be continually on the move, walking the streets of the cities and the byways of Galilee and even down to Jerusalem, and I know not how you could find—"

"Simon," said Gaius, "you fear that I am trying to trap you or the rabbi. The hate of Rome that you Jews always have, even though it may be submerged, makes you cautious. But I assure you that I mean no man any harm. In fact, my Roman friends charge that I have become more Jewish than Roman; they say that I am a follower of this young rabbi." He hesitated. "At any rate, I would like to know more of him."

"I believe you, centurion," said Simon, simply. He turned to John, as if for confirmation, and John nodded. "We are, indeed, followers of this young man of Nazareth. It wasn't of myself so much that I was thinking. But we would have no harm befall him. You see, we love that young man."

"I have heard," Gaius said, "that he has a tremendous capacity to draw his friends to him. I can see that this is true. How do you account for it? What do you make of this man?"

51

"Well, sir—" Simon cleared his throat, set down the fish basket. "That is the question that puzzles us. You have heard aright that he has a great power to attract men to him. Frankly, centurion, we don't understand him. There are some things we know, and then there are other things that puzzle us. Maybe as we continue to be with him and listen to his teachings we shall come to understand him. I cannot say. We have been with him only a short time. We do know that he is a most remarkable man. Is that not so, John?"

John nodded. "Yes," he said. "We have never before seen anyone like him."

"Simon," said Gaius, "I can see that you two are under his spell."

"Yes, centurion, you are right. He has a great power over all of us, especially when we are with him. It is very strange."

The centurion motioned to the bench. "Sit down, men. Stay a moment. I would hear more of this rabbi."

"We must be going too, centurion. We still have much work to do today. My brother Andrew and James will be wondering what has become of us."

"And the rabbi, where is he? Will he be waiting for you, too?"

"I don't exactly know where he is just now," Simon replied. "But he is in Capernaum, and probably down by the lakeside. He seems to enjoy the company of the fishermen and the other plain men who gather there. We'll see him tonight."

"But, being a holy man, he would not wish to consort with the common people, I should think, but would be attracted to the religious people, the group about the synagogue."

This time John spoke. "You are wrong, sir. And that's one of the things that puzzles us. Most rabbis do congregate about the synagogue with the people who dispute about the law. Of course, he does go to the synagogue, and he can dispute with the best of them about the law and the sayings of our ancient prophets of Israel. But he seems to prefer to be with the ordinary people, plain fishermen like us, and even tax collectors like Levi, who sell themselves to work for you Romans against their own people, and even the children. He's a great one to play with the children. And he isn't averse even to passing a word with a woman of the streets."

"It's strange that a rabbi would lower himself—"

"Ah, sir, but you do not understand," said Simon, interrupting. "He doesn't lower himself. He raises up the others. That's what the synagogue crowd can't get into their small heads. They insist that he contaminates himself by consorting with the poor and unfortunate who do not understand all the requirements of the law and wouldn't be in position to carry them out if they understood them. They say that when he talks to Levi, for instance, he pollutes himself. The Jews have a great many very strict rules, and the leaders of our religious affairs have come to put more importance upon carrying out these rules than upon the way you treat your neighbor and the way you worship God. The master doesn't go to much trouble to carry out all these ancient rituals, centurion. He doesn't put much emphasis upon such things as always washing your hands, as the Jewish law requires, before you break a bit of bread."

Simon paused, and a slow grin spread over his grizzled brown face. "You know, centurion," he said, "sometimes I've wondered if the master pays enough attention to our Jewish rules, concerning eating, for instance. You know"—and he lowered his voice— "I wouldn't be surprised some day to see him eating a catfish, or even an eel." Suddenly he was serious. "Don't misunderstand me, centurion. The master wouldn't eat a catfish if he thought that would be a temptation to us. But I don't believe he would consider it wrong—" he hesitated, as if trying to make his words more understandable "—down inside of himself. In other words, he looks deeper than the words of the law; he is concerned with the spirit, and he might hold that there would be nothing wrong in itself in eating even a catfish—"

"There's nothing better than a small catfish cooked quickly in a pot of boiling fat," Gaius interrupted. "It seems a shame that you Jews should always throw them back."

"Anything without scales we throw back. That is the law of the Jews." Quickly his round face broke into a grin. "But we have a sufficient choice left, centurion. This lake is filled with fish. I

53

doubt if there's as many kinds in the Great Sea. We have probably a dozen or more peculiar to the Sea of Galilee, and there's more than forty different kinds in it, all told, many of them belonging to the carp family. So, centurion, there's not likely a time will come when the master will have to eat a catfish or go hungry, and that's one thing the Temple crowd probably won't have to charge against him."

"He must stay in trouble with the strict Pharisees and Sadducees, the synagogue leaders—"

"Yes, they contend he's trying to destroy the law. But I think the reason they don't like him is really jealousy. He's getting such a strong hold on the common people."

"I suspect there's truth in what you say. But, tell me this. Most rabbis, I understand, are rather soft. They sit around and study the ancient laws or dispute among themselves some fine point of the law. But I've heard that your rabbi is a strong fellow. I saw him one day down by the shore, but it was at a distance. And I have had a few other glimpses of him. He appeared to me to be a strong, tough-muscled fellow."

"Strong!" Simon's big voice boomed. "Look at me, centurion." He thrust a powerful hairy arm from beneath his robe, revealing muscles that knotted under the deeply tanned skin. "I'm a pretty tough fellow myself. I'm still young, and I'm used to hard work. If you fish all day and half the night it will either make a strong man of you or kill you. Well, I'll tell you this. The master is a better man than I am. I don't know whether he's any stronger—I can pull a fish net with the best of them—but the master has more endurance, I'd wager my boat. He can walk all day—and if you tramp over these Galilee roads, centurion, you've done a day's work—and then he can fish all night. Many a day we've had to call on him to stop and let us rest." He nudged John. "Isn't that right?"

"Yes," John agreed. "There's nothing of the weakling about him."

"And still, I'd say he was a philosophical person primarily, wouldn't you two?"

"Yes, sir, he's principally interested in his teaching. But he's certainly no weakling physically." The younger Zebedee cleared his throat. "He seems to live closer to nature than the rest of us.

Not that we aren't outdoor fellows. But he seems to understand nature better somehow, and he gets more enjoyment out of it. He likes storms on the sea, seems to get pleasure out of the spray blowing across his face. He talks to us when we are tramping across the hills about the way the clouds look when the sun is setting, or as it is coming up out of the sea on mornings when we have been fishing all night. He notices the flowers and birds and trees. But people, centurion, they're his main interest. He even seems to get much enjoyment out of fellows like us."

"John, I thought you and Simon said you didn't understand him and were puzzled about him. It seems to me that you two understand him very well."

"Oh," Simon spoke up, "it wasn't those things that puzzle us. It's—" He hesitated. "Have you heard of the belief of the Jews that a Messiah would be sent by God to deliver his people? Do you know that story? It is an ancient belief of our people."

"Yes, I have heard the story. I am more interested in Jewish beliefs—your religious views, you know—than most Romans. I have made quite a study of Hebrew religious lore. Do you believe that this young rabbi is the Messiah, Simon?"

"I—I—we—" Simon, betraying his momentary confusion, looked quickly toward John. "Centurion, that is the question. We Jews have long looked for a deliverer. But we have always thought that he would be a powerful king and a great warrior who would drive out the Romans with his sword and set up a kingdom mightier even than our father David's. Maybe we have been looking for the wrong sort of Messiah. It may be that our deliverance will come not through the sword but through the strength of his teaching. I am just a fisherman, centurion. I am too quick to speak and too slow of thought. But this I do know; the master is of a different mold. He is one of us, yet he is different from us. He has the command of great power, and yet he steps aside to avoid crushing a worm in his path. Maybe after we have been with him longer we'll be able to answer your question. But this I know even now. I know that his way is the right way."

For a moment the centurion was silent. "Your demeanor proves your devotion to him. But tell me this, how did you happen to become one of his band?"

55

"I hardly know, centurion. It was shortly after he came to Capernaum from Nazareth. I had seen him, and I'd heard others speak of him. He was a follower of that fellow John who was exhorting the people down in the Jordan valley and baptizing them with water.

"Then one day we were busy with the nets down at the shore, my brother Andrew and I and Zebedee's boys. We usually fish together and help each other out with the nets when we get a big haul. Well, we were down there when he came walking along the beach. He came right up to us, and we got to talking."

"What did you talk about?"

"Well, centurion, I don't remember it all. Just ordinary talking, like a bunch of men would likely be saying to each other. Mostly about fishing. I remember he was interested in the boats. Looked them over closely. He said he was a carpenter and he seemed to be interested in the way the timbers were fitted. And he gave us a hand with the nets. That's when I noticed his muscles, and the way he handled himself."

"But how did you happen to join with him, Simon?"

"He got to talking of what he called his way, and of God. He called him 'the Father,' and he said he wanted to show the children of the earth the way this 'Father' had laid out for them to travel. And he talked about fishing and what success we were having, and after a while he asked us to help him to spread the news he was trying to bring to our Jewish brethren. 'Follow me,' he said, 'and I'll make you fishers of men.' Those are the very words he said, centurion. I'll never forget them. He has a way of saying things so that they stay in your mind. 'Fishers of men.' That's the way he put it, wasn't it, Zebedee?"

John nodded.

"That was a unique way of saying it, Simon. And what did you do?"

"We went with him."

"How about your boats and nets and the servants?"

Simon laughed. "We just up and left everything. Zebedee didn't like it when his boys left, eh, John, but he couldn't do anything about it." Simon's face showed his sincerity. "You know, centurion, if you once really get up close to the master, and look in his face, and hear him speak—well, sir, you'll never be the same again."

"It's amazing. He must be a man possessed of tremendous personal magnetism. How do you explain him?"

"I can't. I don't understand him. I'm just a fisherman. I'm not one of those men wise in the laws of our fathers. I've had little schooling, and I'm not what you'd call a religious man. But I do know that the master knows, sir, and that what he calls his way is the right way. It's—it's hard to explain. You see, I want to be on his side. And I am on his side."

He gestured with his big knotty hand. "Oh, I'm no holy man of the synagogue. And I'm not such a brave fellow either. I don't mind a little fighting, and I can usually look after myself with those fellows down along the beach. And if things start getting rough with him—and I have an idea the crowd down at Jerusalem, old Annas and that bunch of hypocrites who pretend to be fighting Rome but really are working with you Romans—" he paused, smiling "—I have an idea they won't like what he's teaching. Well, if things start getting bad, I may have to do some fighting. I'm his man. I can't get away from him. Once he gets a hold on you you'll never be able to get away from him." He picked up the basket. "We've got to be going, centurion. And I shouldn't have talked so much. That's my trouble. I'm always talking."

"Don't be afraid of talking with me," said Gaius. "But what of his mysterious power to heal? I was going to tell you about my young servant boy. He is grievously ill. He seems to be afflicted with a serious palsy. I was wondering if the rabbi—"

"He has great power to heal, if one but has faith in him."

"How does he do it, Simon? What is the source of his power?"

"He says it is the 'Father' working through him. He says all his strength is of the 'Father.' He seems at all times to be in close communication with this 'Father.' I do not know how it is. All I know is that he heals the sick, and lame people, and the blind, and the palsied. This servant boy, sir, is he a Jew?"

"No, he's a Greek, from Thracia."

"The master was sent to bring deliverance to the children of the household of Israel—"

"But, Simon, if—"

"I am not sure of these things, centurion," Simon hastily explained. "That is my understanding. But why do you not yourself approach the master—"

"But I am a Roman soldier, Simon. Would he permit me to approach him?"

"I have never seen him turn any man away, sir. And tonight—" He hesitated, looked over his shoulder.

"No one else listens, Simon," said Gaius. "You can speak freely to me."

"Tonight the master will be at my house. There will likely be a great throng, for they press him closely now that the word has gone out that he heals the sick. Could you not come to my house?"

"But, Simon, would not the motive be misinterpreted? Would I not make him fearful?"

"No man, sir, makes him fearful," John spoke up quickly. "He knows not fear."

"My friends, you are generous. I appreciate it. I have learned much from your talk. If there is a way—"

"I hope you can come, sir."

"And I thank you both for the fish. You have not entirely deserted your work to go with the rabbi?"

"Oh, no. We work all the harder. We came back to our nets that same day we left them. But now there's a difference. We aren't absorbed in fishing. You understand what I mean, sir? It's not the principal thing."

"I believe I understand. And with this new interest, it appears, you have become even better fishermen—of fishes, I mean."

"Maybe so, sir. But perhaps he has a hand in that too."

"How is that, Simon?"

"Well, these fish I am bringing you today—they're part of the biggest haul we ever made, and we've been fishing since we were boys. The other night we fished all night long and caught nothing. The fish weren't running. Then shortly after sunrise the master came walking along the beach. We were bringing the boats in to shore. He seemed in fine spirit, but we were glum. I suppose he noticed it." Simon set the basket down. "By the time we got the nets out on the beach to dry, the people started coming. You see, sir, he can never get away from them; they tread upon his heels."

"He must have a tremendous following," Gaius interrupted. "But go ahead."

"Yes, he does. And it is increasing every day. Well, sir, to get back to the story about the fish, the people were pressing so closely around him that he asked me to push my boat a little way out from the shore. We didn't raise the sails; we just shoved her out a short way. Then he stood up in the boat and talked with them. And when he had tired of speaking, he asked me to get my nets. 'We will do some fishing, Simon,' he said.

"'But master,' I said to him, 'we have been fishing all night long, and we are worn out. The fish aren't running.'"

"What did he say?"

"He just smiled and told me I had little faith. He often tells me that. 'You have been fishing in the wrong place, Simon,' he said. 'The fish are out there. Launch out where the water's deeper.'

"I was still half grumbling. 'Master,' I said to him again, 'I am tired. But nevertheless, if you insist, I'll go out there and cast down the nets.'"

"And you did?"

"Yes, and we caught the greatest haul of fish I ever saw. I called to John here and James, and they brought their boat over and helped with the nets. All of us tugged until we were almost exhausted, and the nets started breaking. In fact, centurion, the fish almost sank the boats before we could get them on the beach. Isn't it so, Zebedee?"

John smiled, nodded. "And what did the rabbi say?"

"Nothing, centurion. But he seemed to be greatly amused at our struggling with all those fish. He even helped us pull them in."

"That is remarkable. How do you explain it? Was he just a better fisherman and knew where the fish would be running, or did he put the fish out there?"

"I don't know. All I know is that we got the fish."

7

Simon's house sat behind a stone wall at the end of a narrow way that ran out to the cobblestone street pushing up the slope from the lakeside. The house was near the stretch of beach where Simon and the Zebedees dried their nets. At the foot of this street, where it joined the broader one that ran beside the waterfront, was the customs house in which Levi the tax collector received the tribute money.

Fish nets were spread along the wall to make them more easily handled in repairing them. The nets proclaimed by looks and odors that the house was the home of a fisherman. The house was old and long ago had settled into a drab complacency. Whitewash was peeling from its walls, and in many places the lime and sand binders between the stones had fallen from the joints.

On one side a giant fig tree completely filled the small space that separated Simon's house from a dwelling that appeared even more ancient and unappreciated, so much so that it was difficult when the figs ripened to push into this space and gather them, for the limbs and the thick leaves of the fig were almost a barricade between the tiny front yard and the court in the rear.

It was already night when Gaius neared the house. He had put off his centurion's uniform and was wearing a simple tunic that would be less noticed. But readily available should it be needed he carried a short dagger, for along the lakeside after nightfall prowled many desperate men who would slit a throat for a penny.

As Gaius approached this wall in front of Simon's house, he saw a throng that had pushed into a small front yard out as far as the wall and over to the great fig tree. Some men lounged against the wall, unmindful of the stench or not caring, and a few flickering lamps left on the wall by their owners who had thrust themselves nearer the doorway threw leaping, grotesque shadows.

Others were lost in the deep gloom of the gnarled and ancient olive tree at the other end of the house.

Just as the centurion reached the opening in the wall that gave entrance into the small front court, a man extricated himself from the crowd and came out into the narrow way in front of the wall.

"It's the same way in the back," he said. "The courtyard's full, too. I couldn't even get a glimpse of the rabbi." Gaius could not see the man's face, but there was defeat in his voice.

"But we can't give up now after we have brought him this far."

Gaius, looking in the direction of the new voice, saw another man, who in the shadows appeared to be a squat Jew. Then he caught sight of a dim form lying stretched at the man's feet. The man bent over the improvised bed.

"Don't lose heart, father," the man said. "We'll find a way to get you to him."

"Maybe you'd best take me home—" Gaius pushed nearer, strained his ears to hear the feeble voice. "I—I—it's no use."

"Father, you must not give up hope. They say that the rabbi demands faith."

"But I've waited so long. Could I but see him—but always the crowds—if I could walk, if I could get to him—" He had partially raised his head, but now he fell back, exhausted.

"Whom are you trying to see?' Gaius now asked.

"The rabbi who teaches and heals," said the man, as he straightened up. "But they press about him so closely that we cannot get my father to him."

"But what would this rabbi do were you to get your father before him?"

"Do you not know of the great rabbi of Galilee, have you not heard them speak of the wonders?" The man leaned forward, peered into the centurion's face. "You are a Roman soldier?"

"Yes, but don't be alarmed. I too would see this strange rabbi."

"To mock him? Perhaps to carry him a prisoner before your centurion?"

"No," said Gaius. "I would do him no harm. Nor would the centurion."

"That is true, Zadok," said the other man. "Have you not heard how the centurion is a friend of the Jews of Capernaum and helped them build the new synagogue?"

"I have also heard it said that one should never trust a Roman."

Gaius ignored the hostile manner. "Perhaps I could help you get the sick man into the house. Maybe we can go in through the door that must open into the courtyard in the rear."

"The courtyard itself is filled—"

"There is but one way," said the first man. "I have been back there. One could not even get to the door for the great press. But I walked up the stairs that lead to the top of the house, and I caught a glimpse of the throng inside. It must be that he is seated somewhere in their midst. I could see them through the lattice."

"I'll help you make a way," said Gaius. "Bring him and follow me."

The roof was low, and after they had pushed through the crowd to the bottom of the steps, it was not difficult to get the man up the stairway.

"What are you going to do now?" Gaius asked, when they had set the man down.

"If we could get the rabbi to come up to the roof—"

"But that he could not do," the man on the mat said, and his voice was weak and despairing. "He is down there disputing with the scribes. He will have no time for this poor outcast son of Israel. He will never even see me up here."

"Perhaps we could let him down into the presence of the rabbi," said Gaius. "The roof is not high. And with helping hands below—"

"But we would not dare," said the son of the afflicted man. "This is not our house, and we have no money with which to repay the damage—"

"Simon would not hold you to paying for such a trifle—"

"Then you know Simon, soldier?"

"Yes, I have bought fish of him. He is a generous man. And he is one of the rabbi's followers."

"It is the only way, indeed. While I pull away a section of the

62

lattice, Zadok, you step down and bring two others to help us lower him."

The latticework had been laid above an open-air court between the two short wings of the house, as a defense against the hot sunshine, and by the time Zadok had returned with two men a section large enough to admit the afflicted man had been removed.

Gaius stood back in the shadows and with straining eye sought out the rabbi. After a moment he saw him, for the people massed below were watching him so intently that none appeared to notice what was happening on the roof. The rabbi, his serious, intense expression heightened by the flickering light of the lamps, was talking calmly, not passionately, and Gaius could distinguish only an occasional word. And then the vision was obscured entirely by the bed and the afflicted man upon it, for they were lowering it into the opening, and down below arms were being lifted to take the burden.

Gently, Gaius could see from the shadows that framed the opening, they set him down, and the rabbi stopped speaking, and the throng was still, and Gaius felt that the entire assembly around the rabbi had all but ceased to breathe.

And now the afflicted man, gaunt and with heavy beard that seemed to emphasize the impoverished look of his sparse frame, raised a skinny arm and twisted himself around to face the rabbi. "Oh, master," he said, and his voice was high and shrill and frightened, like the cry of a small child lost from his mother, "Oh, master, help me. Long have I sought you, but always the great press of the throng has kept me from you. Oh, master, help me! Help me!"

He tried to hold up his head, but he had not the strength, and he fell back, his frame shook, and his fingers opened and closed, his legs twitched and one leg drew up spasmodically, he lay upon his back, and his eyes, glittering in the frame of his heavy beard, stared upward into the hole through which he had been let down.

Gaius, watching intently from above, saw the rabbi raise his own eyes to the opening, and for an instant, from the darkness of the night outside the small covered court, he found himself looking deep into the warm eyes of the young rabbi. He was transfixed, powerless, gripped by unseen mighty arms.

But only for an instant. The rabbi was looking now at the other faces peering down from the opening in the roof, faces framed in the light that came up to them. He smiled. "What faith, what great faith." He seemed to be talking to himself.

And then his eyes dropped quickly, and he stood up and walked the few steps to the palsied man. Gaius, venturing nearer to the opening, saw him smiling encouragingly upon the afflicted man. And the man smiled too, though it was a twisted, pained smile, and as he looked upon the young rabbi standing calmly above him he seemed to grow quiet, his limbs relaxed and he was still.

The rabbi bent down and with his right hand stroked gently the forehead of the afflicted man. "Great, too, is your faith. Be of good cheer, for your sins are forgiven."

He had hardly spoken before a raucous babbling of voices broke the spell. From one side of the small courtyard, where a group had huddled as in an effort to keep themselves apart from the crowd, an erect, proud Jew spoke. "But, rabbi," he said, "how do you say, 'Your sins are forgiven,' when only God can forgive sins?"

"Who is he?" Gaius whispered to the man nearest him.

"I don't know his name, but he is a scribe," said the man. "That little group over there is made up of Pharisees and scribes who have come forth tonight to dispute with him."

"Blasphemy!" A short middle-aged Jew with a spiked beard pointed a pudgy finger. "He ascribes to himself the powers of God."

"Yes," said another in the group. "We have heard it. He takes to himself power to forgive sins." He faced the rabbi, gestured with trembling hand. "How do you say, rabbi, that you have the authority to forgive sins?"

The babbling among the small band was increasing now, and heads were bobbing and hands were gesturing.

The rabbi stood calmly regarding them, a half-smile, as of sorrow mixed with scorn, upon his bronzed face. And as he looked, their raucous cacklings and babblings ceased, and they stood sullenly confronting him.

"Which is easier to say," he said calmly but in a resonant voice that came clear and strong to Gaius and the others on the roof, "'Your sins be forgiven,' or, 'Take up your bed and walk'?"

There was a hush that stopped every movement, that transfixed those on the rooftop to the spot where they stood. The eyes of the young rabbi swept the assembled throng, looked upward to the newly made opening in the roof, came to settle upon the group of Pharisees and scribes.

"But that you may know that the Son of Man has power on earth to forgive sins"—Gaius sensed a new timbre in his voice, a resonant quality that bespoke defiance and challenge and power and great purpose—"I say to you—" he had turned and was looking down upon the paralytic "—arise, and take up your mat, and return to your house." As the rabbi spoke the command, his voice gained a quality of power and something else—a tone of encouragement, of warmth, of understanding and great love.

"Master—" The old man was looking up appealingly into the face of the rabbi. Slowly he lifted his head, pulled an unsteady arm forward, the palm of the hand dragging along the mat beside his gaunt frame, half turned on his left side, and breathing heavily, raised his body into a sitting position on the mat.

Jesus reached down, his encouraging bright eyes still upon him, took the man's extended hand, helped him to his feet, steadied him. "Now pick up your bed, my brother, and go home."

Slowly the man bent down, grasped the bedding in his thin fingers, and, clutching it up, started walking. The crowd fell back before him as though it had seen a ghost.

"Glory! Praise God!" A man seated in a corner leaped to his feet, shouting. "Praise God!"

Another man jumped into the little cleared space beneath the opening. "Praise God!" He ran behind the man walking toward the doorway, the bed still clutched in his arms. "Wondrous strange things have we seen this day!"

Behind him a woman was screaming, and another. At the door the man who had been afflicted turned. Holding the bed with his left hand, he thrust his right arm aloft. "Glóry be to God!" he shouted. "I walk, I walk! Many years I have lain upon this bed. Now I carry it. Oh, master, master." He held out his arm toward the smiling Jesus. "I thank you! I walk! I walk!" The crowd had opened a way, and he stepped out into the night.

But Gaius had not seen him depart, for he was stumbling down the steps that led from the roof of Simon's house, down again to the solid brown earth, to the darkness of the night now come swiftly out of the east. Light streamed from the doorway through which the people now were surging, and through the opening he could hear the singing and shouting.

But the light and the people and the shouting, all these were ephemeral, transient, unreal. As he made his way down the cobblestone street through the cool sweet darkness, already little remained to him now of this strange experience. Yet he could not lose the vision of the young rabbi looking with compassion upon a poor wretch, and of the lame man casting aside forever the palsy that had bound him.

8

Oh, sir, I am sorry!" Tullus put down his broadsword. "I didn't mean to strike you."

Marcus laughed. "It was a neat thrust, Tullus. But you didn't touch me."

"Yes, I did, sir. And I fear it's a rather bad cut. See—" he pointed to his sword "—there's blood on the blade. And your shoulder." He went up to Marcus, examined the wound high on the left arm near the shoulder, from which the blood was already running freely. "Hold the cut place together while I go for a basin of water, and I'll bandage it. I do hope, sir, that it will not interfere with your journey to Alexandria."

Marcus twisted his left arm around to see the wound. "It is cut, all right, and a pretty neat slice, at that. Strange, I didn't feel it, Tullus." He pinched the gaping flesh together. "And I don't feel it now."

In a moment Tullus was back and with fast fingers was probing into the wound with a swab he had brought. "I'm sorry, sir, I know this is painful, but I must see that the wound is cleansed."

"On the contrary, Tullus, I don't feel a thing. If I did, I'd be flinching."

"It's only your Roman courage, sir. I understand." He smiled. "You are an able actor, sir."

"No, Tullus, I'm not acting. I really feel nothing."

"That is strange, sir. I should think it would be quite painful. I don't understand why it doesn't hurt. Perhaps it was the quickness of the thrust, or maybe you haven't recovered from the shock. But it will likely be painful when the feeling returns. I am very sorry, sir. I should have been more careful."

Marcus laughed. "I should have been more careful, Tullus. You are a better swordsman than I. But don't let this worry you. If you'll tie up the cut now, it will soon mend. It's a small place, and it doesn't hurt. Forget it."

When Marcus removed the bandage two days later the cut was almost healed, but in bathing the area around the slash he noticed a small grayish ring. *Discoloration from the wound*, he said to himself, as he felt gingerly of the place. *Hmmm. Still no feeling. That is strange*. He finished his bath, put on fresh clothing. "I'm lucky at that," he said aloud. "Might have been a nasty slash. But I don't understand about the loss of feeling."

Nor could Tullus, he declared, when Marcus summoned the overseer to discuss with him plans for the journey to Alexandria. "It does seem very strange, sir. It seems that by now it would be painful. I really cannot understand it. And that color—" He examined the spot. "Usually such spots get dark brown and then of a bluish cast, if they are bruises. But there is no reason that it should be bruised. It was not a heavy blow. It was a clean, quick cut."

"Well, anyway, Tullus, it doesn't hurt."

But the strange circle of apparently deadened flesh worried Marcus, and after the cut had healed he almost reopened it in his scrubbing of the spot in an effort to restore feeling. And when two weeks later as his vessel was nearing Alexandria while having his morning's cold bath he discovered another spot farther down on his arm, he was frankly puzzled.

On his dresser lay a writing instrument. He picked it up, tapped the area within the newly discovered ring of grayish flesh. There was no feeling. He tapped the upper ring. The same thing. He pushed harder. But no feeling. He jabbed the instrument into the skin. There was no sensation whatsoever. He might as well have been sticking the instrument into a block of soft wood.

On his return to Tyre he said nothing to Tullus about his discovery of the new spot.

9

Unless my duty interferes, Simon, I'll be there. The main reason I want to go is to get a nearer view of your rabbi. The other night at your house I was so amazed that I ran away almost before I realized what I was doing, and before I had ventured to ask his aid for my servant boy. The man has a strange fascination—"

"That's the way he affects many people, centurion," Simon said. "But perhaps at the feast you will have a better opportunity to speak with him—that is, if Levi doesn't require all his time."

"You don't have much faith in Levi, do you?"

"Well, centurion, I may be wrong. I've been wrong before. But that's the way I feel about him. I—" He stopped abruptly. "I talk too much, centurion. Here I am talking freely to a Roman soldier, and if there's anything in the world I hate, it's Rome."

"But you don't hate me, Simon. What you hate is Rome's domination; you hate the idea of your country's being subject to Rome, but you don't hate any particular Roman. Isn't that a fact?"

"I don't know, centurion. I hate many things. I hate those hypocritical Pharisees and scribes who are always talking of their goodness. And the Sadducees are no better. I put them all in the same boat, and if I could, I'd dump the whole lot of them into the Great Sea. I hate a traitor, and Levi has been a traitor for years, because he has been robbing his countrymen to gather taxes for the Romans, and he has been dipping his hand pretty deep into the treasury. I'd swear to that. In fact, he admits it. And yet the master makes him a member of his band. I believe it was a mistake, centurion. That fellow is probably figuring on selling him out to the Romans."

"What makes you think that, Simon?"

"Well, sir, he has been collecting taxes a long time. He's deep in his devilment. I don't believe a man changes like that overnight. Yet he's now one of our group, and he's giving the feast tonight in honor of the master and to celebrate his sudden forsaking of his job with the Romans. So he says, anyway."

"How did it happen, Simon, this sudden reversal of his whole way of living? Were you with the rabbi when it happened?"

'Yes, centurion, I saw it all. We were walking along the road beside the lake. When we got opposite the customs house I saw the master raise his hand in greeting, and then I looked through the office window and there was Levi bowing and smirking and rubbing his hands as if he had just robbed a rich widow. I didn't speak to him. I despise these Rome-lovers. But what do you suppose the master did?"

"What?"

"He walked over to the window and motioned to Levi. 'You've had enough of this way of living, haven't you?' he asked him.

"'Yes, rabbi,' Levi answered. 'How did you know?'

"'I have been watching you,' the master said.

"'What shall I do, rabbi?' he asked.

"'Leave it,' said the master. 'Come with me.'"

"What did Levi do?" Gaius asked.

"He had been accepting the tax on a boatload of fish. He put the money in the money-box. 'Boys,' he said to his two helpers, 'you take charge of the office. You understand how it operates. I'm through.'"

"Did he really quit?"

"Yes, sir, he walked right out with us. He hasn't been back. But I have a feeling that sooner or later he will go back to his job with the Romans."

"Maybe not, Simon. What happened after he left the customs house?"

"He has been with us ever since. It's still new with him. When the excitement wears off, he'll be wanting his old job back." He shrugged his shoulders. "Anyway, centurion, he's still excited, and tonight he's giving the biggest feast Capernaum has seen in a long time. He can do it, too. He's rich with money he has wrung out of Jews for the Romans but let stick to his own hands."

"Nevertheless, his food and wine will probably be of the best and will taste as good as though it were earned by selling fish, eh, Simon?" Gaius laughed. "At any rate, I hope I can come. Tell Levi I thank him, and I hope I may have an opportunity to speak to the rabbi about Andreas. I—I wonder, Simon. Does your rabbi require that all his followers be Jews?"

"I—I suppose so, centurion." His round grizzled face lighted quickly. "But don't hesitate to ask him about the boy. I understand how you feel. Many people hesitate. And you are a Roman. But, sir"—his face brightened even more—"have no fear of him. He is so understanding. And if you'd like, I'll be glad to speak to him also of the boy."

"Would you, Simon? It might be that he could—that he would —restore the boy. I—I understand so little of him and his ways."

"None of us, centurion, understands him too well."

Nor did the memorable happenings that evening add to the centurion's understanding of the strange young rabbi whom he had seen the other night at Simon's house.

Unforseen duties kept Gaius at his post longer than he had anticipated, and the narrow cobblestone street on which Levi's great house stood was a darkened canyon when he arrived at the entrance gate in the wall. The yellow flame from an oil lamp hanging above the doorway lighted the street a few paces in each direction. Its light flickered along the unbroken first story wall and the underside of the balcony that extended above the street.

Gaius had met the tax collector, but their few contacts had been official, and he had never been to his house. As he paused at the door in the wall he wondered if he would find it barred, for he was late and the feast must already be underway. But before he could try the latch, the heavy door opened and a servant stepped into the semicircle of light.

"Enter, centurion," he said. "The master is expecting you, and he bade me await you here and conduct you to the balcony where the feast is now in progress."

Gaius nodded, stepped through the opening in the stone wall. "Business detained me longer than I had foreseen," he said. "I am sorry I am late." He hesitated. "Tell me," he said, after a moment, "is the young rabbi who lately has been teaching in Capernaum—is he attending the feast tonight?"

The servant smiled. "He is the honored guest, sir," he said.

They walked several paces through a vaulted stone passageway lighted by a lamp supported on a wall bracket. Then they entered a large, open court in the center of which was a pool enclosed within a low parapet and surrounded by green plants and flowers of gorgeous colors. They turned left to skirt the pool and walk along a colonnaded terrace that dropped off to a lower and much larger courtyard.

The servant, sensing that the centurion had caught the pungent, musty odor of hay and grain and stabled animals, pointed to his right with a quick, sweeping gesture. "Over there, sir, is the service area. From here onward this wall screens that section from the living quarters."

The wall, Gaius could see, ran out at right angles from the colonnaded walkway they were moving along toward the swelling sound of feasting, and as they passed the end of the wall the centurion saw by the light of the suspended lamps a sunken garden, perhaps four feet below the terrace upon which they were walking and embracing at least a half acre. In the center stood a large fountain, and walkways ran from the center in a symmetrical design. Gaius admired the evergreen shrubs and beds of gay flowers that filled the plots bordering the walkways.

"Your master is a very rich man, is he not?" He swept his arm outward in an embracing gesture.

"One of the richest in Capernaum, sir," the man replied. "But since he fell in with this rabbi he has been giving away money very freely—restoring it, he calls it—and this feast will likewise cost him many a shekel. I know not how long he will remain rich."

By now they had come near the end of the passageway and through the colonnades had a clear view of the great throng feasting on the wide terrace overlooking the garden.

"You can see for yourself, sir," said the servant, "that half Capernaum must be here tonight."

"Levi has invited with a lavish hand," Gaius agreed.

"And it's a mixed crowd if I ever saw one, sir. Everybody's here—proprietors of shops, fishermen, farm people, vineyard dressers, shepherds, magistrates, rubbing shoulders too with Pharisees and Sadducees and scribes, the washed with the unwashed, and now a Roman soldier—pardon me, sir, I meant no offense."

"I understand. Go ahead."

"Thank you, sir. Yes, and even women of the street. But the master would invite everybody. And even those who were not invited to the feast were admitted to stand about and look on and listen to the talk. Most of them came in the hope of hearing that young rabbi." He paused. "We go up these steps, sir, and turn to the right. The master has reserved for you a place at the head of the table, near him and the rabbi. I shall conduct you to it."

They were crossing the great broad terrace toward the long table that stretched almost the length of it. Gaius stopped. "No, I thank you, and I appreciate your master's thoughtfulness. But I am late, and I would not wish to disturb him. He is busy entertaining the rabbi. I shall sit here, where I can watch without being noticed. I'd prefer it that way."

"But, sir—" The servant showed his embarrassment. "My master bade me fetch you—"

"That's all right," Gaius assured him. "I shall explain it to your master. He will understand."

"Then, sir, " the servant said, quickly, "I shall make it my task to see that you are well served."

From the place where he sat Gaius could look directly into the face of the rabbi, who appeared to be enjoying the food Levi had spread so lavishly upon the long table. "Perhaps he doesn't often have a chance at such a wealth of food," Gaius said to himself. "He probably lives on coarse fare."

But the company seemed to be more stimulating to the rabbi even than the food, and it was quickly evident to Gaius that the rabbi was the center of the crowd's interest. Those who were eating and drinking, as well as the uninvited group that had thronged into Levi's great establishment to watch the merrymaking, were watching him and listening to catch any word he might say. And Jesus, too, apparently was relishing the fact that he was the figure upon which the crowd's regard and affection seemed to be centering.

His dark face, deeply tanned by the Galilean sun, was lighted with an inner happiness, and when he spoke to Levi, seated beside him, his words seemed charged with a new enthusiasm and warmed with an almost womanly tenderness.

He is a strange man, Gaius said to himself, though the words never reached his lips. *He is a Jew, and not only a Jew but a rabbi. And here he is sitting beside a hated tax collector, a renegade Jew who has become rich robbing his countrymen, sitting beside him as his honored guest, and all about him are Jews who do not observe the strict rituals of their race, and even hated publicans, and women of the streets—and a Roman soldier. And he seems to be immensely happy in doing it.*

But not all those at the feast, and especially among the groups standing about the table, the centurion soon observed, were following with approval the behavior and conversation of the Galilean. Some paces away, knotted about one of the entrances that opened upon the terrace, a group of scowling Pharisees stood apart from the others as if to avoid the contamination of contact with those who through ignorance or indifference or inability might not be conforming strictly to the letter of the Jewish law. These men, Gaius realized, had come to spy upon Jesus, to criticize and find fault and mock him.

Hardly had he noticed them before one old Pharisee, whose voice and manner were as unctuous as his heavily anointed and braided long beard, pointed a skinny forefinger at one of the men at the table, a bronzed young man Gaius supposed to be a follower of the rabbi. "Why does your master," he asked in a loud voice so that the rabbi himself would hear him, "sit down to eat and drink with publicans and sinners?"

It was a pointed question, Gaius realized, and he wondered what the rabbi's man would say. Nor did the fellow answer, for almost before he had time to frame a reply, the Galilean himself turned to the Pharisee.

"A man who is well does not need a physician," said the rabbi, smiling, "but those who need him are the sick. And the duty of the physician is to the sick, not the well." He reminded them that one of Israel's ancient prophets had written that God had said that he desired mercy and not sacrifices, and the knowledge of God more than burnt offerings, and then he raised his arm and pointed directly at the small group about the Pharisee. "Go you and learn what this means," he told them.

The frowning Pharisees, proud in their knowledge of Jewish

law and tradition, said nothing, but their heavy scowls showed the centurion that the strong words of the young Nazarene had deeply offended them.

And then, from behind Gaius, another voice spoke, and turning quickly, he saw the man. In the sickly yellow light that fell upon him from the lamp almost above his head the fellow's matted coarse black hair falling over face and shoulders gaunt and shrunken and burnt to the color of an old chariot harness showed him to be an ascetic from the lost wastes of the wilderness. With him were several much like him.

"We are followers of the Prophet John," the man said. "He taught in the wilderness and baptized many in the waters of the Jordan in the days before Herod imprisoned him in the fortress Machaerus beyond the Dead Sea. He taught us to fast and to avoid the pampering of the appetite. And so do yonder Pharisees—" he raised a skinny forearm to point "—and so the law strictly teaches. How is it then that you, and your rabbi there whom you profess to follow, do not obey this law but instead you give yourselves over to eating and drinking and much stuffing of stomachs, and unrestrained merriment?"

Once more the young rabbi accepted the challenge, made ostensibly to those in his immediate group. Smilingly he turned to the tall gaunt fellow. "A worthy prophet is John," he said. "But John does not teach that he is the bridegroom but rather calls himself the friend of the bridegroom who stands with him and rejoices to hear him speak. And if this be true, then can the followers of the bridegroom mourn, as long as the bridegroom is with them?"

Gaius saw in the light of the lamps that the rabbi was smiling as he spoke to the gaunt and hungry followers of imprisoned John. But, as the centurion watched the rabbi's face, he saw a cloud envelop it, and the words of Jesus were almost a sigh as he added: "But the days will come when the bridegroom shall be taken away from them, and then they shall fast."

Those words, the centurion said to himself, *seem to prophesy his death.*

The words of the rabbi continued to ring in his inner consciousness throughout the feasting, and they echoed in his ears as he walked silently through the streets of Capernaum when the feast had ended. Once again he had slipped from the presence of the young Nazarene without approaching him in behalf of the ailing Andreas.

10

Pontius Pilate set down his wine goblet and fixed his cold gray eyes upon Marcus. "The Tribune Lucius Mallius here—" he nodded his round, closely cropped head in the direction of the tribune "—tells me, sir, that you are a good friend of the prefect Sejanus."

"I know the prefect, procurator, but not too well. It is my father who is his special friend."

Pilate considered a moment. "That should be just as well for my purpose." He smiled, but coldly. "I have asked you to come for two principal reasons. In the first place, I have heard from several sources that you manufacture excellent glassware and also fine woolen textiles. I thought perhaps that I might equip our table with new glassware and purchase a quantity of your purple to be made into wearing apparel. My wife bears with great patience our assignment out here, but she misses tremendously the life of Rome, and this palace, though sumptuous, is fitted out in ill taste. I would like to purchase a sizable order and surprise her with it as a gift on her approaching birthday." He shrugged a shoulder, gestured with white hands.

"But that is hardly a reason to be bringing you to Caesarea. I could have sent a servant to make the purchases and not disturbed you." Hastily he sipped his wine, set down the goblet. "What I wished to discuss with you, sir, is the situation here in Palestine. I am a soldier, and I speak bluntly. Frankly, after having talked with Lucius of your friendship with Sejanus and the great influence of Senator Marcus Calpurnius over him, I came to the conclusion that I might be able to obtain your aid, and through you your father's, in reaching the ear of Sejanus. You see, I am anxious to be transferred from Palestine. I want another assignment."

"But, sir, you are procurator of Judea. It's an important post and one of great honor."

"Yes, but it is one in which there is no peace. One has no time to relax. Every day there is some new annoyance. Palestine is in a continual foment. I firmly believe there's no more restless place in all the empire." He picked up his goblet, sipped the wine again, licked his red lips. "It's the Jews. They are the most obstinate people I have ever seen. Every turn you make in trying to administer the affairs of this rebellious country you run counter to some regulation of their religion. I have never understood their religion, and may the gods protect me from trying to understand it. I would like to get completely away from it." He thudded his fist on the table before him and sent the wine climbing the sides of the tall goblet. "I tell you, sir, I'd rather be a centurion in Spain or Gaul or even Britannia than procurator in Judea. This is one ungovernable race of people, these Jews!"

"Procurator"—Marcus was smiling—"I'll confess that I agree with you. I have no patience with the Jews. They are a smelly, fussy, loud people whose every contact with me annoys me. I am happy that we have comparatively few of them in Tyre. All I want with them is to make all the money I can dealing with them; and you must keep your wits about you if you want to do that, I have found."

"Yes," said Pilate, "they are shrewd traders. They can drive a hard bargain. They make it as difficult as possible for all Romans because they resent being subject to us. They see an affront to them and their jealous god—they have only one god, as you doubtless know"—Marcus nodded—"in everything we do."

Pilate drummed nervously with ringed fingers. "When I came out here three years ago, I marched my legionnaires into Jerusalem. It was one of their feast days, and I thought it would be an excellent time to impress upon them the power of Rome. I contemplated no trouble and meant them no harm. But because we marched with our banners unsheathed they made a tremendous issue of it. They have a religious law that they can display no graven images, and they argued that the eagles on our banners and the likenesses of the emperor constituted graven images. They tried to climb the walls of the Antonia fortress to pull down the banners, and in the fighting many of them were killed. Later when I came back to Caesarea they sent hundreds here to protest. When

I threatened to have them killed if they did not desist and return peaceably to Jerusalem, the insolent Jews fell to the ground, laid their necks bare and declared they would rather die than permit their god to be insulted by those banners. They are a stubborn, contentious people."

"What did you do then, sir?"

"I couldn't kill men lying on the ground defenseless."

"They knew that, procurator," Marcus smiled. "They are clever as well as contentious."

"Yes, but they are also fanatics. They would have suffered my soldiers to hack off their heads before they would have relented—many of them would have, I'm confident. You see,"—Pilate's expression revealed his earnestness—"their religion is bound up with their civil affairs to such an extent that one who is not a Jew finds it impossible to keep the two separate. They are forever protesting that I am violating some strictly religious tenet when I have nothing of the sort in mind. If they are opposed to some purely civil action that I may be inaugurating, they take the position that I am doing something that violates their religious code. The emperor, they know, wishes them not to be disturbed in the carrying on of their purely religious functions, so upon every possible occasion they raise a great commotion in the hope that the noise will get back to the emperor and that he will intervene. It keeps me continually disturbed, and I am sick of it. I long to be relieved of this post in Palestine. I would wash my hands of everything to do with the Jews."

"Procurator," said Marcus, "perhaps were the matter brought to the attention of Sejanus, along with an appropriate present—"

Pontius Pilate laughed, but without warmth. "I see that you know the emperor's chief minister very well," he observed. "I have not been neglectful in that respect. Perhaps I have been too generous. I have required a number of the richer synagogues to share their golden plate with me—" he smiled "—and I in turn have shared the plate with the emperor's minister, although I sold much of it and with the funds I have constructed aqueducts and other public works urgently needed by the Jews. Perhaps the prefect would like for such gifts to continue to arrive in Rome. But were I in some other post I could do better. And, on the other hand, I understand that the emperor is invariably angered when a report reaches him on Capri that the Jews are again in ferment, and that perhaps he may hold me responsible."

"I can see how the situation could be rather trying, procurator."

"It is. I am an exile. I have few friends, and I am surrounded by enemies. Nothing I do pleases the Jews, and even Herod is critical. I get reports that the tetrarch spreads poison about me and the Roman administration generally. Little I can do about it, however, for I would not dare risk an open rupture with Herod. He has the ear of Sejanus and likewise the emperor. His father, I have been told, was a great favorite with Augustus. The Herods seem to be well established. And yet three-fourths of the sedition against Rome arises in Herod's own tetrarchy, Galilee. Of all the Jews, the Galileans are the greatest troublemakers. They even seem to take great delight in fighting with other Jews, as well as the Samaritans, with whom I am continuously having trouble. And Herod resents the slightest interference in the affairs of his tetrarchy. That, perhaps, emboldens the Galileans all the more. I would like to take my legions into Galilee and clean out that whole rebellious nest, but Rome would not approve, I'm convinced. I probably haven't been discreet enough as it is.

"You see why I am anxious to be transferred. I am positively sick of contending with these Jews." He arose, and he straightened his toga. "Should an occasion arise in which you might get a word to Sejanus, or even the emperor, I would appreciate your aid."

"I shall be glad to do what I can," said Marcus. "Perhaps through my father I might be able to have your views receive a sympathetic hearing."

A short while later he took his leave of the procurator. Lucius went with him to the harbor, where he was to catch the boat going northward to Tyre.

"It is a great harbor," said Lucius, "one of the finest in the empire, no doubt."

"Yes," agreed Marcus. "It was built by Herod the Great, father of Herod Antipas, you know. Old Herod spent tremendous sums on building this town and the harbor as a gesture to please Augustus, for whom he named the place. It seems"—he changed his tone to one of mild inquiry—"that Pontius Pilate should find something of interest in all Palestine, doesn't it? But he is really anxious to get away, isn't he?"

"Yes," agreed the tribune, "of all the Romans out here, he appears to hate the Jews most. He certainly is no Gaius. By the way, how is the centurion?"

"I haven't heard from him recently," said Marcus. "I suppose he is too busy going to the synagogue to send me a message."

Lucius laughed. "And have you had any news of the strange rabbi, the faith healer of Galilee?"

"Only indirectly," Marcus replied. "It seems that his fame is spreading. It's a wonder Pilate didn't speak of him. One of these days, and it won't be long, I suspect, Pilate will also have him to contend with."

11

Andreas, you must try to go to sleep and get some rest. That will help you." Gaius dipped the cloth into the bowl of water, wrung it out, spread it across the boy's burning forehead, stood looking down upon the thin, jerking form. The boy's fingers were opening and closing, his legs twitched, he twisted his head sideways grotesquely. His eyes were shut, but the lids seemed to be clamping the eyeballs deeper into his burning face. His lips moved, but they made no sound.

Gaius bent over the boy. "Andreas, listen to me," he said with sudden resolution. "I am going to get help. I know a man who can help you. When I find him, I'll bring him with me."

The boy's eyes opened. For an instant the quivering lids were still, for the moment he forced his twitching lips to frame the words, "The rabbi?"

"Yes, Andreas, I shall find him. He is a good man. He will come."

The boy's anguished features seemed to relax. "If he would but come—"

"He will come to see you, my boy. Just you wait, and try to rest." Gaius spoke quickly to a servant standing by. "Watch him carefully," he said, "until I come back. I am going in search of the rabbi of Galilee."

Nor was it difficult to find him, so great had his fame become in Capernaum and throughout all Galilee. "He went by this door only this morning," a tailor sitting cross-legged on his bench told him when he inquired if he had seen the rabbi. "A multitude was following. I would have gone too had I not promised this coat for a wedding tomorrow. He has many followers." He suddenly grew cautious. "Are you not the centurion who helped them build the new synagogue?"

"Yes," said Gaius. "I intend him no harm. In fact, I would beg of him aid for my ailing servant boy."

The man nodded, pointed with his needle. "He was going that way. I suspect he went out to the hillside, or else down to the lake. But anyone can tell you, sir. His every movement nowadays is common knowledge."

"They have gone out to the hill beyond the gates," said a man he encountered down the street. "A great throng is with him. Such a spell he casts over them that they will all stay there as long as he is willing to talk to them."

So after much walking Gaius came to the foot of the rounded hill and slipped almost unnoticed into the throng that had come out with the rabbi. Unobtrusively he pushed forward until he could distinguish the words the rabbi was saying.

Jesus stood upon a small smooth boulder that thrust outward through the rocky hillside to raise him somewhat above the crowd. His robe, now colored with a fine dust from the parched roads he had been traveling, was thrown back to expose his bronzed chest beneath the straight rounded stem of his neck. His brown reddish hair, which behind fell down to his shoulders in soft curls and above his ears was brushed back from the temples, was damp with perspiration and glinted in the bright sunlight. Perspiration creased his forehead and ran down his cheeks to drip from the twin points of his double-spiked beard.

From time to time to emphasize his words he raised his arm to gesture, and his robe fell back from his naked brown arm to reveal the smooth swell of the muscles.

"Simon was right," Gaius said to himself. "The rabbi is no weakling." Then he caught sight of Simon and the younger Zebedee in the little group that pressed closely about the rabbi. He edged nearer the rabbi, impelled by an urge to hear him better and driven by his anxiety because of the stricken Andreas, and yet fearful that he might approach too near.

Another voice was speaking now. Gaius peeked from behind the broad back of a short, swarthy Jew. Down the slope a few feet from the rabbi and off to his right stood a tall, haughty Jew, a robe of finest texture wrapped closely about him as if to shield him from the contamination of the sweating multitude. Another Pharisee, Gaius saw. They were always heckling the rabbi. This one evidently had been questioning him about some interpretation of the Jewish law. He had finished speaking just as Gaius had located him in the throng, and now he stood with arms folded, a cold smile upon his sneering face.

Jesus evidently had been listening calmly as the Pharisee had framed his question. Now he spoke, and his voice was unruffled. "You are wrong, my brother," he said to the man. "You do not interpret my words aright." He was speaking gently, in the plain Aramaic of the Galilean countryside. "Think not that I come to destroy the law, or the prophets; I have not come to destroy, but to fulfill. For I say to you truthfully that as long as the heaven and the earth endure the law likewise will endure and not one jot or tittle shall be taken from it until it has all been fulfilled."

Gaius, leaning forward to hear every word, found himself intrigued with the words and the tone and the gentle warm smile of the rabbi, standing there on the small boulder with the perspiration streaming down his face. The law, the rabbi went on to say, was not a cold inanimate thing upon a table of stone or a sheet of papyrus; the law was a living, breathing way of life that was meant to lead man to his Father, and it was not so much the word of the law that was important as it was the spirit. Men should strive to teach and show other men the way of the law and to uphold it. "Whosoever therefore shall break one of the least commandments," he went on, "and shall by his example teach other men to do so, shall be called the least in the kingdom of heaven; but whosoever shall do and teach them, the same shall be called great in the kingdom of heaven."

When he referred to the commandments, one of the Pharisees, standing erect and haughty and confident, interrupted him: "Master," said he, "which is the greatest commandment in the law?"

"Why must these smug Pharisees always be quizzing the rabbi, and annoying him, and seeking to trap him?" Gaius whispered to the man beside him, for he had lost his caution under the spell of the young rabbi's words.

"Because they are Pharisees," replied the man, grinning. "That is their nature."

But the Pharisee's question did not disturb Jesus. He turned to face his questioner, and not a sound broke the deep silence except the twittering of a small bird in a shrub on the hillside just beyond the rabbi. "You shall love the Lord your God with all your heart, and with all your soul, and with all your mind. This is the first and greatest commandment. And the second is like it. You shall love your neighbor as yourself. On these two commandments hang all the law and the prophets."

"A simple answer," Gaius said to himself. "A proper answer, too. Again he has confounded his critics."

Jesus turned from the sneering Pharisee to continue his discourse upon the law. Obedience to God, obedience to the law, he said, was not a matter of upholding the cold, dead letter of the scriptures, but of yielding one's self in heart and mind to the spirit of the law. Then he turned to the Pharisee who had interrupted him. "And I tell you"—Gaius sensed a new strength in his voice, a challenge, a command—"that unless your righteousness exceeds that of the scribes and Pharisees, you will never enter the kingdom of heaven."

And now, his voice gentler, he returned to the exposition of his views. He spoke of the commandment in the old Mosaic law against murder. "You have heard that it was said to the men of old, 'Thou shalt not kill,' and whosoever kills shall be liable to judgment. But one may murder his neighbor in his heart without actually thrusting a dagger into him," the rabbi said, "and whosoever is angry with his neighbor without cause is breaking the law whether or not he lays a finger upon him. The same thing is true of other evils, nor can a man approach God unless he is free of evil thoughts," the rabbi continued. "If you come to the altar to offer your sacrifice to God upon it," said Jesus, "and you remember that you have done harm to your brother, leave it and go to your brother, and right the wrong you have done him, and be reconciled, and then come back to the altar and offer your gift to God."

"There can be no reservations in man's reconciliation with man if he wishes to be reconciled with God," Jesus declared.

"One must hold back nothing. You cannot hold to old evils and old wrongs, to evil thinking, if you would approach God," he said. "You must give them up, cast them away utterly, abandon them forever. Even if your right eye causes you to sin, pluck it out, and cast it from you, for it is better for you to lose your eye than for your whole body to be ruined. And if your right hand causes you to sin, cut it off and throw it away, for it is better that you lose one member than your whole body."

He is a powerful speaker, Gaius said to himself. *Never have I heard an orator in the forum with such power of persuasion. Is it his manner of speaking, the soft cadenced words of the Galilean countryman, is it the power, the logic, the dramatic force, of his message? What is the source of his power?* The people were listening intently, straining to hear every word that came from the earnest young preacher standing there under the afternoon sun, his face flushed and wet from the heat of the midsummer day. But Gaius abruptly dismissed his own thoughts, for now a man in the crowd was asking the rabbi's interpretation of the old Jewish law of an eye for an eye and a tooth for a tooth.

"Master," the man was saying, "is that the proper method of dealing with one's enemies?"

"How would one defeat his enemy?" the rabbi replied with his own question. "The ancient law would say that if a man strikes you unjustly then you should strike him in return. And then what would your enemy do?" The rabbi smiled. "He would smite you again, and then you in turn would smite him." He stopped a moment. The he spoke quickly. "Who would profit? Would not both you and your enemy suffer, and what would be the end?"

For a moment he allowed the Jewish heads before him to bob. Then he cut short the babbling that was about to get started. "But I say unto you that the way to defeat your enemy is not to strike back. Striking back is the law of vengeance. But it is not the law of love, and has not the Father all power? I say rather turn your other cheek, and let him strike it also. By so doing, you will show him a superior strength. Soon he will leave off striking you, for he will see that you have found a better way, and he will be reconciled, and will seek your pardon, and you will walk away with him reconciled. Now, I ask you, what has become of your enemy? Has he not been defeated? Have you not overcome him? In truth, you have defeated him and overwhelmed him and utterly discomforted him, for you have transformed him from an enemy into a friend." Gaius, turning away a moment from the rabbi's glowing countenance, let his eyes rest upon the perspiring face of the younger of the Zebedees. Jesus, seeming to sense John's inner conflict, at the same moment turned his head and spoke to him: "I ask you, my brother, is there any other way?"

Quickly John replied, and though it was the first time Gaius had heard him speak since the day he and Simon had brought the fish, he felt that John's voice had a tenseness about it that betrayed a great emotion.

"Truly, master, yours is the proper way. But it would be a great burden upon me not to strike him back."

On the fringe of the inner circle about Jesus a man ventured to ask the rabbi a question. Hesitant and uneasy at first, under the smiling eyes of the rabbi he seemed to grow more confident, and soon he was talking freely.

"But, master, how can we, the little people of earth, learn the way and travel along it? We are not wise in the laws of the fathers, and there is none to tell us. We transgress the law daily, we break its commandments, for how can we obey when we know not the intricacies of the law? We are not wise as are the priests in the synagogues and the great Temple, we are not learned in the law as are the Pharisees"—he pointed toward the group over beyond the rabbi—"and the Sadducees and the scribes. We are poor and have not money for the purchase of a lamb for the sacrificial altar; some of us cannot even buy a brace of pigeons. We are not welcomed among the people of God who know His way to do it, and there is none to show us the way. What, oh, master, is there for us, the little people of the earth who are poor and fearful and seek the way of the righteous, who wish to dwell in peace with our fellow man and our God, but are reviled among the great of the earth who understand the law and have money for the sacrifices?" The man, gaunt and thin and displaying in his dress and his frame the poverty that he must have known all his days, stepped a pace nearer the rabbi. "What is there for us, the cast-off of God and man?" There was pain in his voice, and bitterness.

The rabbi said not a word. For a long moment he looked into the sad, starved face of the man, and it seemed to Gaius, watching him intently, that he drew into his own countenance all the sorrow and poverty and pain of suffering mankind. And then swiftly, as the sunshine coming quickly sends the shadow of the cloud racing fast across the brightening fields and forests, the sadness was swept clear of his face and a smile transformed it, a smile of confidence and strength and power to warm and nourish all the cold and hungry of earth. Then he spoke.

"There is none cast off of the Father," said Jesus. "No, not one. He sees every sparrow that falls from the limb, and His heart is grieved. He loves all, for He is love. He loves the high and great of earth, but it is more difficult for them to love Him, for they are busy with their affairs and they exclude Him from their hearts, for they have not time for Him. He loves the rich, but for them it is hard to find the way to the Father. It is hard for those who trust in riches to enter the kingdom of heaven. It is easier for a laden camel to go through the needle's eye in the gate than for a rich man to enter the kingdom of God, for often the rich man is unwilling to lay down the burden of his riches in order to present himself before the Father." He had glanced toward the group of Pharisees. But now he turned to look directly upon the poor man who had spoken out with such feeling.

"But you of the countless little men of earth have no such burden to keep you from the Father. You are free to love Him and to serve Him. For you there is nothing that stands in the way to separate you from the Father. You are free to come to Him and abide with Him and be gladdened and sustained in His great love. Oh, blessed, thrice blessed are you, my brothers the little men of earth."

And now the rabbi lifted his eyes and looked out across the people upon the hillside, and he raised his arms as though he would take them all to his heart, and when he spoke again his words came forth strong and clear and melodious as the tones of a bell of fine metal.

"Blessed are the lowly of spirit," he said, "for theirs is the kingdom of heaven. Blessed are they who mourn, for they shall be comforted. Blessed are the meek, for they shall inherit the earth.

Blessed are they who hunger and thirst after righteousness, for they shall be filled. Blessed are the merciful, for they shall obtain mercy. Blessed are the pure in heart, for they shall see God. Blessed are they who are persecuted for righteousness' sake, for theirs is the kingdom of heaven—"

John, standing almost within arm's length of the rabbi, was looking up into his face, an enraptured expression upon his countenance. Near John stood Simon, leaning upon his knotted staff, oblivious to everything except the words falling from the rabbi's lips. And not far away, Gaius saw, stood the new member of the little band, Levi the publican, his gorgeous robes gone now and only a plain brown Galilean homespun about his squat, well-fleshed frame.

It is sheer poetry, Gaius said to himself. *It is fabulous beauty translated into words. What meaning! What power! What magic!*

The rabbi had paused for the moment to give emphasis to what he was about to say, Gaius reasoned. For now he turned again to look into the eyes of the gaunt man who had questioned him, eyes now no longer lusterless but glowing with a new excitement. "Blessed are you, though men shall revile you, and persecute you, and shall say all manner of evil against you falsely on my account," said he. "Rejoice, and be exceeding glad, for great is your reward in heaven, for even so they persecuted the prophets which lived in the days before your time." He hesitated a moment. Then he lifted his arm and swept it in a half-circle before the people ranged upon the side of the hill. "You are the salt of the earth," he declared, and there was a ring of assurance in his tone, almost of defiance, as he said it. "But if the salt has lost its taste, how shall its saltiness be restored? It is thenceforth good for nothing but to be thrown out and trodden under foot by men."

Again he raised his arms, so that the robe fell back and the sunshine glinted along the reddish brown hair that grew heavy upon his forearm, and he pointed with a swift thrust of his hand toward the multitude. "You are the light of the world. You must interpret to the world the way of the Father. You must show the way into the kingdom. And how must you do it?" He paused, changed his tone, spoke more gently. "A city that is built upon a hill cannot be hid. Neither do men light a candle and put it under a bushel measure. They put it on a candlestick, and it provides light for all who are in the house." Now he raised his voice again.

"You must light the way. You must be an example to the world. Let your light so shine before men that they may see your good works and, knowing that you are children of the Father, may glorify your Father which is in heaven."

"But master,"—it was the thin, gaunt man speaking—"how can we light the way when we know not the way, and who is there to point us the way?" His haggard face was puzzled, and little lines creased his bony forehead as he stared, mouth open and revealing broken, discolored teeth.

"The way I point out to you, my brother, is the way to the Father. His way and my way are the same. It is my mission in life to show the way to the throne of the Father; for this purpose was I born." He said it simply, without dramatic effect, but to Gaius the rabbi's utter sincerity was more effective than any startling oratory could have been.

"But master, our enemies would keep us from the way of life, and we are weak, and we cannot overcome them; we have no weapons with which to smite them."

"You have the greatest weapon of them all, if you would but command it. It is more powerful, more devastating than a two-edged sword—"

"Master, I cannot understand. I am a poor man of the earth. I own nothing. I could never buy even a sword."

"This weapon is free for the seeking," said Jesus. "You have heard it was said of old that one should love his neighbor and hate his enemy. But I say unto you that such is not the way to overcome one's enemy. I say unto you that the only weapon that will truly strike down one's enemy is the weapon of love." Now the rabbi was smiling again, for he was coming to an exposition, Gaius sensed it, of his favorite theme. "The law of vengeance, the law of hating one's neighbor," said he, "is the law of force. And the law of force is an unsound law. A man who lives by force lives only so long as he is stronger than his neighbor. A nation that lives by the strength of its arms endures only so long as it is more powerful in armaments and in soldiers than its neighbor nation. The law of force leads to turmoil between man and man, and nation and nation. Nor is there any end to such struggle for mastery.

"But a new law, my brothers"—the rabbi's eyes swept the throng, and he raised his voice—"I commend unto you. I say unto you, love your enemies, bless them that curse you, do good to them that hate you, and pray for those who persecute you. To do this is the law of the Father and in doing this you show you are children of the Father. Nor is this the law of weakness; it is the law of strength, for there is nothing stronger than love. The father himself is not stronger than love, for God is love. Love is the only thing that endures, love is the only thing that conquers. These other things are transient, they perish, they are gone.

"Lay not up for yourself treasures upon earth, where moth and rust consume and where thieves break the locks and steal it away. But lay up for yourselves treasures in heaven, where neither moth nor rust consumes and where thieves do not break in to steal it away. For where your treasure is there your heart will be also."

Gaius stood entranced as he listened to the smoothly flowing words of the young rabbi standing there upon the hillside under a summer's sun. "He speaks of his God as though he were really his father," Gaius thought, and the idea came to him as forcefully as though he had spoken the words aloud. "He has an entirely different conception of his God from what we Romans have of ours, or the Greeks have of theirs, or even the Jews have of their Yahweh. His God has infinite power and strength, but he is a God of love and understanding and sympathy. It is a beautiful idea, a tremendous conception, the force and strength of love as opposed to the power of force."

He wondered, fleetingly, what Marcus would have to say of this philosophy. Or Lucius, firm in his belief that the Roman army was the ultimate power. Marcus would sneer at his exhortation to lay up treasures in some ethereal heaven. He could hear Marcus now. "I'll take my beautiful glassware, and my gorgeous textiles, and my sweating slaves that make them for me, and my ships, and my warehouses and sheds. Ha! I'll take these tangible things, these things that I can see and feel and hold in my hands, and you and your rabbi can have all the treasures of your heaven, wherever and whatever it is, if it's anywhere!" He could hear Marcus now,

Marcus the prophet of the practical, the worshiper of the material, the man of money.

But what is more practical, Gaius thought, *than the teaching of this young rabbi? After all, how can you whip a man and keep him whipped, how can you defeat a nation with the sword and keep it a subject nation? Rome has been doing it these many years, yet some day even proud Rome will be overcome. Force begets greater force, vengeance begets sharper vengeance. And what does love beget? Only love.*

By the immortals, said Gaius to himself, *this man speaks sense. His message, his philosophy—it's practical, workable. And beautiful. What Roman philosopher has equaled this Galilean of the hill country? What Greek? He goes beyond them all in his conception. He—he seems to have tapped the source of truth.*

Gaius recalled the rabbi's declaration "His way and my way are the same." And the centurion concluded the young Jew was not expounding some philosophy that he had devised out of a clever brain and with a fluent tongue. *No, he is speaking the truth. He knows it. He is walking in the way. He knows where he walks. It must be. Yes, by the immortals—* Suddenly it came to him. How incongruous this old familiar expression of a Roman: "by the immortals." Man must worship. There is more to man than flesh and bone. There is something about man that looks upward to the source from which man came. *The father! That is what this Jesus calls his god. And he talks with assurance. He has been with his father, he lives with him, he walks the way with him day by day.*

But Jesus was speaking, and Gaius, who momentarily had been lost in his own thinking, moved a pace nearer to hear the better. The rabbi was talking in lower tones now, as if he were addressing the tall gaunt man alone.

"No man can serve two masters," he was saying, "for either he will love the one and hate the other, or else he will hold to the one and despise the other. You cannot serve God and money. Serve God and be his child. Live in his love and put your hand in his. Does not your earthly father care for his child? So will our Father care for his children. Be not worried and distraught with life, my brother. Don't fret about what you may have to eat or what garments you may have for your back. There is more to living than eating rich foods and wearing fine garments. Be as the birds of the air. Do they worry and fret? They sow not, neither reap, nor gather their harvests into barns. Yet the heavenly Father feeds them. And are you not more precious in his sight than they? Will worry help you to grow one bit?

"And consider the lilies of the field." He pointed down the slope. "Look at them. See how beautiful they are clothed. They neither toil nor spin. And yet Solomon in all his glory was not clothed as gorgeously as any one of yonder lilies. Wherefore, if God cares for the birds and feeds them and sustains them and if He clothes even the grass of the fields, will he not nourish you and clothe you, oh, you men of little faith?"

He raised his eyes, and Gaius saw that he was tiring, for he had been speaking long and the sun was strong upon him.

"Rather, my brothers, put the emphasis of your life upon the things that are important. Seek first the kingdom of God and his righteousness, and these other things will come in their due time. Be not anxious about the morrow, for when the morrow comes it will bring its own anxieties. Consider rather today, for each day has its own trials. Have faith in the Father. Cease not to call upon him in meekness and sincerity, remembering all the while that whatsoever you would have your brother do unto you, do you likewise unto him."

Simon walked up to the rabbi, was speaking to him in low tones. The rabbi nodded his head. Gaius surmised that Simon was urging him to cease speaking because of his evident fatigue and the heat of the sun.

Jesus seemed reluctant to stop, but after he had spoken a moment longer, he raised his hands and lifting his face toward the sky, closed his eyes and prayed to his Father, beseeching for them his Father's tender care.

Instinctively, Gaius dropped his eyes to the earth and listened reverently, and when the rabbi ceased speaking, the centurion looked up again. The thought came to him suddenly and with clarity that he, too, had been in communion with some power greater than himself.

12

The crowd was surging about Jesus now, and Simon had locked his hairy arm in the arm of the rabbi, and John and Levi and others who Gaius supposed were members of the rabbi's little band were attempting to shield him from the press of the people as they started down the hillside toward Capernaum.

Already Gaius was walking rapidly, almost running, as he had rushed away that night from Simon's house. His mind was in a turmoil, for the words and the manner and the deep sincerity of the rabbi had stirred him. Almost before he realized where he was going he had reached the gates of the city and was starting down the narrow street that led toward the Roman garrison. He was turning a corner when he almost collided with a man running.

"I was running to fetch you, sir," said the servant from his household, panting for breath. "Andreas, sir, is very sick. We are afraid he is dying. I had set out to find you, and someone told me that you had gone to the hill where the strange rabbi was teaching."

The centurion had entirely forgot his mission. He had gone to find the rabbi to implore help for his dying servant boy. And under the strange spell of the rabbi, he had forgot all about little Andreas.

"Return quickly," Gaius said, "and tell Andreas that I will bring the rabbi to him."

"Yes, sir." The man saluted and started on the run.

Gaius walked back toward the gate through which he had just entered. As he drew near he knew by the multitude that met him that the rabbi was coming into the city. At the gate he met the little group.

Gaius walked boldly toward Jesus. Simon saw him, sensed his mission. "But the master is so tired," he said, not unkindly. "Perhaps another time—" He hesitated. "I'll speak to him about the boy."

Jesus, who had been talking with John, turned to face the centurion. "What is it?" His eyes were upon Gaius now, and Gaius knew this time that the rabbi was looking upon him alone. Quickly he dropped his gaze, but only for a moment, and when he raised his eyes and looked at Jesus, he saw that the rabbi was smiling.

He could say nothing. A numbness seemed to have overspread his whole frame. This was not the first time he had been in the presence of people of importance. He had conferred more than once with the legate Vitellius at Antioch. Once in Rome he had even been in a comparatively small group to which Tiberius had given an audience. He had talked with Pontius Pilate, had even provided an escort for the procurator as he had crossed Galilee on a visit to Vitellius. Nor was this Jew a man of standing. Was he not a poor man, the son of a carpenter, a man of earth from the unprepossessing little village of Nazareth? His name was becoming known in Galilee and even down in Judea, but aside from a very few men of influence, such as Nicodemus of the Sanhedrin, were not his followers recruited from the poor and ignorant and forsaken? Yet now as he stood before the rabbi he was speechless.

Jesus understood. He stepped forward two paces, put his hand upon the centurion's shoulder. "What is it you wish, my brother?"

His deep brown eyes were warm and friendly, and Gaius found his speech. "Rabbi," he said, "it is my servant boy. He is very sick with the palsy. We are afraid that he is dying."

Jesus smiled and spoke again: "Show me the way to your home. I will come and heal him."

"Rabbi," said Gaius, "I am not worthy that you should come under my roof. But if you would only speak the word here, my servant boy will be healed. I understand authority. For I am a man of some authority myself; I have soldiers and servants at my command, and when I speak they know to obey."

The face of the young rabbi seemed to light now with a great rapture, and he turned to the group with him. "Truly," he said to them, "I have not found in all Israel so great a faith as this Roman has shown. I declare to you that many shall come from the east and the west and sit down with our fathers Abraham and Isaac and Jacob in the kingdom of heaven. But many of the chosen of God shall be cast out and there shall be among them sorrowing and great mourning, for their faith shall not be as the faith of this man."

Then he turned to Gaius, and his voice was now calm, and there was quiet joy in it, and healing. "Go your way," said Jesus. "Be no longer worried or sorrowful, for as you have believed, so be it done unto you."

Gaius stammered his thanks, hardly knowing what he said; and Simon smiled, and John, and the others. But of them all, the young rabbi seemed happiest.

As Gaius neared his own gate, a servant came rushing to meet him. "Andreas, sir," the servant declared, "is recovering rapidly. His jerking limbs are quiet now. He is talking with scarcely a stutter. It is amazing how quickly he has mended. None of us understands it, sir."

Nor did Gaius. But he was not surprised.

13

Marcus rolled up the papyrus. "That's a good report, Tullus. It's well prepared, comprehensive." He smiled broadly. "And it shows we're steadily increasing our trade."

"Yes, sir, it has been good this summer. Your trips to Alexandria were profitable, and you perhaps will agree that while you were selling our products we at home were producing steadily. The looms have stopped little during that period, sir; we have kept the slaves busy."

"Have we lost many from overwork, Tullus?"

"Not many, sir, of those who came to us physically fit. Of course, we haven't dallied long with those who were ill or otherwise incapacitated. I have found that it's cheaper to replace them with slaves who can maintain our pace."

"Tullus, you know," Marcus declared, "I believe you could operate the business for quite a period without me. Even if I should be away for months—"

"But you aren't contemplating leaving, sir?"

"Oh, no. No plans like that. But it's good to have a man upon whom one can depend. But remember this, Tullus; it is important. Don't be niggardly with Sejanus. Keep him pleased. He is still the power in Rome. It's good business to keep him satisfied."

"Yes, sir, I have always understood the prefect expected handsome tribute."

"Don't ever forget that, Tullus. As long as he occupies the office he does, keep him satisfied."

"Perhaps, sir, if you gave him more—"

"No, I think not. Then he would know that we were making more, and he would expect more."

"Yes, sir, I suppose so. I thought, though, that were you to increase your gratuities, perhaps he would increase the subsidies, send us more slaves—"

He hesitated, and Marcus, looking up, saw that he was staring at the two spots on his arm, the grayish-brown circles in which for weeks not there had been no feeling.

"I beg your pardon, sir," Tullus said, embarrassed. "I was just noticing that the wound seems to be healed completely, although the bruise mark still remains."

"Yes," Marcus said, "it was only a scratch you gave me." But instinctively he pulled his left leg further under him against the couch, for only two days before he had discovered an identical spot on the leg, a graying deadened place in which there was no feeling when he jabbed his fingernail into it.

14

The next afternoon Gaius sent Andreas to Simon's house on the pretext of buying fish. His real purpose in sending the boy, however, was to impress Simon with the slave's recovery so that the fisherman would come to his house and talk with him about it.

Gaius was greatly puzzled at the sudden healing of Andreas. Yesterday the boy had been helpless, a twitching, jerking, pitiable victim of the palsy that seemed completely to possess him. And now Andreas was walking down the street erect, calm, proud. What had happened to the boy?

Had the young rabbi, still sweating and tired from his long discourse, actually commanded the palsy to leave the boy? Or had the malady run its course, had the inherent strength of the youth chosen that moment to overcome the enemy that had invaded his body? How would Marcus explain it? What would the tribune Lucius Mallius say?

Gaius wanted to talk with Simon. Simon was a rough fisherman, with little wisdom that comes from sitting at the feet of the learned. But Simon had a quick perception of things, a nimble mind, even though it was not so nimble as his tongue. And Simon had spent many hours with Jesus.

But Simon was not at home. "He set off this morning," Simon's mother-in-law told Andreas. "The master wanted to make a journey down into southern Galilee, and he wanted Simon to go along. Of course, that's all he had to do, say the word, and Simon would drop everything and start out. And the Zebedees, they are the same way. I think that publican Levi went with them, too, and probably some of the others. And there's no knowing when they'll be back."

The old woman, Andreas thought, was probably thinking of the added work to be done and the fact that while Simon was away no money would be coming in.

"And the rabbi healed her of a severe fever," Gaius observed, when the boy reported to him. "But people soon forget the good that one does them."

Andreas looked up quickly. "But I shall never forget him," he said, "or you, sir."

A week later the tribune Lucius Mallius walked into the centurion's office. Gaius was standing at the window, looking out across the Sea of Galilee toward a group of fishing boats low on the horizon. He turned around as the door opened.

"Tribune Lucius Mallius!" he exclaimed. "Welcome. But what brings you to Capernaum?"

"Thank you, centurion," said Lucius. "I had to come to Tiberias on a mission for Pilate. I came to see Tetrarch Herod. And since I was close by, I came up to see you. How are you?"

"I'm well, tribune, and I trust you are."

"Yes, things go very well with me."

"And how is the procurator?"

"He's well, but he is continually exasperated because of the bickerings of the Jews." Lucius smiled. "I was about to say 'you Jews.' I wonder how our good friend Marcus is. I haven't seen him in some time."

"Nor have I," said Gaius, smiling. "He's probably with that fellow Tullus counting his money."

"And if he isn't careful, these Jews will have it all yet," Lucius observed. "I have learned already that they love it. They certainly pay their taxes reluctantly. That's one thing that keeps Pilate annoyed. I don't believe he'd be so prone to dip into the treasuries of their synagogues—" He stopped short, for Andreas had entered the room with an earthen pitcher of water and glasses. "By the gods, centurion, isn't that the slave Marcus gave you, the one who was jerking and stammering? No, by Jupiter, it can't be!"

"You're right, tribune." Gaius laughed. "He's well again."

"You don't mean it, centurion. He seemed to be hopeless. I wouldn't have given a denarius for him that day. You must have taken him to that faith healer. I remember Marcus challenged you to get the fellow to heal him."

"Yes, so Marcus did," said Gaius. "And the rabbi did it."

"What! By the gods, you don't mean it?"

100

"But he did, tribune. I do not know how or why. All I know is that he did. You saw the boy at Tyre. You see him now."

Lucius slowly surveyed Andreas. "He seems fit enough," he said. "And he's not jerking and twitching. Centurion, this is remarkable. What do you make of it?"

"I hardly know, tribune. The man has tremendous power. He uses it only to restore. He seems to have some peculiar contact with a supernatural power. I do not understand him. But this much I do know, the boy has been restored. That is the important thing."

"Yes, you can't ignore that," said the tribune. "By the way, what did Marcus think of it? I wish I had seen him when he found out. Or has he?"

"No, he doesn't know."

"He would ascribe it to natural processes of recovery, I suppose. And that reminds me, centurion. The other day as I was coming across lower Galilee from Caesarea to Tiberias I stopped for the night at an inn at Nain. There I found that everybody seemed to be excited over a most unusual occurrence in that town the day before. I can't understand the Galilean tongue well, of course, but I was able to get the main points of the story. It seems that the son of a widow of that town had died and they were carrying him out to lay him away in a tomb just beyond the city gate. The boy had been well esteemed, and it was quite a procession. There was much wailing and screaming.

"At the gate they met a group coming in. The leader of this band walked boldly up to the men carrying the dead boy. It appears that the mother's weeping had stirred him. So he stopped them, and then he spoke to the dead boy. Yes, that's what they said. They told me—and the fellow there at the inn who did most of the talking declared he saw it all—they said this man spoke to the dead boy and told him to get up."

"And what did the boy do?" Gaius' eyes were studying the tribune's face.

"By the immortals, the boy sat up on the bier on which they were carrying him, rubbed his eyes, looked around, and then started talking." Lucius laughed. "The fellow told me that about half that crowd took to their heels when that dead boy sat up."

101

"What did the man then do?"

"They said he took the boy by the hand, steadied him as he stood up, and led him over to his mother."

"I suppose that really did cause much excitement at Nain."

"Yes. In fact, that was the only thing anybody would talk about. And there was considerable debate about it. Some of them seemed to think that the boy wasn't really dead; they suggested that he had fallen into a deep trance, that he had become so weak that they mistakenly judged him to be dead. They said that the visitor in stopping the funeral procession and speaking in a firm yet commanding tone had awakened the boy out of his trance. I don't know, centurion; I wasn't there, of course. But as to the practical results, it's very much like your little slave boy. That widow's boy is alive today." He smiled.

"I was amused at the comment of an old Jew there at the inn. When some of the more talkative ones suggested that the boy had been merely in a deep sleep, the old man glared at them. 'They were on their way to put him in the tomb, weren't they?' he demanded, and when one of them nodded, he said, 'Well, if they had put him in there he'd be dead by now anyway, wouldn't he?'

"'I guess you're right, old man,' one of them agreed.

"'Well, he isn't dead now, is he? Then he gave the boy his life back, didn't he? He raised him to a new life.' The old man glared at the group. 'That was more than you did. You didn't know he was not dead, if he wasn't. You—!' He pointed his finger at them, sneered '—You were going to bury the boy!'"

"What was the name of the man who saved the widow's son at Nain?"

"Centurion, I meant to remember that name. I wondered if he was the man you told Marcus and me about. Perhaps if you'd—"

"Was the man's name Jesus?"

"That was the name. Jesus."

15

I'm a plain speaking man," Simon said. "I don't know whether you would or could give us any aid. Some contend that John is a revolutionary; and Rome isn't disposed to tolerate a revolutionary. Nor is old Herod, who pretends to be a loyal Jew, though he would go against his own people in a minute for a smile from your emperor."

"But what do you think I might be able to do?" Gaius asked the fisherman.

"Centurion, you must have considerable influence with Pontius Pilate, or even with Legate Vitellius at Antioch. We thought you might say a word in behalf of John, who is rotting away down in that forsaken hot hole at Machaerus."

"But he is Herod's prisoner, Simon. Where would Rome get a hand in it?"

"Rome gets a hand in anything she wants to," said Simon. "We thought that you might urge Herod to order John released. He is not conspiring against either Rome or Herod. The man's a prophet; he is not concerned with politics." Simon was talking with mounting feeling. "He knew that Herod had stolen his half-brother's wife and was living in sin. He condemned him for it, and it made Herodias angry. She is the one who caused him to be imprisoned. We want to get him released before she causes him more harm."

"How did you learn this, Simon?"

"Last summer when the master was teaching in the cities in Galilee—several months ago, centurion, about the time the late figs were beginning to ripen, I recall—two men who said they had been sent by John came to see the master. John was allowed to have visitors, they said, and many of his friends were crossing the Dead Sea and venturing through the desert to Machaerus to see him."

"But why did the messengers come from John?" Gaius asked.

"John had been hearing much of the work of the master, whose fame has spread far. Poor old John had probably been doing much thinking during the long nights alone. So he sent the men to see the master and inquire of him one thing."

"What was that, Simon?"

"Well, sir, it's the same old question that we have talked about before. We have been hesitant about asking the master. But John's messengers asked him to his face."

"But what did the messengers ask the rabbi, Simon?"

"I was there the day they came. We were all a bit shocked by their boldness. They had been watching him doing his work, and when there was a lull they pressed forward and introduced themselves. 'John the Baptizer has sent us to you,' they said. 'He has had many tidings of the work you have been doing. He sent us to inquire of you if you are the Messiah sent to redeem Israel. He has reason to hope that you are indeed the Messiah.' The men, though bold, spoke with great courtesy and reverence. 'He wishes to know if you are the long promised hope of Israel, or must we look forward to the coming of another?'"

"Simon, that was a bold question. What did your rabbi reply?"

"'Return to John,' he said, 'and tell him what you have seen and heard, how the blind see and the lame walk, how the lepers are cleansed and the deaf hear again, how the dead are raised to new life, how the poor have the good tidings preached to them.' Then he smiled, and added, 'And bear to him my love.'"

"What did they say then, Simon?"

"They seemed content with his answer. They went away in humility. And when they were gone some of those about the master began to murmur at John's lack of faith. Someone said something about his weakness. The master promptly challenged them. 'When you went out to the wilderness where John was teaching, what did you expect to see? A reed shaken in the wind? Or a man clothed in silks and soft purples? Those soft men you find in the courts of kings. Or did you go out to the wilderness to find a prophet, a bold man unafraid to proclaim the ways of the Father? You found a prophet, and more than a prophet. You found there in the wilderness that man of whom the ancient prophets wrote, "Behold I send my messenger before thy face, who shall prepare thy way before thee."' Then his voice mounted in strength and he spoke in renewed emphasis: 'For I say unto you that among those born of women there has not risen up a greater man than John the Baptizer!'"

Simon paused. "It was a pity poor old John down there in the dungeon couldn't have heard what the master said of him. It would have brought him much comfort." Again the fisherman was silent. Then he spoke: "Centurion, that was months ago and John is still in the Machaerus dungeon."

Gaius reflected. "Simon, I don't believe that Herod will harm the prophet. The tetrarch is superstitious. I suspect he is afraid that John may have some supernatural power. I believe that he imprisoned him to silence him. Perhaps Herodias drove him to it. But I do not believe that even she, as much power as she has over him, could drive him into doing John bodily harm. If John stops condemning the tetrarch and his wife and acts discreetly, the tetrarch, I believe, will quietly release him."

"Centurion, John will continue to denounce what he considers wickedness and sin if it costs him his head. He's afraid of nobody. Even should he be released, he'd soon be in trouble again with Herod."

"Then what do you think I might do, Simon?"

"I don't know, sir. But I fear for him at Machaerus. There's always the chance as long as he is imprisoned that Herodias might find an opportunity to harm him. If you could persuade Herod to give him his liberty, his friends might prevail upon him to let his scourgings for a while fall upon sinners other than Herod and his wife."

"Would it please the rabbi for John to be released?"

"I cannot speak for the master, centurion, but I know the baptist is one of his dearest friends."

"Simon, I may be able to help. I owe much to the rabbi, and I would like to do something for him and you. The tribune Lucius Mallius and I have a mission to perform for the army that may provide an opportunity. We have an engagement with the tetrarch Herod at Tiberias. And Herod, of course, is always anxious to please Rome."

16

Tullus, this is an important mission. I want you to do your best to carry out the assignment. Here's what I want. I am going on an extended visit to the tetrarch Herod Antipas at his fortress palace across the Dead Sea on the frontiers of Arabia. My friend the centurion at Capernaum and the tribune Lucius at Caesarea will be there. The three of us will meet at Herod's palace at Tiberias and make the journey southward with the royal party. It is going to be a holiday outing, but I intend to make money as a result of the trip. I want you to select pieces of our choicest glassware in all the patterns we make and pack it for travel by pack asses, and arrange it so that it can be displayed without too much difficulty. I also want you to select some of our best textiles in the finest grades of purple."

He smiled, tugged at his ear. "I'm going to take the samples to Machaerus, Tullus, and catch old Herod when he's drunkest, and I'm going to sell him a tremendous order. And then, having sold him, I'm going to stop at Jerusalem on the way back and show the samples to the rich Jews there, including the high priest Caiaphas and his father-in-law, old Annas. When they learn that Herod and Pontius Pilate are our customers, they will rush to buy. Don't you think so, Tullus?"

"Yes, sir, the leaders of the Jews seek to please the Romans. And there's no place they could obtain more beautiful glassware or purples."

"I agree, Tullus. Now will you see to it that the samples are selected and made ready for strenuous travel? I expect to be leaving in another week. And I will need servants to accompany me to look after the samples, as well as others to provide for my own needs. Will you arrange all those things?"

"Yes, sir," Tullus said. "I shall see that your orders are carried out promptly." He paused, and Marcus, looking up quickly, saw that Tullus was staring at him with an expression between amazement and horror.

"What's the trouble?" he asked.

"Your eyebrow, sir—the left one—it's gone, the hair fallen out."

"Oh, that," said Marcus, and he tried to make his voice sound casual. "Singed it the other night when I bent over too near the lamp. I can paint an eyebrow until the hairs grow out again."

Marcus, watching Tullus, saw his expression change subtly. Then Tullus spoke. "Don't worry, sir. I shall see that the samples of the glassware and the purples are ready when you leave, and the necessary pack asses, horses, and servants. And I hope the journey will be profitable, sir, and enjoyable, and that you will return refreshed and—recovered."

But the expression on the overseer's face left Marcus feeling vaguely disquieted. Tullus had stared that way last fall, Marcus remembered, when he had first seen the graying circle on his arm.

17

Machaerus sat high upon the scourged and punished tableland that for centuries had baked in the sun. For several days the caravan had moved down the green valley of the little Jordan, meandering its slow way toward death in the Dead Sea far below Herod's hide-away here in the Peraean wastelands. The traveling had been pleasant in the valley, for it was March now and the air was crisp though not too cold for comfortable riding; but after the royal train with its horses and camels and pack asses had crossed the Jordan at the head of the Dead Sea it had come into a region of gravel that skirted the shores of the great salt lake. Away to the left at the foot of Mount Nebo they had got glimpses now and again of trees that mantled the foothills. And then they had crossed a small valley with a willow-bordered stream in its center and abruptly had begun the sharp ascent that had brought them worn and short of breath into the high, thin air of this forsaken region of fused granite and basalt. On occasion, the lavalike rocks thrust out from thin soil caught their attention.

They had been at Machaerus four days. Soon now, Gaius reasoned, Herod would tire of this orgy and be ready to begin the return to Tiberias. Tonight the tetrarch was honoring his Roman guests with a banquet celebrating his own birthday; it would excel in exuberance the banquets he had already given, and Herod would doubtless drink himself into a stupor.

It has been an interesting experience, Gaius reflected, as he stood on one of the terraces of Machaerus and faced westward toward the Dead Sea blazing like a giant mirror far off and below Herod's fortress-retreat. Herod and Herodias have revealed themselves. He had talked with Herod on occasional official visits to Tiberias and had met the tetrarchess. But he had known them only superficially. Now he had had an opportunity to study them.

Herodias was more Roman than Jewess, he judged, but that

was perhaps the result of her schooling in Rome and her long residence there. And Herod, too, looked more like a Roman general than a Jewish governor of a province, but that was because he was clean-shaven and kept his grizzled hair closely cropped.

Herodias had been eager, likewise, to affect Roman ways because she was bent upon having her husband made a king rather than a tetrarch, and she has been entertaining in the Roman manner, Gaius reasoned.

Old Herod, here at Machaerus, had revealed himself clearly. Not simply his inclination to debaucheries—his fondness for loose women, his many concubines, his heavy drinking, and gorging of rich foods. Standing on the terrace at Machaerus, Gaius pictured Herod also as a man ruled by superstition and fear, afraid of the future as a child is afraid of the dark, a man fearful of spirits and soothsayers, astrologers, and prophets, those who deal with the unseen, the intangible.

Perhaps that was why it had not been difficult for Gaius to arrange for the release of the strange prophet. Herod had seemed glad of an excuse for ridding himself of the man of thundering wild words, angry bright eyes, and flailing skinny brown arms now bleached white by long imprisonment away from the scorching sun of his beloved desert.

Gaius has descended into the dungeon hewn from the rocks beneath Machaerus and had seen John, though he had not spoken to the prophet. And he had not been impressed by him, even though he had recalled Simon's story of the young rabbi's defense of the desert preacher.

But nevertheless the centurion had urged Herod to release John. He had assured himself, he told the tetrarch, that the man contemplated no sedition against Rome. "He is an ascetic," he had declared, "he is not a revolutionary. He is concerned with men's personal lives. He isn't interested in how Galilee is governed. I can see, sir, how his tirade angered you and was an even greater insult to your wife. But I believe the course calculated to silence his tongue and the tongues of all gossipers who repeat his words would be the releasing of this mad prophet. As long as he is in prison, it keeps alive the issue; it rubs salt into the wound.

Release him with a stern warning, and I believe you will accomplish what you desire."

Herod had agreed. He had not been as angry at the prophet's bitter words as had his wife, he confessed; it was Herodias who was bent upon vengeance, Herodias and her daughter Salome. But he could persuade the two that the centurion had spoken with wisdom, and whether it pleased them or not he would release the prophet.

Tribune Lucius Mallius had been agreeable to the release of the prophet after Gaius had assured him that the man was not a revolutionary. "As far as his preaching is concerned," Lucius had said, "I care not a fig. But I would not countenance any inflaming of the people against the government. Herod is a part of the Roman government, though he may be a poor administrator. I have not been out here long enough to get a fair estimate of his work. And you know much more of Galilee than I do, for my work, as you are aware, is concerned principally with affairs in Judea. Rome cares not how many wives Herod has, where he got them, or what he does with them, so long as he operates the government of Galilee efficiently for Rome. But I think it hardly conducive to good government for a fanatic to be allowed to condemn the tetrarch and his wife and try to bring them into disrepute. But if you feel that this man if released will rant no more of Herod and his family affairs, then I'll join you in suggesting that he be released. It may be, as you suggest, that keeping him confined serves only to aggravate the situation. Were I handling the case, I would either have him executed at once, or exiled, or released upon the condition that he keep his silence."

Marcus had declined to intercede for the prophet. "I care not what he does with him," he had said, impatiently. "That is your mission, centurion. You should handle all affairs concerning Jews and religion. I think you alone are qualified to deal with such matters. But you might call in your faith-healing Jew to advise you. That's an idea." Then he had feigned an air of humility. "But I should not speak lightly of your rabbi. Did he not heal your slave boy?"

Marcus's manner annoyed Gaius, but he held his tongue, for he knew that Marcus was seeking an argument.

"I'm sorry, centurion," Marcus said, when he saw that Gaius resented the remark but was not going to challenge it. "But I am simply not interested in this wild prophet. I came here for one thing, to do business with the tetrarch. Let this fellow in the dungeon look to his own head. I care not whether he keeps it or loses it. Nor does the emperor, by the immortals! Nor even"—he raised his arm in mock salute—"the prefect Sejanus, as long as I keep the money going his way."

18

The tables had been arranged to form three sides of a square in the great dining room at Machaerus. The open end was toward the terrace from which in the daytime one might have an impressive view of Mount Nebo twelve miles off to the northeast. A corridor ran along each side and doors opened into these corridors to provide a passageway from the inner rooms of the palace, including the kitchens at the rear.

The couches were ranged about the U-shaped banquet table with the couch of the tetrarch Herod, of heavier build to support his great frame, in the center. On his right was Herodias and next to her the tribune Lucius, who as representative of the procurator Pontius Pilate deserved a special place of honor at the banqueting board. At the right of Lucius was Salome and then came the centurion Gaius, and beside Gaius was one of the dark-haired beauties of Herod's court.

But as Marcus glanced quickly around the three sides of the great table he saw none whose beauty was as breathtaking as the creature between him and the tetrarch. "I am tremendously honored," he whispered to her. "My couch is not only close to the tetrarch's but also I have been placed beside the most beautiful of a host of beautiful women. I wonder to what I should attribute my good fortune."

The girl laughed, so merrily that Marcus feared it might arouse the jealousy of old Herod. "I have heard"—she had turned discreetly to say it into his ear—"that you have the double virtue of being both rich and a close friend of Sejanus in Rome."

"Without admitting either of the charges," Marcus said to her, under his breath, "would it mean anything to you?"

The girl's deep blue eyes opened wide, with evident amazement, but she was careful to keep her head turned away from the tetrarch, who at the moment was busy with his wine goblet. "No," she replied, "not particularly, though the riches might. But you are very bold—or else foolhardy." Now she spoke in lower tones. "Talk also with the girl on your left. He might resent your being too attentive. You see, I'm—" She paused.

"I understand," Marcus replied. "He's a lucky man." Herod had set down his goblet, was wiping his thick lips with the back of his hand. Marcus raised his goblet. "I propose a toast," said he, "to the tetrarch Herod Antipas." Instantly the guests raised aloft their glasses. Herod remained reclining, a pleased smile lighting his already reddening face. "Let us drink to the health of our mighty tetrarch Herod Antipas upon the occasion of his birthday anniversary," Marcus said; "to our gracious ruler, friend of Tiberius the emperor, friend of the prefect Sejanus, protector of the provinces of Galilee and Peraea, defender of religion, guardian of morals, savior of his people"— he raised the glass higher—"our gracious Herod Antipas!" He downed the wine, as did the others ringed about the three-sided board, and Herod beamed his satisfaction.

"You are clever, as well as rich—and bold," the girl whispered. "Later we shall have an opportunity to talk with more freedom."

Now the tetrarch straightened his heavy frame and then bowed. "I thank you, my friends," he said. It was evident that Herod's debaucheries of the last several days were beginning to tell upon even his rugged physique. He raised his goblet. "Now let us drink," said he, and the guests raised their wine glasses, "to His Imperial Majesty the emperor Tiberius, mighty monarch of the Roman Empire, protector of Palestine, our defender and our friend." He drank the wine, and along the three sides of the board elbows bent as the purple liquor poured down still thirsty throats. Hastily servants stationed in the hollow square filled the glasses again. The tetrarch reached for his, held it high upon slender stem. "And now," he said, "let us drink to the health"—the glasses went up along the line—"of the great prefect Sejanus, able, patriotic, sacrificing friend and minster to His Imperial Highness the emperor." He swallowed the wine, and the guests drank theirs.

But the tetrarch did not recline. Instead, when the glasses had been filled again, he raised his a third time. "Now let us drink to the health—" he paused, as the diners reached for their goblets "—to the health of our Roman friends—" he glanced to his left "—the manufacturer of Tyre and friend of the great Sejanus—" he turned toward the right "—the tribune from Caesarea, able aide to the great procurator of Judea, Pontius Pilate—" he craned his fat neck forward, nodded toward Gaius "—and the centurion stationed in our own Capernaum, able commandant of the garrison there and befriender of our people. To them, my friends, let us drink their good health." Now the tetrarch and the others, with the exception of the three Romans, drank their wine, and Marcus, Lucius, and Gaius bowed low their acknowledgment of the compliment.

But even yet the tetrarch remained upright on his couch, though Marcus noted with a feeling of satisfaction, anticipating, perhaps, that Herod was steadying himself with his left hand. Once more he reached for his glass. "Today is my birthday," said Herod. "This toast I shall drink alone." He drank the wine, licked his lips, leaned back on his couch, closed his eyes.

But in a moment he opened them, waved an impatient arm. "It's my birthday, isn't it?" he shouted. "Cannot even a tetrarch do what he wishes to do on his birthday? It is my command that all of you be merry with me tonight." Herod's face was reddening. He reached for his glass, held it up. It shook once, but he steadied it. "And now," he said, "I shall drink a toast to the health of you my friends who join with me in celebrating my birthday." His round, clean-shaven face lighted with a crooked smile that more wine would soon turn into a leer. "This is the only way I can get one more drink than you." He laughed loudly, swallowed his wine, and wiped his purple lips with the back of his hand, as the guests bowed low before him.

When they had reclined again, Herod waved his hands impatiently. "Now eat, my friends, eat well and drink all the wine you can hold." He laughed again. "This is my birthday, and there's still a bountiful stock of food at Machaerus. Even pork for our Roman friends, if they can get their hands on it before some of you Jews grab it!" He threw his head back and laughed loudly. "Go ahead and taste a bit of pork, you Jews, if you like. We're a long way from Jerusalem, my friends, and what old Annas doesn't see won't hurt him!"

The tetrarch reached for his goblet, and the glass lurched so that some of the purple liquid spilled. But then he clasped his great hand about the slender stem, lifted it to his mouth, and drained it. He waved the empty goblet. "Eat, my friends. Eat. This is my birthday! Have a good time." He stopped, seemed to be trying to recall something that had eluded him.

"We will have some entertainment. Dancing by the Egyptian women. Ha! The dark women with the fat, shaking hips. Yes. We will have entertainment soon. But now you must eat and drink, my friends. For this is my birthday. And who knows whether I shall have another?" He was serious again. "Yes, and there will be other entertainment, a special treat, my friends. I shall display the great magnanimity of the tetrarch of Galilee and Peraea. But that must wait." He took another swallow from the glass, which a slave had promptly refilled. "Now we must eat and drink, and have a great time, my friends."

He set down his glass unsteadily, so that the edge of the crystal balanced precariously upon the high rim of the golden plate in front of him, and it fell over, spilling what remained of the wine across the embroidered linen table covering.

Herodias turned to Lucius. "I trust you will forgive the behavior of the tetrarch tonight. He is really not himself. He has been drinking steadily since we came to Machaerus. It has got the better of him. When he comes here he seems to take upon himself the wildness of this dreary place."

"Then you do not like Machaerus?" Lucius asked, avoiding a reference to the drunken condition of his host.

"I hate it," Herodias said. "It is so desolate, so unlike Rome, for instance." She smiled coyly. "You know, I have spent much time in Rome."

"Yes, so I have heard, Your Majesty."

"And what else—" Herodias looked down demurely into her plate, fluttered her darkened eyelids "—have you heard about me, pray, tribune?"

"I have heard that you were a most delightful hostess, Your Majesty," Lucius lied gallantly, "and now I know it for a fact."

"You speak most flatteringly, tribune," Herodias replied. "And it gratifies me immensely. But surely you must have heard derogatory gossip concerning my marriage to the tetrarch. I understand that it was the subject of much talk in Rome—"

"But, Your Majesty, I have not been in Rome, you understand, for quite some time, and—"

Salome, who had been listening, turned abruptly to confront Lucius. "You do not realize, tribune, that my mother adores hearing her matrimonial conquests discussed. Of course you know that she left my father, who is her uncle, to marry Antipas, who is her half-uncle, in the belief that my dear stepfather there would be a king." She pointed with quick forefinger that flashed the light from a giant amethyst. "Isn't he the regal figure, tribune?" Her laugh was high and shrill and, Lucius felt, as cold and sharp as an icicle.

"Tonight," said Herodias calmly, "is not one of the tetrarch's best moments. But—" she looked quickly at her daughter, and Lucius saw a flash of defiance "—he will yet be a king."

"Perhaps," said Salome. "Certainly if you can arrange it, my dear mother." She winked at Lucius. "And she's a great arranger." All at once she laughed again, high, shrill, this time with the tone of real merriment. "She can arrange everybody, it seems, except that wild wilderness preacher. And he—" she burst into a veritable gale of laughter "—he put her very neatly in her place."

She twisted around to confront Gaius. "Have you heard of the mad preacher of the desert, centurion, and what he said about my dear mother and my dear stepfather?" She winked. "It was a good story. Too good, in fact, and shall I say—" she rolled her black eyes "—too true? At any rate, though Antipas—" she lowered her voice "—is deathly afraid of the man, he had him thrown into"— she pointed with stabbing forefinger toward the floor—"the dungeon down there."

Gaius laughed. "Yes, I've heard that this fellow talked bluntly to the tetrarch. That's why it's all the more magnanimous for the tetrarch to be releasing him."

"Releasing him?" Salome wheeled about on the couch, sat upright. "What do you mean, releasing him?"

"You hadn't heard? I thought the tetrarch had discussed the matter with your mother and you."

"No! Never a word. When, pray, centurion?"

"Tonight, so I understand. Was not that what he meant when he said that he would display his magnanimity?"

"By Yahweh in Israel and the immortal Jupiter!" Salome swung her feet to the floor, slipped around the couch on which Lucius was reclining upon his elbow, and began whispering in her mother's ear.

Gaius, watching Herodias, saw the tetrarchess wince. Her hand, outstretched upon the table, knotted into a small fist, and Gaius could see the knuckles whiten as she clenched the ring-covered fingers. After a moment's low talk between the mother and the daughter, Herodias leaned over and whispered something to the tetrarch.

"Heh? John? The mad prophet of the desert? Oh, no, my dear." Herod's voice boomed. "Oh, no, no, indeed my dear. Not yet, no—" He reached a great hairy hand across his disordered plate and patted his wife's hand. "We must have some dancing. Yes, ho, heh, heh. Dancing we must have. Women. Bring them on." Sharply he cupped his big hands together. "Bring on the Egyptians and the Arabs! Strike up the drums!" He was arousing from his stupor. "Ho, ho." He banged his palms together. "Bring on the dark women." He belched loudly. "It's my birthday, isn't it?"

His hand lunged forward to grasp the wine glass, but he failed to clutch it, and the glass spun off the table and shattered on the floor. But few heard it, for already the drums were throbbing, and a stream of women, tall and statuesque and dark, with only gaudy thin veils about their middles, was pouring through the doors into the hollow square between the tables.

"Most of them were given to him by King Aretas of Arabia," the girl beside Marcus whispered. "The rumor is that Aretas is incensed at Herod because of what the tetrarch did to his daughter; we hear that one of these days he may start a war with Herod; he may come take his beauties back."

"As far as I am concerned, he could have them," Marcus said, leaning over to whisper into her ear, for now the throbbing of the drums and the rhythm of the dancers had made ordinary conversation impossible. He watched them a moment as the throbbing grew louder and faster and the twistings and bendings of the

117

dancers grew more sensual. "They can dance," he admitted, "but I can see no other charms in them."

"Your eyes are not the eyes of Herod," said the girl. She lowered her voice even more. "He's at times a barbarian." Watching her, Marcus saw a shadow cross her face.

"But you—"

"Oh," she said bitterly, "I too am his property, just like those poor women. In fact, I am more to be pitied." Then she laughed, and picking up her goblet, drank the wine. "Look," she said gaily, pointing to one of the women who to Herod's great delight had just executed a neck-to-toe twist almost against the table in front of the Tetrarch, "that one really knows how to wriggle."

But just as quickly she was silent and sat watching the voluptuous movements of the women.

Suddenly Herod picked up his knife of heavy, figured silver, and banged the handle sharply against the table. "Enough, enough!" he shouted. "Hold the drums! Stop the dancing!" In a moment the great room had dropped away into dreadful silence. The women stood in their tracks, the sweat running down their naked limbs in tiny streams.

But Herod was not angry. "Wonderful dancing, my beauties," he said. "Beautiful music. I am greatly indebted to my dear former father-in-law." Gaius caught the sarcasm. "Now let them be fed bountifully and supply them plentifully with wine." He waved his arm. "Out with you, my dark beauties. Quickly. We have more novel entertainment awaiting us." Already the women were grabbing up the discarded or lost veils and hurrying from the great room.

And now Herod arose to his feet heavily. "Keep your seats!" he commanded, as the diners began to rise. "Isn't this my birthday?" As they resumed their places on the couches, he steadied himself against the table. "It is the custom of many great kings of this day and aforetimes," he began, "to grant boons upon their birthdays. It is the occasion for showing magnanimity—" He labored somewhat over the word, but then he went on. "So tonight I have decided to do a deed of charity that will demonstrate my forgiving spirit. I have decided, my friends—" he cleared his throat

"—to release him whom they call the mad prophet of the desert, the man John."

Gaius glanced at Herodias as the tetrarch finished his pronouncement. Her face seemed instantly to drain of all color. He saw her lips move, but he could understand nothing she said. Salome quickly put her hand upon the back of his. "By all the gods, centurion," she said under her breath, "you were right. The old fool. The silly old fool."

"Go, fetch him," the tetrarch commanded, nodding his head toward the detachment of guards standing near the main entrance doors. "Tell him I command him to be the guest of the tetrarch on his birthday anniversary."

Herod sat down, and Marcus, bending forward, saw Herodias lean over and begin talking with the tetrarch. As she talked color returned to her pallid cheeks and ran along the slender white stem of her neck and spread across her forehead, and though Marcus could not hear her words, he sensed that they were coming fast and angry from her thin lips.

"She hates the mad prophet with a consuming hatred," the girl whispered to Marcus, when he had sat back. "The fellow told the truth about her, and it incensed her. She could very happily cut off the fellow's head."

"I can see how she would be vindictive," Marcus observed.

"Yes, and jealous. Who knows better than I?"

Abruptly now Herodias ceased speaking, turned her back upon the tetrarch. Herod, already befuddled with gorging and heavy drinking, shook his head, as if to clear it, blinking his bloodshot eyes. Then he turned to the girl and smiled, as if he had suddenly come upon someone who would prove sympathetic.

"The tetrarchess is very angry at me," said he. "She doesn't think that a man should be magnanimous on his birthday. She spoke very harshly to me." His thick lips were pouting. But quickly he relaxed, and his round dark face beamed. "But you, my pretty chicken, you are not angry with me?"

The girl leaned forward, patted the great hairy fist of Herod. "I think it is fine and generous and altogether worthy of the great tetrarch Herod that he be magnanimous to the mad prophet."

Then she leaned over and whispered in his ear. "But don't tell the tetrarchess I said so."

Herod laughed, patted the girl under the chin. "Ah, my little chicken," said he, bending over until Marcus caught the alcoholic stench of his breath, "what the tetrarchess doesn't know won't—"

Suddenly he broke off speaking, for now the guards were returning, and in the center of the small group was a tall, heavily bearded, gaunt man whom Gaius recognized as the prophet of the desert.

19

The guards escorted the prophet to the center of the open space before Herod and then, bowing low to the tetrarch, withdrew to their station near the doorway. The tall man left alone now before the Tetrarch stood blinking his eyes in the brightness of the great lamps, for he had come from long confinement and doubtless had been awakened from heavy slumber.

Under the searching glare of the lamps, his spare frame seemed covered with little more than skin, now drained of the leathery brown burn of the desert sun. But he stood evenly upon his feet and faced the tetrarch without the slightest evidence of fear or embarrassment. His eyes were becoming accustomed now to the brightness of the great hall, and Gaius, looking into his lean strong face, saw that they were bright and piercing, and he thought of the eyes of the rabbi back in Galilee. But this man was an ascetic, whose eyes gleamed with the first strength of the zealot, while those of the rabbi burned with a different power, an impelling, warming, sustaining strength.

On his feet were coarse sandals, and Gaius, glancing down at them, saw that they had done long service. The soles at the front and on the sides were worn away, and the straps were frayed. His discolored brown robe, too, was old and thin, and where the fold crossed his left shoulder there was a long rent. Save for the robe, held about him at the waist by a rope belt, he wore only a large loincloth. His uncombed hair fell below his gaunt shoulders to frame his bearded face in a tangle of black matted locks. Gaius, looking at this unattractive figure a few paces there in front of him, wondered at the power of the man to attract such throngs to his desert home and to hold them faithful to him through his long confinement.

"You are the man whom they call John the Baptizer?"

For one long moment the wilderness preacher calmly surveyed the tetrarch, and Gaius had the feeling that the prophet was measuring Herod. "Can it be, oh Herod, that I am so changed by my imprisonment that you no longer recognize me?"

"No," replied the tetrarch, "I know you. The question was an idle one. You have long been in prison?"

Again there was a tone of challenge in the even words of the gaunt tall man. "Did you not cause me to be cast into your dungeon? Is your memory no longer than the year I have been your prisoner?"

"Yes, that too was an unnecessary question. But you have fared well during your confinement, have you not?" Herod, Gaius felt, was trying to justify himself, and he sensed in the tetrarch's manner of speaking a certain fear of the strange prophet.

"For a dungeon prisoner I have fared well, for I have had food and drink and visitors have been permitted to see me. But to a free spirit all imprisonment is a heavy stone about his neck."

Herod under the fierce eyes of the prophet had forgot his wine, seemed even oblivious of his guests. Gaius surmised that the tetrarch had come under his spell. He was looking upon John, it seemed to the the centurion, in reversed role; he was the prisoner appealing to his jailer, the accused standing before the bar of his judge.

"But you need not be longer imprisoned," Herod hastened to assure the prophet. "Today is the tetrarch's birthday; today he wishes to demonstrate before his guests"—he swept his arm before him—"that he is the soul of magnanimity. You have spoken harshly of the tetrarch and the tetrarchess. But you doubtless spoke your fierce words in passion. You have not incited your followers to rebel against our government; your offense has been against us personally. But you have paid your debt for the crime against our persons. And now my gracious wife, the tetrarchess" —he glanced quickly toward Herodias but his eyes dwelt only for an instant upon her scowling face—"and I are willing to forgive—"

"Hear me, oh, Herod!" The mad prophet had advanced a pace nearer the table in front of the tetrarch, leveled a lean forefinger. "There is none who can forgive, save God. How say you then, 'I will forgive,' when I have done no sin against you? I have sinned against God in many ways, and He alone can forgive my

122

sinning against Him, but I have not sinned against you—" he turned slightly upon the worn soles of his sandals to stab his long finger at Herodias "—nor against this woman, the most sinful of your concubines!"

One long gasp, as if in chorus, swept around the three sections of the table. Herodias, her face flushing, her lips moving with unheard words, half arose from her couch. "I shall not permit him to say such—"

"Sit down, you sinning daughter of death!" John's eyes were flaming. "You will hear my words. My God has commanded me that I warn you against the wrath to come, oh, Herod and this lustful woman whom you have stolen from your brother to warm your unholy bed! Repent while there is time! The hour grows short. Soon the kingdom will come, and God's children will be delivered."

"Sedition!" Lucius was furious. "The man is mad, tetrarch. You should not permit him—"

"Hear me!" The prophet whirled upon Lucius. "The Messiah sent by God to deliver his children is come! I have seen him. I, John of the wilderness and the desert and the great silent places, have baptized with the water of our Jordan him whose shoe laces I am not worthy to unloose! Even now he goes about Galilee and Judea doing the will of God, teaching and healing and restoring from the dead. To me in this foul dungeon"—he pointed downward—"he has sent his message, and now I know that our Redeemer has come." He waggled his great lean distended fingers at Herod. "Repent, oh, Herod! Repent, lustful daughter of Satan! Repent of your evil ambitions and your lewdness. Call upon God for forgiveness while yet there is time! For the sun is low in the west, and your time grows short. You, if you cast your lot with sin and lusting, must be cut down quickly when the Messiah comes to set up his kingdom. Repent, seek the Lord in his righteousness and his strength, cease your dependence upon the power of the evil one, for his days are growing few, and soon the Chosen One of God—"

Lucius, his face livid now, leaned across in front of Herodias. "Tetrarch, I insist that this man be required to cease his rebellious utterances. Should it come to the ear of the emperor or the prefect

123

Sejanus that the tetrarch Herod Antipas was permitting this madman to speak thus with impunity—"

Herod had sat as if in a daze as the prophet had shouted his denunciation. But when Lucius spoke, Herod shook off the inertia. "You are right, tribune," said he. "I cannot longer countenance his inflamed words. Perhaps his imprisonment has impaired his mind." He faced the prophet. "I had planned to release you," said he. "I had hoped that your days in the dungeon had sobered you, but it appears that your ill-temper has only been all the more increased. Perhaps further imprisonment under more rigorous discipline—"

"He deserves only death!" Herodias hissed the words in the ear of her husband. "Let him be taken out now and beheaded!"

John stood before Herod, his deep-set black eyes staring straight into the tetrarch's sobered face. And once again Gaius, watching the drama, had the impression that Herod was the frightened prisoner awaiting the verdict of a calm but vindictive judge. But only for a moment did Herod hesitate under the stern flashing eyes of the mad prophet. The guards still stood near the entrance doors, and raising his arm to signal them, he called out: "Return this man to his cell."

In a moment they had surrounded John and were walking with him toward the doorway. When they were gone, Herod appeared to relax. He reached for his second wine glass and filled it; he had briefly forgotten about drink during the prophet's thundering denunciation. "Drink, my friends. Let us forget the impolite words of the desert preacher. Drink, and fall to upon the food." He clapped his hands together. "Waiters, see that the vessels are refilled. And now, more entertainment! Is it not my birthday? Ha! More dancing! More music!" His glass had been refilled. He drained it, wiped his thick lips with the back of his hand.

The girl leaned toward Marcus. "Soon he will be drunk," she said. "He is afraid of that madman. Did you not see how frightened he was? Now he is so relieved that the man has been taken away that he will get drunk—and quickly. And when he is drunk enough, he will try to—to interest Salome—"

"You don't mean—" Marcus broke off abruptly. "Why, she's his stepdaughter."

The girl laughed. Then she leaned over so that she wouldn't be overheard. "Isn't Herodias the daughter of his half-brother, and wasn't her other husband, Philip, her full uncle? Salome is Philip's daughter—or she's supposed to be—and also his grandniece. Close blood relationship in Herod's family is no bar to—to romance." She whispered, "He's after Salome now. He's crazy for her. I can tell. He's always seeking new adventure—with women, I mean. He quickly tires of us who—"

But Marcus couldn't hear the remainder of the sentence, for the drums had begun their throbbing, and other dancing women, sultry Arabs with flashing dark eyes and hair as black as crows' wings, came prancing into the great hall and danced their way into the opening between the tables.

Herod watched them for a few minutes, drinking his wine and nibbling at the fruit the servants had now placed before him. But quickly his interest began to pall, though the women went through their voluptuous motions with an abandon that earlier in the evening would have excited him. Suddenly he sat upright upon his couch, waved his hands palms outward rapidly in front of his face as a signal for the dancing to stop. "Hold!" he shouted. "Stop the drums! Cease the dance!"

The throbbing stopped immediately. The women paused in their dancing. "Away with the wenches!" the tetrarch hooted. "Feed them, and give them wine. Let them have all they want. They have danced well, but now I crave a different sight, my friends. And is this not my birthday?" He swallowed the purple wine, wiped his purple lips. "Yes, it is the birthday of the tetrarch of Galilee and Peraea. Shall not the tetrarch have what he wishes on his birthday?" He turned toward Salome, who from her place between Lucius and Gaius was watching him.

Marcus, his eyes upon the tetrarch, whose face was now turned away from him, felt the girl's hand close upon his in the shadows and heard her whisper: "He's about drunk enough now to get brave." He squeezed her hand. "I loathe him," she said, too loudly.

But Herod's thoughts now were far from her. He was looking squarely at Salome. "What the tetrarch of Galilee and Peraea craves to see now," he said, "is white flesh. White and smooth as

125

velvet and soft as satin, with muscles that ripple beneath; I would see white flesh exhibited in a swift dance of unrestrained youth. Away with the raw and the unrefined; let us now feast upon perfection. It would be my great pleasure now if our beloved Salome would honor us with a dance." He smote his hands together, and the diners joined in the applauding.

But Salome, when the applause had quieted, did not stir from her place. She smiled in a half-pout, said nothing. Herodias, too, smiled and remained silent.

"Come, my dear," said Herod, his mouth half open, his thick lips thicker now with desire and purple with his draughts of wine, "please the tetrarch upon his birthday by letting him see you—" he hesitated, grinned drunkenly "—dance."

Salome shrugged her white shoulders. "I could not dance to please the tetrarch," she said. "I am a poor dancer."

"Oh, come now, my dear girl. All Palestine knows that you are a most excellent dancer, that you possess movements that would embolden even the bashful Adonis."

"He fancies himself cosmopolitan," the girl said to Marcus. But she did not enlarge upon the remark.

Herod was pleading with Salome, but she was resisting coyly. "The tetrarch would make sport of me before his guests," she declared, with enough spirit to whet Herod's desire all the more. "He would show off my poor frailties before all these discerning people."

"Oh, no, my dear," he remonstrated. "To the contrary, I would have my guests more fully appreciate the—the—" he smiled, licked his heavy lips "—heretofore undisplayed virtues of our beautiful Salome. I would have her perfection of form and rhythm displayed as the chief attraction of our evening's entertainment. I crave beyond all things—"

"Just how much does the tetrarch crave to see me dance?" Salome's question cut short Herod's pleading.

"Indeed—" He spoke now with new spirit, for he apprehended her question as the forerunner of her yielding. "Indeed, my dearest Salome, what would the tetrarch not give? A beautiful palace of marble in Tiberias, with a great terrace supported by columns carved from cedars of Lebanon, and walls hung with tapestries, and great chests filled with the finest linens—" he turned to face Marcus "—from the looms of our friend of Tyre, and glassware from his furnaces, yes, and plates of gold, and carriages and horses and servants in finest livery—ah, my dear, only let our little Salome name her most lavish desire and it will be the joy of the tetrarch to fulfill—"

"But the tetrarch is now light of heart and happy because of his birthday," Salome countered. "He has drunk much of strong wine, and he might not remember. And besides, I need not a great palace, and carriages and horses, nor"—she leaned forward, glanced quickly in the direction of Marcus, who was leaning close to the girl—"glass and linens from Tyre." She turned her head away, with a toss.

"Ah," said the girl, whispering, "the proud Salome is jealous even of me. She is a vicious, unfeeling, cold-blooded snake. But by the gods, what a figure! One can hardly blame him, the way she flaunts it before him!"

"She is clever," Marcus said. "She is preparing to drive a hard bargain."

"The palace at Tiberias was just a thought," Herod was saying. "It need not be that. It could be other things, my dear. A great ship fitted out with slaves to carry you over the Great Sea, though it would break my heart to have you out of my sight. Anything, my dear girl, anything—" Herod was feeling his wine now. He arose unsteadily, motioned to the guests with unsteady hands to keep their seats. "Anything, indeed, to the half of my kingdom. I would divide it equally with you for one dance." His words were reckless, but the wine had not thickened his tongue. He was frankly pleading.

"But the tetrarch—" Salome paused, for her mother was whispering in her ear. A moment Herodias talked, as the tetrarch waited, and then Salome spoke again. "If the tetrarch would not forget his promise—"

"Never! Never! My dear!" Herod was emphatic. "I have drunk much wine, but I know what I am saying, and I know what I do. I swear it, and these my friends hear me and are witnesses to my oath." That she should display her physical charms tonight at his birthday feast had become the most important thing in his life. He had been upon the point of defeat, but now he sensed victory. He had overcome the gorgeous Salome; even she had succumbed to his will. He raised his hand aloft. "Hear me," he shouted, "if our beloved Salome will dance before us tonight, the tetrarch of Galilee and Peraea will regard her every wish even to the half of his kingdom!" He turned to Salome, bowed. "And now, my dear, will you honor us?"

The girl dropped her eyes demurely. "As the tetrarch of Galilee and Peraea wills," she said. "I shall do my best to entertain the tetrarch and his guests."

"My dear girl," said Herod, his round face glowing, "you shall not regret it!" He backed from the table between his couch and the one upon which Herodias now reclined languidly, walked ponderously behind Lucius, and stood beaming down upon Salome. Then he took her hand, helped her to her feet. Still holding her hand, he bowed to the diners. "And now, my friends, as the climax of our entertainment for which we have all been waiting with such eagerness, our daughter Salome will dance!" He bowed to her, she bowed low, and then she moved around the table behind Gaius toward the little knot of musicians in the corner near the entrance doors at the right.

"By the gods!" exclaimed Marcus, "What a figure! What a woman! I can't say that I blame the old fellow. Can she dance as well as she looks, pray the gods?"

"Wait and decide for yourself." She said it petulantly, he thought, but he did not dwell upon what she had said, for he was watching Salome gliding noiselessly across the floor with the slithering grace of a tiger. And so were all the guests about the great table.

Herod, seated again now, was watching her too. His fat lower lip hung down, revealing large, ill-kept teeth. His eyes, following every movement of Salome's undulating hips as she walked, seemed to be divesting her of her clothing.

Marcus felt the girl's hand upon his. "It won't be long now," she said, "until she'll have the tetrarch drooling."

"Maybe I'll be drooling myself," Marcus said. "By the immortals, what a woman!"

The girl's lips rounded in a pout. Without glancing toward

Salome, she reached for a fig, pulled out the stem, split it in half, bit a tiny segment of the tender pink flesh. "You had better stay away from her," she said casually, "while he's looking."

Marcus laughed, patted her hand. "It's all right to look, isn't it?"

She laughed then. "So long as that's all you do, I suppose. Maybe I'm getting jealous."

Salome was talking with the leader of the musicians. She turned and spoke to the young woman who played the harp, and then to the Egyptian flute-player. "She's giving them instructions," the girl explained. "She's planning to make him—" she nodded toward Herod, whose eyes were still upon Salome "—fall off his couch foaming at the mouth."

Now the girl walked away from the musicians and entered the hollow square. She stood a moment facing the tetrarch and her mother. In the instant she was motionless. Like a Grecian goddess in white marble she stood before Herod and his guests.

"So help me Hercules," Marcus murmured. "What a woman!"

Salome was tall, inches taller than most of the women watching her, a great many of them out of jealousy inwardly disapproving. But her litheness, her graceful carriage, her slim, beautifully proportioned figure accentuated her appearance of tallness.

"She is more Roman than Jewess," Marcus said.

"Yes, and more Oriental than Roman," said the girl. "As soon you will see."

Slowly Salome turned a complete circle. Her black hair had been combed back loosely into a large knot that sat upon the back of her graceful neck, and the knot was held in a bag fashioned of what appeared to be a fine net of gold. The net was attached at its open end to a narrow band of woven golden threads in which were embedded an immense number of stones that sparkled brilliantly with the reflected light of the lamps. One large red gem at the top, Marcus reasoned, served as the clasp that held the band together.

Her gown, Marcus saw with quick appraisal, for he appreciated textiles as well as figures, appeared to have been fashioned of finest silk from the Orient, worth its weight in Herod's gold. Cut almost to the waistline behind to expose her straight, sculptured back, it came up high in front in two sections split likewise nearly to the waist and tapered out at the throat into narrow bands that crossed and went around the neck to be held by an enormous gold pin in the shape of a Roman eagle with wings outspread. At the waist it was held close to her lithe figure by an enormous belt of gold mesh fastened at the front with a pin attached to a tremendous red stone like the one that secured the band about her hair. Below the belt the skirt was full and fell away almost to her jeweled sandals, but above it the gown was modeled to fit snugly.

And now, having pivoted around slowly to reveal her costume and her figure to the guests about the three-sided great table, she turned and, looking over her left shoulder, signaled with a nod of her head to the musicians.

The harp began first. In measured, rhythmical soft notes the harpist stroked the instrument, and as Salome almost imperceptibly extended her left foot forward, raised her right arm and bent her graceful body in a line that ran straight with the line of her left leg, and began to tap the floor gently with her foot in time with the music of the harp, the drums started their low throbbing. Now the volume was increasing, and the tetrarch's guests, their eyes upon the slim girl in the shimmering white gown, saw her foot weaving, and watching, they saw the sinuous movement travel upward as her leg, its modeled shapeliness outlined beneath the gown, began to stir to the rhythm of the drums and the mellow throatiness of the harp. Nor did it stop until it had moved along the slimness of her waist upward to pass along her weaving arm and out her fingers. Then she extended the right foot forward, raised the left arm and repeated the movement.

The throbbing of the drums grew more insistent and now the sharp notes of the flute joined the music of the harp and the drums, and Salome began to circle the open space before the tetrarch, and suddenly her whole body seemed vibrant and her hips swayed and her arms rose and fell in sinuous rhythm. And now she threw her head back and half closed her eyes so that the long black lashes spread fanlike in a dark half circle, and she gave her whole body to the voluptuous movements of the dance. Back and forth, swaying from side to side, now turning her white back upon the tetrarch, now whirling to face him, she moved on light feet as

130

the drums and the harp and the shrill high flute poured forth their maddening oriental rhythm.

Salome now was dancing in the center of the open space. All at once, she clapped her hands together, kicked high, and her dainty sandal, the jewels sparkling as they caught the lights of the lamps, flew from her foot and went spinning heel over toe straight toward the tetrarch. Herod grabbed for it, but he had drunk too much of the wine, and it sailed almost through his hands to skid along the floor behind him. Almost by the time it landed, an Arab woman, one of Salome's maids, picked it up.

The other sandal she sent whirling toward Marcus, but it was high and he could not touch it. "Ah," said the girl, "now she dares show an interest in you. Perhaps she thinks you have more to offer than the tetrarch." She laughed, and Marcus hoped he detected a tone of jealousy.

"I could give her some fine cloth for gowns, and some pretty glass."

"You fancy yourself clever," said the girl.

But Marcus was watching Salome, for the music was increasing in volume, and the drums were throbbing faster, and now the guests were leaning over the tables to get a better view of the girl's waving, twisting, sinuous figure. But they hardly saw it, so fast did her arm fly to her head as she flipped the golden net from her hair, gave her head a fling that sent her black hair tumbling to her waist, and slung the golden net across the hall, where an Ethiopian maid quickly recovered it.

She came tripping upon noiseless bare feet up to the table of the tetrarch, her body undulating as every muscle from toe to neck seemed to pulse with the throbbing, beating rhythm of the drums and the shrill shrieks of the flute. Herod started to rise, but Herodias, watching with frozen smile that failed to soften her cold countenance, restrained him, and he sank back upon the couch. Around the square Salome danced, her torso following in sensual wrigglings and sinuations the wild abandoned rhythm of the music. Now he raised a white hand, and the musicians understood, for they bent nearer their instruments and the music grew faster and faster, until the vast hall seemed to be leaping and rolling with the wild throbbing of the strangely exciting rhythm.

Salome, too, was leaping into the air. Somehow she had removed the bottom portion of her gown to reveal a short, white skirt. The girl, leaping and wheeling, spun the transparent skirt high upon her whirling legs; the skirt spun outward like a fast revolving top. Faster and faster she whirled upon the balls of her flying feet as she moved almost imperceptibly toward the open end of the square, and the tetrarch's guests, watching her spinning form, fancied themselves spinning too around the fast rotating axis of her revolving body.

Now she had reached the ends of the tables that ran down on either side of the cross section at which the tetrarch and Herodias and the honor guests sat. The music had attained a frenzied tempo, and the great hall was reverberating with sound. The air was sultry with the heaviness of the incense and the smell from the burning lamps, and the odors of the food and the wine, and the clashing fragrances of the perfumes and the oils. Herod sat hunched over on his couch, his elbows resting upon the table, his empty wine glass in front of him, his eyes fastened upon the spinning figure of the dancer.

Her hands held high above her head, her skirt now almost parallel with the floor wheeling beneath her, she spun giddily as the diners tried by the power of their eyes to slow her whirling. The drums increased their rhythmical thumping, the flute shrilled above the heavy bass of the drums and the harp strings. Salome lowered an arm as she maintained her giddy wheeling; and suddenly, before the watchers realized what she was about, the shimmering skirt went flying across the open space.

Abruptly, the music ended, Salome stopped spinning, and before Marcus and the others could recover, had run around the table at the right and out the door, her long waving black hair falling protectingly around her slim white shoulders.

Behind her trailed two black maids, her sandals and the recovered pieces of her costume in their hands.

In a short moment, even before the wild applause had subsided, Salome had slipped into her place between Lucius and Gaius. Her white gown gave no indication of having been so precipitately discarded, her wild black hair was again rolled neatly into an enormous knot that reposed serenely in the golden mesh of the

132

bag held at the top of her head by the large red stone clasp.

Herod wheeled his ponderous frame around, put his feet upon the floor, sat up unsteadily, raised his hand, and immediately the vast hall was silent. "Wonderful, my dear Salome," he said, and he licked his puffy lips, "wonderful, marvelous, great dancing, my dear, gorgeous display, wonderful evening, wonderful party, wonderful birthday."

"Soon he will be doing some wonderful snoring," observed the girl to Marcus. "And then maybe I'll get some wonderful rest from him."

Marcus leaned over, whispered in her ear: "And I'll continue to have a wonderful night with you, yes?"

She slapped his hand on the couch in the shadows of the table. Then she squeezed it. "Silly," she said, and winked. "But sweet."

"Yes, glorious dancing," the tetrarch was saying. "Good of you, my dear, to dance at my birthday party." He grinned, wiped his mouth with his hand. "Waked up some of these old fellows about our festive board—" he turned toward Marcus, then to Lucius and Gaius "—eh, my Roman friends? Yes, great party, thanks to you, my dear Salome." He coughed, reached for his wine glass. And when he had swallowed the wine, he coughed again, wiped his purple lips. "And now, my dear daughter, what is your pleasure? The tetrarch of Galilee and Peraea is not one to forget a promise once made. Speak up, Salome. It is for you but to name your wish, and it shall be granted. I have sworn it, have I not?"

Salome threw back her head and laughed. It was a merry laugh, Gaius thought, a friendly gesture in appreciation of the tetrarch's lavish thanks. "Yes," she said, "and I thank the tetrarch for his kind words. But I think not that the tetrarch will grant my wish."

"What! Have I not promised? Have I not sworn before"—he waved his hand— "this great company of friends here to do me honor on my birthday? Think you, my dear girl, I would dishonor them and myself by refusing you? Speak. Name your wish. Palaces, ships, slaves galore, gorgeous raiment, anything, yes, anything to the half of my possessions and sovereignty."

"But the tetrarch would not dare!" Salome spoke loudly, and the assembled guests heard it down both lines of tables, even to the end of the banqueting hall. "The tetrarch would be afraid!"

"Afraid!" Herod shouted. "Never! Of what am I afraid, pray, my girl?"

"The tetrarch has already shown his fear in this case. He is not afraid of the king of Arabia, though Aretas threatens bloody vengeance; he is not even afraid of the emperor, for he is a friend of the great Tiberius and the great prefect Sejanus. But still I am convinced that he will never grant me my wish." Salome reached for a grape, chewed the meat, picked the seeds from her mouth with dainty fingers.

Herod arose, swaying, supported himself against the table. "The tetrarch is afraid of nothing!" He spoke sharply, though his tongue was thickening. "Be done with this nonsensical talk. What does Salome wish in recompense for her dancing?"

"Does the tetrarch promise to give it to me?" Salome's eyes were shining, and her smile was bright. "Will he really fulfill his promise so rashly made?"

"I have sworn it, Salome. I swear it again. Only name it."

Gaius, turning now to watch Salome, saw her expression change. All the warmth, the apparent friendliness she had been showing in her tilt with the tetrarch, was suddenly washed from her countenance, and now it seemed utterly cold, and when she spoke her tone was deadly serious.

"My desire is that you have the head of the mad prophet brought to me on a platter."

The eyes of Herod's guests, the centurion saw and even more strongly sensed as he looked up quickly, were centered upon the girl beside him, and the expressions on their faces ranged from amazement and shock to cold horror.

"What!" Herod swayed but sustained himself by bracing his knees against the couch and his hands upon the table. "Did I hear you aright, my dear? The head of John the Baptizer? You wish his head cut off and brought here?"

"Indeed. It is a simple wish."

"But, Salome, you don't mean you wish the mad prophet beheaded and his head—you cannot mean—"

Salome's high shrill laugh rang out across the silent hall. "I knew you would not grant my wish! I knew you were afraid! I knew you would refuse me my only request."

Herod's eyes were upon his golden plate. "Salome, I thought you would want something gorgeous—palaces, ships, servants, clothes, my dear child." He was sobering. "I had no idea that you would want the head of a man. Such a strange, unearthly request, such an abnormal desire for a beautiful young girl, such a terrible—"

"I knew you would not stand by your oath. I knew you would be frightened, fearful, afraid—" she leveled her outstretched white forefinger at the tetrarch, raised her voice, spoke in her most sarcastic tone "—afraid of the mad prophet, who would insult you and your wife, my mother, before these guests and these representatives of Rome, against whom he inflames his miserable followers. I knew you were fearful, frightened, superstitious—"

"Silence, Salome!" His face was flaming now, his voice shrill with anger. For an instant he looked at the girl, and she dropped her eyes. "It is a hellish, unwomanly request," he said, and his tone was more subdued.

"I am utterly surprised, and disappointed." He paused for a moment. When he spoke again, his voice was calm. "But I have promised. I have given my word. The word of the tetrarch of Galilee and Peraea is law. It is binding upon him as well as his subjects." He raised his voice. "Guards!" The men near the entrance came sharply to attention. "You have heard the request of our daughter Salome. Go you at once into the dungeon and fulfill that request. It is my command."

He sank upon the couch, covered his face in his hands. The dining hall was silent. There was only the diminishing sound of the guards' footsteps.

After a while footsteps were heard along the passageway. Now all eyes were upon the entrance. The tetrarch Herod raised his head. The guards were at the door. One bore a large silver platter. Herod turned his head. "Fetch it to the table and place it before our daughter Salome," said the tetrarch. The little procession moved forward through the open space in which Salome had danced. The guard set down the platter.

"The tetrarch's rash promise is fulfilled," said Herod, without glancing toward the platter. "My word remains law."

The head of John the Baptizer lay upon its left ear. Beneath the head was a linen napkin edged with lace, now crimson with the blood that had drained from the severed neck. The face lay toward Gaius. The mouth was half open, and the fierce black eyes were set in a wild stare. The great tangle of blood-soaked black hair heightened the pallor of the bearded face, and the thin, bloodless blue lips were frozen now in a thin, startled smile.

Nausea gnawed at Gaius's middle and mounted to his throat. He turned his eyes away.

Herodias calmly studied the platter's gory burden. Salome, inclining her head slightly to the right so that she might get a more nearly parallel view of the shriveling face, idly reached for a grape, chewed the pink flesh.

Herod risked a glance toward the platter, quickly turned his eyes away. "He is not dead," said the tetrarch. "He watches me. He shall always watch me. I am undone. This night I have sinned greatly. I will never rid myself of this great burden of sinning." The tetrarch, erect now and sobering, appeared oblivious of all in the great hall save himself and the severed head of the mad prophet. "Never for me will there ever be peace again!" He covered his face in his hairy hands.

Salome, her voice entirely calm, turned to whisper to Gaius. "The tetrarch seems somewhat indisposed now that we have been avenged," she said. "He has always been afraid of the mad prophet. And he still is. He thinks there's something supernatural about him. He sees a mystery in everything; he's highly superstitious." She laughed, the cold cynical laugh of the assassin about to thrust the dagger, Gaius felt. "He's afraid of that!" She pointed to the pallid head lying in the center of the reddening circle. "But my pet wouldn't harm poor Herod, would he?" Herod's guests seated near her were aghast. "No, indeed, he wouldn't harm anybody. He wouldn't say a word against even little Salome." Her lips rounded in a half-pout. "But Salome is losing her manners. She has let her pet come to the banquet and has given him no food. The poor darling must be very hungry, for his mouth is open!"

She picked up a fig and, leaning forward across the table, with her own dainty ringed fingers wedged the fig between the rigid teeth of the gory severed head.

Herod at that instant looked up, turned his eyes to the right, full upon the profaned pitiful face. For a long hushed moment the wide eyes of the dead prophet, set and staring and glistening in the flickering light of the lamps, held the tetrarch. Then Herod seemed to wrench himself free of the power of the eyes.

"Oh, God in Israel!" he screamed. "He is not dead! His eyes moved! They haunt me! Always, always to the end of my hard days they will haunt me! I am—I am—" Suddenly his big hands clutched at his middle, he half arose from his couch, his hands pushing frantically against his tremendous paunch. "I am sick! Air! Air! I must have air! Get me out! I am about to—uugh-h-h—quick! Air!—" Servants came racing. With one on each side supporting him as he held his heaving middle, and others trailing behind, they unceremoniously hustled the tetrarch toward the great doors opening upon the terrace.

But they were not fast enough. Three paces short of the quickly opened doors Herod's sorely punished huge stomach could carry its burden no longer. And there, in the full view of all his guests assembled for his birthday feast, it revolted.

Quickly the servants helped the tetrarch through the great doors, and other servants came running with basins of water, towels, mops.

20

She lay now, her head in the crook of his arm, while outside the March winds howled and whistled in boisterous rage as they flung themselves impotently against the stone might of Herod's Machaerus fortress-palace.

"Naamah—" He pronounced it slowly, rolling the name out on his tongue. "Naamah. It is a lovely name, though not so lovely as you."

She stirred, so that the fragrance of her hair, its dark beauty lost now in the blackness of the unadorned, severe bedchamber, came renewed to him. "That's what it means," she said, "loveliness. Herod gave me the name. He said it was the name of a beautiful woman who came into the establishment of King Solomon long ago. He thought it appropriate that he name me for her, he said. The name is Jewish, and I am of Jewish descent. And so that's what he calls me."

"How did she happen to be in the establishment of King Solomon?"

"I don't know anything of her except her name. Perhaps her story parallels mine. She was doubtless sent as a slave to King Solomon as I was to Herod. Nothing survives of her but her name, as nothing will be remembered of me, except that we were playthings of kings."

"A slave! So help me Hercules, Naamah, I didn't know—"

"No, I didn't think you did!" He sensed the bitterness in her laugh. "You didn't know you were sharing your bed with a slave woman. And now you'll be sending me away." She moved, as if to sit up. He held her, gently.

"Silly Naamah!" he scolded. "What difference is it? Aren't you still a gorgeous woman?"

"Then all women are alike to you, so long as they are beautiful, and have what you describe as gorgeous bodies?"

"Well, all women, I would say, are equipped in the same way"—he said it teasingly—"though, of course, there are differences. But how, pray, would the matter of being slave or freeborn change one's womanly equipment—"

"I hate you!" she snapped. "And I would have you to know that I was just as freeborn as you! Had it not been for a damnable rich Roman—"

"I'm sorry, little one," he said, and his tone was sincere, and even pleading, "I was only teasing." In the quiet darkness of the great palace, he patted her shoulder gently. "Tell me, how came you to be sent to Herod? Perhaps I could—"

But she lay silent, and he supposed she was pouting.

"Tell me, Naamah, what of the rich Roman? I might be able—"

"I have turned those pages," she said. "There is no turning back to read them again. I don't like even to think of those other days, when things—when I was different."

"But the rich Roman, Naamah, what—"

"I like not to think of him," she said. "When I think of him, I begin to go blind with rage and repressed fury. I—I loathe him more than—than—"

"Than old Herod?"

"Far more, yes. Herod is a wild barbarian, a slave of his desires. He takes what he wants, but he does it openly, without pretending to be something he isn't. If he sees a woman and wants her, he tries to get her. That's why he was so determined to have Salome, and he would have had her if he hadn't been scared out of his wits by the strange way the party turned out. He'll have her yet, after he recovers from his fright. But when he wants a woman, he wants her because she is a woman, a pretty plaything with which to satisfy himself. He doesn't want her as a means of accomplishing something else—to make money or obtain someone's favors or carry out some other purpose. He at least honors her to the extent of admitting that she is a woman and not just property." She was silent, spent with the indignation her voice had revealed.

"But this Roman? What did he look like? How about him?"

"I have never seen him. If I ever do, I will claw his eyes out, by all the gods!"

139

"But, Naamah, my dear girl, you have not told me anything about yourself yet."

"I was not always a slave, a plaything of men, a mere object," she said, and the bitterness sharpened her voice. "I was once— and not so long ago—as free as you are, yes, and as clean as your sister, if you have one. I lived in the southern region of Dacia, and I was of the ancient aristocracy of that land. My Jewish forebears had gone there many years ago. But we Dacians were peaceful, and we had no army comparable to Rome's. And then the Romans came, and they raped, and pillaged, and slaughtered—oh, by the gods, how I despise the Romans, though I was sent to Rome to study as a young girl and though I know the capital well, and though I am even now talking with a Roman—"

"Cannot you forget all that, Naamah, just for tonight anyway? Cannot you close your eyes to my being a Roman and the wrong done you by the Romans, cannot you—"

"No," she interrupted. "But now I must finish the story, for having told it thus far, I must rid myself of it entirely!" She paused, moved slightly, so that the fragrance of her hair once more rose around him. "I was captured by ruffians who used me wantonly and cruelly, and then I was put upon the slave block, and sold—" She hesitated, and when she spoke again her voice was almost a hissing. "Bah! What knows the cold, dead heart of Rome about civilization? What cares Rome for the rights of other peoples, for common decencies? They stood me up, with hardly any clothes on my back, and displayed me, and gave me over to the sneering, superior-feeling Roman men to be ogled over and felt of and studied as though I were a brood mare or a common woman of the streets. And I stood there in shame and anger and wretchedness until finally a proud rich Roman, a senator, paid the price and bought me! And then I was sent away, not into service as a laborer but into further degradation, and in the foul hold of a ship I was brought to Tyre, and there, without ever seeing me, the man who was to receive me had me sent as a gift from him to Herod at Tiberias, and—"

"By all the gods! I—"

"You what?"

Marcus lay upon his back, his eyes staring wide open toward

the ceiling lost now in the chamber's darkness. "I—I had no idea that you had been so shamefully treated." He was thankful that the girl could not see his face. "That man at Tyre, did you know him? His name, I mean? Did you ever see him?"

"No. And it is good for him that he is lost to me. If I ever find him, I will kill him! I would not have done this, I would not have talked this way only two years ago, for then I was different. Now I am hardened; I could kill him without the flicker of an eyelash!"

"I doubt it, Naamah," Marcus said. "You paled considerably when those guards walked in with that wild fellow's head on the platter. You didn't appear particularly composed then. Salome, I would say, is the cold-blooded one, not you."

"But the mad prophet had done them no harm. He had only told the truth about them, and not half the truth, at that. They had no cause to kill him." He felt her warm body stiffen slightly, her hand clench into a little fist. "That's just it!" she said, with emphasis. "Can't you understand, even though you are a Roman of the upper class? Can't you see that a man, a woman, just any man or woman, has no rights under the Roman system?"

"But, Naamah, if Rome is powerful enough—"

"That's what you Romans believe. Yes. But is it right? Just because Rome has a powerful army, many weapons, many resources, much wealth, great power, is it right for Rome to invade Dacia and plunder and kill and rape? Is it right that I should be a slave and you a free man? Where are you better than I am? Why should I be forced to share your bed?"

"But I have not forced you to do anything, have I? In fact, I had fancied that you had been finding my company pleasant."

"Yes, but as a beggar enjoys the crumbs that fall from the table. Don't you see? Can't you understand? I am a slave, though they did not punch my ear because it would have robbed me of a part of my commercial worth. I am at the call of Herod. If he tires of me, he can do with me as he wishes, cast me upon the street, even kill me. Just now I am petted and pampered. But that is of the moment. The point is, I am not my own. And there are thousands, countless thousands, like me, more miserable by far, in fact, than I am. And it is not right. The gods did not ordain it."

"The gods, Naamah; who are the gods? You are an intelligent

woman. What are the gods? Do you not know that they were invented by men to give approval to the acts of men? Do you not know that the gods rule as men would have them rule? The gods! Bah! I put no faith in them!"

"What, pray, do you put faith in? Anything?"

"Yes, money. Money is the gateway to power. With money one can purchase anything he desires."

"I do not know. And I am not sure about the gods being only an invention of men. It seems that something must oversee the acts of men."

"But you just said that men were unfair, that right is being trampled in the dust, that thousands are miserable, downtrodden—"

"Yes, I did. I am confused in my thinking. Perhaps there are no gods. Perhaps I just devoutly wish there were. Perhaps it is just that there should be." She lay silent for a long moment. "I should not have burdened you," she said, after a while. "But that is my story. And now once again I am closing the door upon it, I—I hope." In the darkness she felt for his hand, squeezed his fingers. "I shall even forget—until morning—that you are a Roman."

"Naamah, as a Roman I feel that I owe you a debt," Marcus said. "My nation has evilly used you. Very soon I must leave for Jerusalem, where I have business. But before I go I shall see Herod and purchase your freedom. I will have your emancipation from his own hand. I can do that much to make amends."

"But would Herod permit you to purchase my freedom? Has he tired of me that much? Do you think he is enamored so much of Salome that he would let me go?"

"I do not think he is enamored of Salome anymore," Marcus answered. "He is too afraid of Salome. I think Herod will shy from her as from a leper. And I am sure he will want you all the more. But, Naamah, the tetrarch will not dare refuse me. He knows that my father yet has great influence with Sejanus. And my father is wealthy. Money speaks powerfully, as I told you. Rest assured that I will be able to obtain your freedom."

"And then?"

"You can go with me to Jerusalem. Afterwards we can make further plans. But that is not for tonight, my dear. Tonight is for—tonight. Never worry about the future, when there is the bright and

142

glowing present. Has not one of our poets written something about enjoying the day, for tomorrow we die?"

He pulled her close. Her head was against his chest. He buried his nose in the compelling warm, fragrant softness of her tumbled hair.

21

He seemed to be floating upward out of the dungeons of sleep, drawn by some strange, impelling power, and suddenly he was fully awake though caution kept him feigning sleep. Carelessly, as though he were stirring in sleep, he moved his arm across his eyes and from the shadow of his arm ventured to peep cautiously.

Naamah was sitting up beside him. Bright sunshine was streaming in the windows and he lay quiet a moment to allow the slits in his eyes to adjust to the light. Then he moved his arm again and his eyes traveled up her body until he could see her face.

He was so shocked by the expression of surprise and horror or fright with which the girl was regarding his bare left arm that he opened his eyes wide, and she saw that he was awake. Instantly her expression changed.

"Good morning," she said brightly. "Did you sleep well?"

"Yes," he said. "And you?"

"Very well, thank you."

"You didn't dream of that Roman who sent you to old Herod?"

"No." She laughed. "I have forgot that horrible man. The sun is too bright. It is going to be another wonderful day." Her voice was so merry that he wondered if he had been really awake or if he had only fancied he had seen that expression of horror twisting her beautiful face. "And last night was such a gorgeous night."

"Herod's party?"

"No, after Herod's party," she said.

He sat up, kissed her lightly on the cheek. "You are so sweet."

"You are sweet," she said. "It is a pity you are a Roman. It is a greater pity that you are rich."

"Why does being rich damage me, pray?"

"Because it makes you want to be richer."

"Ha. A woman's reasoning."

"It is true. You are not content with what you now have, but want more. And when you get more you will want to pile up even greater riches. But you may miss the really important things of life in your mad striving for what you consider riches. You may miss the real riches, unless you change your thinking. Do you see what I mean?"

"Yes, but I do not agree. I know what I want, and I'm getting it. The more I get the more I want, it is true; but the more I get the more able I am to buy what I want and lack. But you, dear girl, what do you want?"

She sighed. "Let us not talk about me," she said. "The things I hoped to have are irretrievably lost."

"But today I shall purchase your freedom."

Her laugh had a tone of bitterness. "Your money could never restore what I have lost." She whirled about, slipped her feet from the covers, placed them gingerly upon the floor. "But we must be getting up. It is late. If you are to set out today for Jerusalem—"

"Naamah," he said, ignoring her suggestion, "when I awakened a moment ago, you were looking at me as if I might have been a ghost. Your expression was almost like Herod's last night when Salome put that fig in the mouth of that bloody head. What were you so afraid of?"

"Afraid of? Why, I wasn't—what do you mean? Afraid of?"

"You had a startled, horrified look. Was it—was it these?" With his right hand he pointed to the spots on his left arm.

"Yes," she said slowly, "and the eyebrows. They—they have fallen out. I had not noticed them before. And your tunic sleeve covered the spots. But this morning, lying here in the bright sunlight—"

"It is an extraordinary thing," Marcus said. "But don't let those spots or my lack of eyebrows worry you. No doubt, it's some passing disorder, a skin ailment of some sort." He laughed, but it was forced. "Probably from working too hard to get too rich to appreciate your noble philosophy."

Naamah's face clouded. "It couldn't be—" She hesitated.

"It couldn't be what?"

"It couldn't be that serious, could it? The spots—they don't hurt?"

"Oh, no. As a matter of fact there is no feeling in them. It's just as though the flesh were dead—" The fleeting look of terror that crossed her face stopped him. "May have been caused by a cut from a sword during a fencing bout. I don't know. But it doesn't hurt, and it doesn't bother me." He pinched her chin. "So don't give it another thought. The eyebrows will grow back soon, no doubt, and the spots on my arm will gradually disappear." He tossed the covers toward the foot of the couch. "So help me Hercules!" he said. "We must be getting up, my beautiful one"—he grinned—"as reluctant as I am to do so. But there's much to be done today if we are to start tomorrow for Jerusalem."

"We?"

"Of course. You are going with me, Naamah. Aren't you?"

Her eyes were upon the cold floor, from which she had lifted her feet to slip them into her sandals. Then she looked up, coyly. "I would like to," she said.

22

All day the train of horses, camels, and pack asses had been making the tortuous slow descent from the bald upflung headland upon which Machaerus sat, and now the sun, with its dying rays, gilded the gaunt, scarred rocks as if to taunt Herod with his remembrance of the murdered prophet.

But down here in the green valley of the Jordan the shadows were already long, and night was coming fast and cold. So in a smooth spot they halted for the night and made camp, and when the sun rose again over the eastern headlands they prepared to resume their journey, for the tetrarch was anxious to be leaving Machaerus far behind.

Gaius and Lucius took leave of Marcus, for they were going on Herod's train, while Marcus and the girl, with his servants, were turning westward to swing around the head of the Dead Sea and strike the Jericho road to Jerusalem. Gaius would go all the way to Tiberias with the tetrarch and from there would continue his journey to Capernaum. But Lucius planned to go with them up the Jordan valley only to the point where the waters of the Aenon entered the Jordan. He would then follow the valley of that stream as it cut through the mountains and coming out upon the Plain of Shefelah just south of Mount Ebal would continue northwestward to Caesarea.

"I'll see you both in the early summer," Marcus said. "I'll come by Caesarea on my way to Tyre, and I'll make a journey into Galilee and see you then, centurion. And later I'll expect to have you both visit me at Tyre. I'll try to entertain you well, but I'll promise no dances equal to Salome's and no heads on silver platters. And, tribune," he said, "give my regards to Pontius Pilate and Claudia and tell them to send me word if they need any more glass or textiles."

"Always looking out to get an honest penny," said Lucius,

laughing. "I'll give your regards to the procurator and his wife. And come to see us."

"Speaking of money, Marcus," said Gaius, "you are carrying a tempting treasure in those chests. Many robbers in these parts would like to get their hands on that money Herod paid you. You must be careful. The road up from Jericho is steep and difficult traveling, and many desperate men lurk among the rocks. I suggest that you send a servant ahead to keep a sharp lookout."

"Don't be alarmed about me, centurion," Marcus reassured Gaius. "We are well armed, and we will take care."

So here at the head of the Dead Sea in the fertile valley of the meandering River Jordan, pushing slowly southward from the Sea of Galilee, they parted, and Marcus went west while the remainder of Herod's party struck north.

He rode beside Naamah, and it was pleasant riding here in the valley, for the winds off the great eastern headlands almost a mile above the valley's floor blew above their heads and they escaped their greater fury. And it was warm, too, as the sun climbed higher above the great tableland, though it was March and though the nights came swift and cold with the setting of the sun.

"Do you feel different today?" he asked her as they rode quietly along beside the winding slight depression of a small stream that in wet weather emptied its waters into the Jordan.

"Yes," she said, "I feel relieved to be free of Herod, though I know not what lies ahead. Is that what you mean?"

"Yesterday you were a slave," he said, apparently ignoring her question. "Today you are free. You carry with you your emancipation. Do you feel different today?"

"Oh, that," she replied. "No, I cannot say that I do. I have never been a slave in my heart. It isn't that. Let us say that I feel today as I did yesterday—except for being rid of Herod, of course —but that neither today nor yesterday did I feel as I did before I was made a slave. Do you see what I mean? My experiences, my cruel treatment, the indignities, the depravities—these have changed me, have left scars that can never be erased, wounds that will not heal. Don't you see? Yesterday I was a slave, today I am free. But it is not that simple. Today can never wipe clean yesterday. Put it the other way: yesterday I was free, today I am a slave.

148

"I must sound foolish. Here is what I am trying to say: I have always been free in my mind, during the days I was a slave just as much as during the days before my enslavement, and yet, now that I am free, I remain just as much a slave as I was during the period of my bondage."

"Naamah," he said, "I believe I understand what you mean. You feel that because you have been harshly treated and subjected to indignities, that because you have been forced to make your bed with men, and were given to old Herod and forced by him to share his bed—"

"That I feel befouled, you mean? No, it isn't that, I think." She smiled. "Did I not share your bed the last two nights? And did you force me? Of course not. And will I not share it again tonight?" She looked toward him, coyly, out of the corner of her eyes. "I am inviting myself even before I am invited. I am—"

"My dear girl. I—"

"No," she interrupted, as if she had not even heard, "it is not that. Half the women in Rome, so I understand, will crawl into a strange bed for a smile and a squeeze of the fingers. No, I do not feel soiled because of any act, or any series of acts, I think. I don't know just how to explain it. Perhaps it is the weight pressing upon me, the weight of evil and intolerance and imbecility and utter depravity that I have seen in my days; perhaps it is the state of the world today; perhaps it is that I have seen so much of suffering and evil and so little of charity and simple joys." She paused, was silent for a long moment. Nor did Marcus say anything. Then she spoke, slowly, as though she were measuring her thoughts. "Where shall one find a man who is not selfish, who is not cruel, who is not intolerant of the rights of others?"

She meditated, as if seeking an answer to her own question. "My father came nearer to being it than any other man I have ever known. Yet I did not know him well, because I was so long away from home, and it was shortly after my return that the Romans came and—" She stopped abruptly. "But that page is turned." She smiled brightly. "And you have been kind to me, and gentle. But even you are selfish, you have said it yourself, and believe only in the power of money, and you have the arrogance of the high-born

149

Roman, and I'm afraid you'd be intolerant of poverty and weakness and perhaps even of simplicity or humility."

They rode again in silence, and now they had climbed above the green valley of the Jordan and had come again into a region of gravel, and about them no longer were there vegetation and the signs of awakening life but only desert sands and shriveled, dwarfed things clinging desperately to a frail existence.

Thus they were riding silently when one of the servants approached Marcus. "Master," he said, "we are nearing the Jericho road and soon we shall be climbing into the hills. There are many robbers in these parts, and we carry much treasure. Would it not be well for me to ride a few miles ahead so that if highwaymen appear they will not be able to take us by surprise?"

"Indeed, yes," said Marcus. "Select one other to go with you and keep a sharp lookout on either side of the trail, especially where there are outcroppings of rocks among which they could conceal themselves."

"It would perhaps be better, sir, if I placed this other man between me and the main column so that he could send back the alarm quickly should I discover approaching robbers," the man countered.

"Well, as you think best," Marcus replied. "Just so you do not permit us to be taken by surprise."

He saluted, rode off. Marcus and the girl, now abreast, now one behind the other, according to the smoothness and width of the way, rode toward the junction with the Jericho road, and after a time they came to it, and turning left, began the steep climb toward Jerusalem high upon the hills toward the southwest.

The sun had now crossed the sky and was fast dropping toward the hills above them. "Soon it will be time to stop and make camp for the night," said Marcus. "I doubt if there is an inn in this desolate land."

"The nights are cold, for the heat quickly lifts from the gravel, and I shall be frightened when the wolves howl among the rocks, and sometimes even a lion grows bold and comes prowling in search of an unwary sheep or ass, and—" She was looking at him under lowered lids, through her long black eyelashes.

"And so you'd like for me to post a guard near your bed to see that no wolf or lion—"

"You can be so teasing," she said, her lips pouting.

He laughed, so that the servants following behind looked up quickly to discover why their master had suddenly become so merry. "You are a tantalizing morsel," said he. "But I had already planned tonight's arrangements. It's tomorrow night and the next night, and all the other nights, that I have already begun to worry about. I wonder, my dear"—and now his tone was serious—"how I shall be able to go back to Tyre and leave you in Jerusalem. It's strange what a hold you have upon me already, Naamah. I cannot understand it. It's not that I have never had any women. Yet you are a new experience for me. You are more than they have been. I started off with you as I had with those others; you were a pretty plaything with which to idle away a few hours. You were an interesting dinner companion, and most wonderful to be with; but that wasn't all. There's something about you that intrigues me, tantalizes me, makes me wish to be with you and hear you talk, and watch your quick mind work. Naamah, why don't you go on with me to Tyre? What is there for you in Jerusalem? You know no one there, do you? How would you live?"

"I have always managed to live," she said, not without a tinge of sadness in her voice. "I suppose I could go on living. Perhaps there is little promise for me anyway."

"But at Tyre—"

"I do not like to think of Tyre. There my degradation touched bottom. Before I had been put upon the block and sold after sharp bidding; but at Tyre I was given away. How could I be happy in Tyre?"

A long time they rode again in silence; the trail narrowed as it led between high upthrust boulders. "Naamah," Marcus said when they had climbed yards higher on the trail, "why could you not be happy at Tyre? I have money, and you could have all your heart wished. And I would try to make amends for the wrongs that have been done you."

"And be the mistress of an arrogant rich Roman instead of a half-Jewish, half-pagan tetrarch? Where would be the difference?"

"Would there be no difference in being the mistress of Herod and the wife of the proud rich Roman?"

"Yes," she said, "all the difference in the world. Yet, even then, I fear, there would remain the canker in my heart, the remembrance of things lost irretrievably, the knowledge that the better part of me had been left somewhere along the way, the fear—"

"Naamah, your argument is without reason," said Marcus. "You would be withholding nothing, you would have lost nothing that could not be restored, for you have spoken frankly of your past, and in revealing it you have been restored. You are free, you are young and intelligent and beautiful. A bath will cleanse you of the grime of travel and then you will be clean—clean all through. But I—I have not cleansed myself in revealing myself to you. I am the one to make amends, to seek pardon, to restore myself. Yet I dare not, Naamah, I dare not tell—"

"I would hear nothing of your women," she said, interrupting. "I care not a fig for how many you have had. That is not what I am talking about. I have had men, too, men other than Herod—and you—in the months since I was sent by that black-hearted wretch to be the plaything of the tetrarch. We shall soon be going our ways, no doubt, and I shall be having other men—"

"It is not that, Naamah, not women. It is something else. I have not the courage to tell you, and yet I—I so much want your understanding, your forgiveness—" He was riding now close to her, so that he could almost put his arm about her waist.

"My forgiveness!" she said. "You have added no weight to my burden. You have made it lighter. Did I not invite and welcome the nights with you? Have I not told you it was that—that other—that —oh, I know not what to say, how to express it, how to reveal—"

"But I was not speaking of—of our shared bed, either. It was something else too, Naamah, something dark, and commercialized —yes, I am the better able now to see the depths of depravity—"

"Then that is all the better," said Naamah. "Then we, perhaps, by sharing the blackness could dispel it, by having trod separately the dark valley together could rise to ascend the steep trails—" Her deep black eyes were shining now, and in them Marcus saw new light and hope to start anew, and seeing them now as he had never before seen them, he was sick at heart and at the same moment lifted up and swept to new heights, and a lightness danced along his spine, and he moved nearer to her, and his arm was encircling—

"Hold! Draw rein where you are!"

The harsh, heavy voice was almost in his ear. Whirling in his saddle, he saw the man, a great, hairy, bearded fellow, standing beside the boulder, his huge spear thrust forward.

"Don't move, dog of a Roman!" The fellow advanced a step. "Wriggle so much as an eyebrow, and I'll pin your spindly thigh to the belly of your diseased beast!"

Marcus sat calmly in the saddle. Along the trail now furtive, bushy-headed, bearded squat fellows, their skins burned to a leathery tan, their robes tucked up high on their hairy legs, were slipping from behind the concealing rocks. "You are a plain spoken fellow," said Marcus, contemptuously, "though I think little of your brand of wit. Who are you?"

"You might think better of my brand of cold iron were you to get a taste of it, Roman son of hell. My spear is fairly itching to test the toughness of Roman hide. But to answer your question—" the man bowed low "—oh, proud son of a streetwalker of Rome, you are now being addressed by the leader of a band of revolutionaries who delight in pricking the tough sides of the Roman invader of Israel. Perhaps, oh, foul pig of the sty that is Rome, you have heard of the name—"

"Yes, but nothing good of it, if you are the knave I suspect you to be," Marcus interrupted, looking the leader in the eyes. "But how knew you I was a Roman?"

"It can plainly be seen that you are not of Israel—"

"Yes, the gods be thanked."

"You would strain my good humor, perhaps, to the point where it might break. And then I might proceed to the pleasant task of breaking thick Roman skulls."

"When the procurator hears of this, oh, son of a Jewish swineherd," Marcus retorted, "he will send his legionnaires to seize you and have your bones broken on the cross. Do you not know that the procurator has several legions garrisoned at Caesarea?"

"Ha! Ho! Ho! Hear him, my brave followers! Hear the round-headed, short-haired rat from the Roman gutters! He threatens us

153

with old Pontius Pilate. Hear me, ill-begot cast-off of Rome." He shook his spear almost in Marcus's face. "It will be a long day when that fat-paunched, skin-covered wallow of slimy sewer pipes catches this fox! But enough of this banter. We would have the chests of ill-gotten treasure, and quickly, before our patience draws thin."

"The treasure? What treasure do you speak of, son of unmarried keepers of swine?"

"You would best hold your tongue," said the robber chieftain, testily. "And bring forth the treasure chests quickly. Your servant has told us about them."

"My servant? Did you put him to the torture, foul Jew?"

The leader motioned with his bushy head. "Bring him forth," he said.

Two men stepped from behind the large boulder that had concealed the fellow a moment ago. One was a squat, swarthy Jew. The other was the servant who had gone ahead to serve as lookout. The servant pointed to Marcus. "He brought three chests," he said. "They contain gold and silver given him by Herod in payment for glassware and cloth he plans to deliver the tetrarch."

"Ah, yes," said the leader, "money stolen from the people of Galilee, money taken from the synagogues, money squeezed from the poor people in the villages and on the farms—"

"Did they torture you?" Marcus asked his servant. "I see no marks."

The fellow threw back his head and laughed, and the chief of the robbers and the members of his band standing near him laughed. "Torture me?" the fellow repeated the question, when the laughter subsided. "Of course not. I sought them out." He laughed. "I went in search of them. I knew this was the neighborhood often frequented by Bar Ab—" He stopped quickly, put his hand to his mouth.

Marcus laughed. "I thought this foul Jew was Bar Abbas," he said. And now the scowl on Marcus's face was dark as he glared at the servant who had betrayed him. "If I could just get my hands on you—you—"

The fellow laughed in his face. "But you can't. Never more

will I be beaten and worked to death to put filthy money into the coffers of an arrogant Roman."

Marcus, furious, held his temper. "But how came you to think of this? I thought I had instructed Tullus to select only the most faithful servants to make the journey to Machaerus with me."

The man laughed, this time with real merriment in his voice, and Bar Abbas and his fellow robbers laughed with him. "I was selected because I was one of the most faithful of servants," said he, "one of the most faithful to Tullus. You see, Tullus instructed me carefully how to proceed. It is the idea of Tullus. You see—"

"You mean that Tullus will share in this robbery?" he asked, incredulous.

"These small pickings? By the gods, no! Tullus would plan nothing so trifling. Tullus is taking over the dyeworks, the looms, the glassworks—everything at Tyre and along the Phoenician coast held in your name. You have disappeared, and he will continue the operations—"

"But my father? Sejanus?"

"Ho! Tullus has seen to that. Sejanus will get a much larger share. That will please Sejanus. If your father is not happy over the share he receives, what matters it, so long as Sejanus is pleased?"

Marcus sat calmly, though his thoughts were boiling, and a nausea was creeping into his middle. "So Tullus counseled you to kill me?"

"No, not that. That was my suggestion. I thought it best to bash in your brains and thrown your body, well weighted with rocks, into the Dead Sea. But he thought otherwise."

"What was his suggestion?" He said it evenly, as though it were a matter of small concern to him.

"Tullus was determined to have fuller vengeance—"

"Vengeance upon me. Why, I have never—"

"He said he had suffered for many years under your arrogance, your smug satisfaction with yourself and your growing treasure, your debasing of everybody around you. He said he wanted to see you groveling in the dust, asking for a crumb of stale bread, having the dogs lick your sores, living with lepers—"

"By all the immortal gods! If I could get my hands on his neck, the scoundrelly—"

155

"But you won't. He saw to that."

"What did he propose that—that—you do to me?"

Before he could answer, several of the men, bearing the three chests, came up and dropped them at the feet of the robber chieftain. "Here is the treasure," said one of the men. "The chests must be well filled, too. They are heavy." He nudged one of the chests with his sandaled foot. "And we sent the Roman's servants flying back along the road toward Jericho."

Bar Abbas nodded to the traitor. "Go ahead. Tell him what he wanted to know."

"Tullus said he wanted you to be abased, to feel the misery that you have been causing others through the years. He wanted you to see that your money would do you no good. That would be his own vengeance." He paused, considered a moment. Marcus ventured a glance at Naamah. The girl's face was deathly pale, but she sat erect, proud. Her bearing gave him more courage.

"So he instructed me to arrange for the robbery. He hoped I could find Bar Abbas. He knew Bar Abbas was a revolutionary and had no love for Romans or the smug Jews of the Temple crowd at Jerusalem. The robbers would get all the money, except what they agreed to give me as my share. As for you, your life was to be spared, but your rings were to be removed so that you would have nothing to prove your identity, you were to be stripped of your clothing and left with rags, and then you were to be driven into the leper colony—"

"Leper colony! By all the immortals, did Tullus tell you I had leprosy?"

"Of course not! Do you think I would have come with you to Machaerus had I thought you were a leper? You must be a fool, indeed."

"Did Tullus think I had leprosy? Was that the basis of his damnable scheme to make me a lost man unable to recover my money and my position, even my identity?" He glanced again toward Naamah. The girl's face was deathly white.

"Certainly he did not. Are you a fool?" The fellow's anger was rising. "Don't you know that a man has no dealing with a leper?" The traitor's face suddenly registered uncertainty, doubt. "Why did you think that he might—"

But his words were cut short by Bar Abbas. "Enough of this jabber!" he shouted. "We must be getting back into the rocks. Some of those servants by chance may shortly be coming upon a detachment of those evilly begot legionary sons of Roman pimps!" He turned to the fellow who had betrayed Marcus. "Speak up, man! What do you wish for your share? We must divide it quickly and be gone. Talk fast. Bar Abbas is not one to be quarrelsome over a little money. Open the chests, men. Let us get at the money." Heavy hands were clawing at the fasteners. "Now speak up, fellow. What do you want as your share?"

"I think it would not be too much, Bar Abbas, to ask for one of the horses, a tenth part of the treasure—" he hesitated, grinned, suddenly raised his arm to point to Naamah "—and the Roman's woman!"

Fury, boiling utter rage, swept over Marcus, possessed him. In the instant he sprang from the horse, jumped for the fellow, his fingers outspread, tense, eager to grasp his throat, to choke the life from him.

But he had forgot Bar Abbas. As Marcus clutched for the fellow's throat, the man's great hairy fist swept upward, caught Marcus fairly upon the point of the chin, seemed to lift him clear off the ground.

And now all the upthrust sharp boulders in Judea were tumbling down upon him, pushing into his chin, forcing him down, down, and all the great mountains and the high headland upon which sat forlorn and lost the great fortress-palace of Machaerus and the rounded small rocks and the hot gravel were rolling over him and covering him and blotting out the sun—

Naamah was screaming.

"Quiet, little one," said Bar Abbas. "No one is going to hurt you. Cease your screeching." But Naamah still screamed. Bar Abbas gestured up the trail. "Take her away," he said. "She is raising an infernal din. Send her on the way back to Jericho." He pointed now to the chests on the ground before him. "Get the treasure divided," he commanded, "and quickly. Do you want to hang on Pilate's crosses?"

When they had counted out the traitorous servant's share and he had tied it in a leather bag he evidently had brought for that use, Bar Abbas pointed to the unconscious Marcus. "Get those rings off," he said. "They'll sell for a pretty piece of coin in Jerusalem. And strip him. He wears woolens of finest quality."

"He'll soon freeze in the night air," one of the men observed, as he pulled at the rings.

"No, he won't," Bar Abbas said, laughing. "You'll exchange those vermin-ridden rags with him. Here, hand me his toga. The lepers are around that bend some several yards from the trail. They have a cave back in the hillside. They'll be here as soon as we leave." He reached for the rings, stuck them in the fold of his robe, then took the toga his man had pulled from the unconscious man on the ground. He glowered fiercely at his ruffian band. "Get moving! We have been here too long already. Here, Joab, take his robe, and Abner, see to the treasure chests." He turned to glance at the Roman at his feet. "Strip him! We haven't time to waste. Soon, perhaps, the legionnaires—"

He motioned with his hand. "You fellows, get back into the rocks. We've got to be moving." Already Marcus's servant had mounted, was riding up the trail. Bar Abbas nudged with his foot one of the two men working over the heavily breathing Marcus. "Get his shirt off. Let the loincloth be. Then roll him in your blanket, Jephthah, and drag him to the edge of the road. They'll find him, and if they don't, the vultures will!"

Marcus had fallen on his face. Now two men wheeled him over on his back. Suddenly one of them bent down, to examine him the more closely. "Strange," he muttered, "the Roman doesn't seem to have any eyebrows." He rubbed his big soiled thumb along the eyebrow line, held it up. "See? Blacking, it rubs off."

The other fellow was pulling the tunic over Marcus's head. As it slid free, leaving his body exposed save for the loincloth, the fellow who had noticed the hairless eyebrows pointed to the inner calf of Marcus's left leg. "See," he said, "what a strange spot. Bruise? No—" He was bending over for a closer inspection.

The other robber had seen the spots on the upper arm, now spread to the shoulder and of a greenish-gray, chalky dead look. Bar Abbas turned again to the two men bending over Marcus. "Now roll him in your blanket and—" He saw the spots, bent nearer. "God of Israel!" He hurled the toga from him. The man who had pulled the tunic over his head dropped it across the inert body. The two sprang to their feet. "Unclean! Unclean! Unclean!" they shrieked, and the shout was echoed down the line.

"God of Abraham!" yelled Bar Abbas. "Away from him! Unclean! Get into the rocks!"

But his final screaming command was wasted upon the silent rocks beside the trail, for already the last of the robber band of Bar Abbas had fled. Only Marcus remained, lying naked upon his back on the bare rocks, breathing heavily, his tunic thrown crazily across his chest.

23

Slowly Simon shook his bushy head. "Centurion, that was bad! A hard end for a man to come to. Especially a man like the Prophet John. And those women! They must have been cold-blooded. And you say old Herod was nervous?"

"Yes," said Gaius. "He was badly shaken."

"The son of hell! John was worth a thousand Herods." He shrugged his hunched shoulders. "That's the way of the world. It looks like there's not much changing it. Even the master sometimes gets discouraged—"

"He knows about John?" Gaius interrupted the fisherman.

"Yes, the word outran you. We heard it before we got back to Capernaum from our trip, in fact. Centurion, we have been away, too, down into Galilee and then across the lake to the Gadarenes' country, and down to Nazareth. The master's going to expound the Scriptures on the Sabbath Day at the synagogue, and that's why I came to see you. We thought maybe you'd like to come out to the synagogue."

"I would, Simon. How is the rabbi? Is he still preaching and healing?"

"He's all right, centurion, except that he's tired out from his traveling and the continual press of the multitudes. If he but shows himself, a throng gathers and pushes and shoves to get to him. He seems to hate to disappoint them, but it tires him, and he doesn't get enough rest."

"It seems that you of his band might be able to restrain him from overtaxing his strength—"

"We do try. The Zebedees and I try to stay close by him and shield him as much as we can. Sometimes we put him into one of the boats and push out where they can't shove against him. And he doesn't have to see to the food and lodging. Judas of Kiriot is the steward; he receives what money is given us and sees to giving alms. He always knows where every denarius goes, and he doesn't do any needless spending."

"Simon"—Gaius' expression was thoughtful—"you have just been through Galilee and the Gadarenes' country with the rabbi. What do the people really think of him? Herod, for instance, when he returned to Tiberias had reports of his activities and of the crowds that forever surge around him. He was alarmed. He thinks that Jesus is the spirit of John returned to physical life; he is afraid of the rabbi."

"Well, centurion, many think the master is a great prophet. Others flock to see him because they have heard of his works of healing, and they expect to be entertained. Some believe him to be the Messiah long promised. There are many beliefs about him, centurion."

"What does he seem to think about himself? He must be aware of his great powers."

"I hardly know. The master is a man of mystery. Sometimes I may come upon him seated on a stone gazing out across the little sea, or again high on a hilltop overlooking a field of lilies, or lying on his back, his head upon his folded arms, staring up through the branches of a tree. Sometimes in the midst of a storm on the sea, when the boat is bouncing about like driftwood, one may find him quietly looking out across the churning waters. I often wonder what he is thinking, but I have hesitated to trespass upon his thoughts." Simon reflected a moment. "But I do believe, centurion, that the master feels that he has a great mission, and that his time is growing short. Down in Galilee, after we had visited Nazareth, where the people seemed to see in him only the carpenter boy who had been brought up there, he was in such haste to do his work that he divided the band two by two and sent us out in groups while he himself went another way, and when we all got back here he was anxious to find out what we had accomplished. He seemed pleased and said it was good training against the day when we would no longer have him to lead us."

"What did he mean by that, Simon?"

"I don't know, sir. Here of late he has seemed more thoughtful than usual. Often he says that the kingdom is at hand, and very

161

soon now the kingdom will come, the ancient promise will be fulfilled."

"Simon, do you think that he could be contemplating a rebellion against the authority of Rome?"

"I don't think so, though I confess at times I would almost—" He hesitated. "I was about to say that I almost wish he would lead a rebellion to throw off the authority of Rome."

"But, Simon, it wouldn't succeed. It would cause only needless bloodshed."

"Yes, I suppose you are right. But subjugation to Rome is galling to us. I don't think the master is concerned about political matters, though. He is interested in his kingdom, and his interest is growing. His conviction that he was sent to redeem the world grows stronger every day, but that isn't what many of his followers want. They want him to throw off the yoke of Rome and set up a kingdom of Israel with himself as king. He is popular; the Jews love him, except, of course, the rulers like Annas and Caiaphas and the Temple group who deal with Rome in secret."

"But, Simon, don't you foresee a clash between the rabbi and his followers and the ruling Jews?"

"Centurion, it is bound to come. I think it causes the master much concern. I believe he feels that soon he will have to make a decision—that he will either have to lead a revolt against Rome to set up a new government in Palestine or lose his present great influence over the people. You see, they don't understand him. In fact, centurion, I don't know whether I understand him myself—"

"Simon, what do you think of the rabbi?"

"That is a hard question. We have talked over that question ourselves many a time, too, John, James, Andrew, Levi, and Thomas —Thomas is a hard one to convince about anything that he can't get his fingers into—and the others. Nathaniel seems convinced that the master is the long awaited Messiah. I put much reliance in Nathaniel." For a long minute Simon's round bearded face was reflective. "Jesus is not the sort of man that most Jews believe that God would send to redeem us. We have been looking for a great warrior, centurion, another King David to drive out our enemies."

"Certainly the rabbi is not that sort of man, Simon."

"You're right, centurion, he's not that sort of man."

Simon was looking out through the open doorway toward the blue waters of the little sea. "He's no warrior; he could never lead battles in which people were run through with swords—not the master. He's too tender-hearted for that. And yet, centurion—" he turned to face Gaius, and his eyes were bright and eager, as if with the remembrance of some lively incident "—the master is no mild, spineless man. Never that! He's got plenty of courage. He is capable of a deep and terrible anger at times; indignation seems to rise from his very sandals to the top of his head, and then he is a force to reckon with. In fact, I have never seen a man yet that at such times did not quail before him."

24

All the piercing, sharp boulders along the Jericho road were pushing into his chest now and pressing against his chin and forcing him down and down into the blackness of the cavernous bowels of the earth.

But now he was rising again, pushing aside the boulders, twisting sideways to slip from beneath them, rising and rising and coming nearer the light that must be far above these black and long sunless caverns. And now he had freed himself of the sharp rocks and had moved clear of them and was floating upward and steadily upward through the brackish salt heavy waters of the Dead Sea. But the saltiness of the waters was stinging at his chin, and the cold waters were chilling his face, and sucking at his heavy eyelids, pulling at them, prying them open. And the waters were lighter now and ever lighter, and he was moving more swiftly toward the surface of the lightening waters, and soon he would swim free into the warmth of the sun and the light . . .

Marcus opened his eyes.

Cold water was dripping upon his face from a hand one foot above it. He squinted his eyes in the half light, opened them wide. Two of the fingers were missing from the hand, and it was twisted and drawn.

"My money—" Marcus said, and his voice sounded to him far off and thin. "What have you done with it? When I report this to Pontius Pilate—"

The fellow bending over him laughed, and it was a shrill, mirthless, eerie laugh. "Calm yourself," said the man. "We are not of the band of Bar Abbas. He got your money. Nor will you report anything to Pontius Pilate." He laughed again, and it was almost a screech. "Nor would your money avail you much now."

"But—" Marcus blinked his eyes to clear his vision. "But who are you? Where am I?"

"Who am I?" The man turned his face around, so that the little light remaining revealed its hideousness. He was a squat, shrunken fellow, with a gnomelike head, and Marcus saw with a shudder that the flesh of his nose was gone. "Tell him, my beautiful queen, who I am."

The laugh from the shadow was a cackle, a sepulchral rattle as of dry bones turning themselves in a long-lost, forgotten tomb. "Who are you?" the voice repeated the question. "Who are you, indeed, my handsome prince?" She laughed again, and it was frightful. "You are what he will be soon enough. You are a walking, shriveling, cankering corpse. You are a dead dog abandoned outside the gate of his master's house, spurned even by the vultures. You are a man left too long unburied."

She paused, and when she spoke again it was with less bitterness. "What you are, I am that twofold and more. And what we are, you are bound to become. So welcome to our companionship, stranger."

"But you should not be so—so discouraging to a newly arrived member," the shrunken man scolded.

"No, I should not be so plain spoken. After all, there are compensations. Having reached the bottom, one can sink no lower. Having drained the dregs, one can taste no more bitterness from the cup. When all is lost, there remains no longer the fear of losing. We have come upon peace—the peace of the utterly lost."

Marcus sat up, shook his head to clear his thoughts. "But where—what is this? Where am I?"

"You are in the only place you could find sympathy and companionship," said the man, and his voice was not without tenderness. "Is it possible that you do not know? Could old Bar Abbas have clouted you that hard?" He must have sensed Marcus's bewilderment. "We picked you up a moment after they fled," he said. "We brought you here. We were watching. We would not have brought you had we not known that you belonged with us."

Slowly Marcus looked around. He was sitting almost in the mouth of a cave. Feeble flames from a struggling poor fire inside the cave sent grotesque shadows stirring upon the walls, and looking more closely he saw vague figures that might have been men or wretched lost spirits moving about in the flicker of the sickly flame.

"But I do not understand," he said, his eyes affirming his befuddlement. "We were on the road from Jericho going toward Jerusalem—the caravan—my servants, a girl. I had money—three chests of it. A band of robbers set upon us, I was hit a vicious blow—" he paused, blinked his eyes, shook his head "—I can't seem to remember—"

"We saw it all," said the stooped little man. "We had heard your caravan approaching. It was just over there—" he indicated with the hand from which the fingers were missing "—and we were peering out from behind the rocks. When old Bar Abbas hit you, you went down. Then they started stripping you, and when they saw you were a leper—"

"Saw I was a leper! By the immortals, you don't mean that I—" Marcus stopped, his face a study of amazement and horror. "These spots! The eyebrows—" He raised his hand to his face, covered his eyes with his palm, bent his head forward.

"You don't mean that you didn't know?" the man asked, his face betraying his own amazement. "You must have known, though the servants, the girl—they could not have known, of course, or else they would never have—"

"But she did know," Marcus interrupted him. "She knew of the spots, the loss of eyebrows. She has seen them, remarked about them—"

"Then she must have been a great fool—" he paused, smiled, and the smile made of him a grinning hideous satyr "—or else she loved you greatly."

"Where is she? Did my servant, the faithless one, carry her away?"

"No, when Bar Abbas hit you, she started screaming. She made such a commotion that he was fearful she would bring the Roman soldiers, and so he sent her on up the Jericho road toward Jerusalem. She was already gone when Bar Abbas and those stripping you of your clothes discovered those spots and knew—I am sorry. I had no idea you did not know."

"And these—" Marcus pointed toward the woman, who had withdrawn toward the group nearer the fire, and those around the

166

struggling blaze. "They are—" But he would not say the dread word.

"Yes, we are all lepers," the man said. "We come from far places and different lands. And now you, a Roman, join us. Welcome to our desolate company, but I am sorry you must be one of us."

Marcus got to his feet. "How far is it to Jerusalem?" he asked. "I must be getting there. There I can identify myself and get money with which to return to Tyre. You are wrong about my having leprosy. Those spots, I think, are but some minor skin ailment—"

"Leprosy is a disease of the skin, but often it likewise disturbs the body in general, and the fingers and toes sometimes becomes paralyzed and drawn, and sometimes they fall off—" the man held up his maimed hand, and pointed with the remaining fingers to the frightfully disfigured nose—"and it leaves a man only a poor wreck of himself."

"But in Tyre with my money I shall find a physician—"

"Never, stranger," said the man. "There is no physician to heal you, nor shall your money avail you anything." A note of scorn crept into his tone. "Did not Bar Abbas carry away your money? Show me your money."

"Ha! The money in those chests"—Marcus was recovering his poise, his confidence—"was but a pittance. It was only the price of some goods ordered by the tetrarch Herod. Let those thieves have that money. I can well afford to lose it. When I have found the girl again, I shall go to Tyre and seek a physician."

"I heard the story of your servant who betrayed you. I know you were a great man in Tyre, stranger. But that was long years ago. Now you are a leper. There are many ages between." He paused, reflecting. "I too had money, much money. I had a great house in Athens. I journeyed to Rome, Alexandria, Antioch, and Tyre, and I had servants and houses and a wife and children. I had everything. And then I came to Palestine and I discovered that somewhere I had contracted leprosy—and soon others discovered it." There was a far away look in his eyes. "I never got back, stranger. It was years ago. All that other, I suppose, has gone. It has gone for me, I know. I never returned. I shall never see any of them, any of it again." He shrugged his shoulders. "I am a dead dog. I am a fish that lies dead upon the seashore, cast up by the waves; I am a corpse that has walked forth from the sepulcher and soon—ah, not soon enough—must walk back again."

He pointed to those inside the cave. "And they. Those in there. They were not always walking dead persons. Some had money. Some had families. She—" he gestured with a twist of his head "—the one who was out here—she was once a great one. She sang, she was wildly applauded as she sat in her box in the Circus Maximus at the games, the poets composed poems for her, children followed her in the streets. Now—" He shrugged his stooped shoulders again, lifted his poor hands, palms upward, dropped them in a gesture of futility.

"Some were only beggars from the beginning. But now—now we are all the same. We are the company of the damned, the legion of lost souls. For a time, stranger, it will be a bitter trial. Sometimes it drives men out of their minds. But there is nothing to do but accept the fate the gods have dealt."

"I am not ready to surrender myself, my friend," Marcus said. "I am not certain that I am a leper. I fancy it is only a minor skin ailment that will heal under the treatment of physicians. I shall return to Tyre—"

"Many who are called lepers have not leprosy," said the man. "There are those who only suffer some disorder that gives them the appearance of lepers, no doubt. And some ailments known as leprosy are curable. But that is not important. It is what the world thinks that counts. And that cry of 'Unclean! Unclean!' sends all men scurrying away, unwilling to stand and examine you whether you actually have leprosy or not. When a man sees you, sees those spots, those lost eyebrows, the paralysis that no doubt will follow, perhaps the sloughing off of a finger or a toe—"

"Cease your frightening talk! You would condemn me to your group of the living dead without allowing me even to attempt to escape. If you will return to me my toga—"

"The night air is chill and there are few shelters among these cold rocks."

"Get my toga and I will risk it, my friend. I must be off to Jerusalem."

"You have no toga, stranger," said the other. "They left the toga, it is true, for it was unclean and they would have none of your clothing, but in this companionship what belongs to one belongs to all, and your toga has already been divided among those who had less. Your tunic must serve. But away with this gloom. You in there!" he raised his voice in a rasping shout. "Get you busy with the supper. Don't you see that we have a new member of our band, and must we not put a little more in the pot tonight and make merry around the fire?"

Marcus moved away from the cave's mouth, sat down on a stone. The shadows were growing long upon the rocky hillside, but they were not so dark as those that mounted steadily upward to clutch at his heart.

25

All day and into the night throngs pressed the tall preacher, paler now for the rigors of the winter in Galilee and the mighty tasks of healing and interpreting the words of the Father, more contemplative and reflective now that the significance of his mission seemed to be weighing heavily upon him, of sadder countenance and less quick to wreath his face in a sudden warming smile or break his silence with a merry ripple of laughter.

Through the lengthening spring days and long after the lamps were lighted, the people surged about Simon's house. From along the curve of the western side of Galilee's stormy small lake they brought the lame, the sightless, the paralytic, and the demented, and they laid them in poor pitiful heaps of broken and sinful and sorrowing and suffering humanity at the feet of the young rabbi. From out of the hills of Galilee for miles around, from small hamlets and lonely farms and vineyards sprawled high upon precipitous slopes, from many scattered places in the Esdraelon Plain spreading westward to Mount Carmel jutting out into the Mediterranean and as far to the south as Mount Tabor and Little Hermon and even to Mount Gilboa they came, seeking an end of their burdens of suffering and sin, their tormenting anguishes of the flesh and the spirit.

And as he healed them, speaking a cheering word to this one, a challenging, inspiring word to another, a flaming, vigorously commanding one to yet another, he talked to them of the Father and of his purpose for his children, and he expounded to them the words of the ancient Mosaic law and breathed into the dead words his vibrant new message of faith, hope, and love.

But the many had not ears for his words—only mouths for the food he gave them and eyes for the wondrous acts he performed before them, and he was saddened and grieved for their lack of understanding of him and the mission upon which he had been sent by the Father. And he was tired with his heavy labor.

So on a bright morning in early spring he listened to the repeated requests of his followers, who had been urging him to slip away for a few days of rest from the labor and the multitudes. He got into one of the boats of the Zebedee brothers, and with Simon and Andrew, Philip and dark beetle-browed Judas of Kiriot, the philosophical Nathanael and practical Thomas, and the others of his small group he sailed northeastward five miles across the Sea of Galilee to land east of the point where the Jordan emptied its waters into the lake. It was to be an outing, a pleasant escape from labors and cares.

But they reckoned not with the persistence of the multitude, for hardly had Jesus and his friends gone ashore and walked a mile up the fast greening valley of the Jordan to Bethsaida until the thong was upon them. Hundreds at Capernaum, hearing that Jesus had sailed out across the sea in the early hours of the morning, had started on foot around the rim of the little sea to overtake him, and as they had walked other hundreds and thousands had joined the procession, so that the multitude perhaps would not have been greater had he remained in Capernaum.

The disciples were annoyed and even angered that their plans had come to nothing, but Jesus, seeing the eagerness of the people and their determination to follow him, stood upon a slight knoll and expounded to them his teachings concerning the laws of the ancient ones of Israel, and the love of the Father for his children, and how the children should love each other likewise as they loved the Father. And he healed the sick and the suffering and gave strength to the faint of heart, and throughout the long day he labored with them and healed them and taught them.

As the shadows began to lengthen eastward and climb up the slopes toward the eastern headlands, he saw that they were tired and hungry and faint from the long walk and the day without food. The men in his band noticed it too, and they suggested that he send the multitude forth into the nearby villages and farms to buy bread. "Many have brought no lunches with them, master. It is time they were setting forth to find themselves food, for it will soon be night and they will be hungry."

"But they are already hungry," replied Jesus. "They have

walked a long way, and many were weary even before they started from Capernaum. Now they are faint, and were we to send them forth searching for food, many would fall by the roadside. I know a better plan." He turned to Philip. "How much bread would it take to feed this great throng?"

"Master," said Philip, "two hundred pennies' worth would hardly give each one a small crumb. There are thousands here. Nor could we likely find so much bread on so short notice."

"Have them sit down by groups," said Jesus. "Now is there not someone among all this great company who will share his food with his neighbor?"

A small boy heard Jesus. He ran to Andrew, handed him his little basket of woven rushes. "Take it to him," said the boy, pointing to Jesus. Andrew looked in the basket.

"Master," he reported, "this lad brings five little barley loaves and two small fishes. But what help will this pittance be among so great a crowd?"

"Andrew," said Jesus, "be not contemptuous of the small thing." He took the boy's lunch basket and held it aloft for the throng of people seated upon the ground about him to see. Then he raised his right arm high above his head to signal to the people that he was about to lift his voice in prayer to the Father. He turned his face heavenward, and when the great multitude had settled itself into utter silence, he closed his eyes.

Jesus prayed.

He thanked God for the sincere and beautiful faith of a child. He asked the Father to restore all men, tired and worn with labor and sin and disappointments and betrayals, to the innocence of little children. He implored God the Father to enter into the hearts of men to make them share themselves and all their possessions with each other as sons of God in the same way that children give of themselves and their playthings to their own small brothers and sisters.

As Jesus prayed his words rose and floated above the great throng, and they were words spoken in simplicity and utter sincerity, and the people listening felt that a loving noble son was sending forth majestic phrases to an understanding, proud father. And for them space fell away and the fingers of time ceased their drumming and were immobile, for Jesus was speaking now to his Father. When he had ceased his prayer, many eyes were filled with tears, but they were not tears of sorrow; they were tears drawn forth from the deep well of their emotions.

Now Jesus opened his eyes, and smiling he began breaking the little loaves and handing them to the members of his band and pulling apart the two small fishes. And Simon, Andrew, the Zebedees, and the others in their turn passed them forth among the people.

When all had eaten their fill and were refreshed and strengthened, the members of the rabbi's band went among them and gathered up the food that had remained uneaten so that nothing would be wasted. And soon the concourse of people, now that they were finished eating, and ready to talk at great length, began to remark upon the strange way in which the rabbi from Capernaum had provided the great feast, for countless hundreds had been bountifully fed.

Some said that they had watched and that all the food had come from the two little fishes and the five small barley loaves; they said that, as the rabbi had blessed the food of the boy and had begun to divide it, the loaves and the fishes kept renewing themselves through the power of Jesus with his Father. Others maintained that the miracle of the feast had been wrought in another manner; they contended that the loaves and fishes of the generous small boy had not renewed themselves but that they had been used by the rabbi even more skillfully to show the virtue of being willing and anxious to share one's portion with one's neighbor. Many of those who had come forth to follow the rabbi, they declared, had come prepared with food against a long visit into the country north of the Sea of Galilee, but seeing the great throng, each who had brought food had been reluctant to fetch it forth because he thought his neighbor would beg it of him.

Those who offered this explanation of the great feast declared further that the example of the small boy, used so happily by the rabbi to show the beauty of sharing and woven so skillfully into his beautiful prayer to his Father, had touched the hearts of the multitude, so that each had brought forth his food and shared with his neighbor who had none, and so all had been filled and

173

great baskets of uneaten fish and bread had remained.

Others had no version of the feast to offer, except that they had been bountifully supplied. "It makes no difference to me how the rabbi provided the food," said an ancient Jew who had walked all the way from Capernaum. "All I know is that I was near famishing from hunger and now I am filled and my stomach groans with the weight of food. If he caused the loaves and the fishes to be continuously renewed, that was a miracle indeed. I could not see, for I sat well back in the midst of the multitude. And on the other hand, if he so well played upon the hearts of some of my miserly neighbors at Capernaum that they brought forth their food and shared it with those about them, it was an even greater miracle." He chuckled, and rubbed his bald head with the palm of his hairy coarse hand. "Let it be either way; I care not. But this I can say: I was faint from hunger, and he fed me."

"Right you are, my friend," agreed the sparse man beside him. "He fed me, too. But where I am ahead of you is that I was confident that he would feed us. So I saved my pennies, and I brought no food. And whether I ate the renewed flesh of the boy's small fishes and the increased bread of his barley cakes or whether I gorged upon the flesh and loaves of those rich Jews in Capernaum who came with their robes swelled out with food I care not. I got mine." He clasped his bony thin fingers across the rounded paunch of his stomach. "My belly sings with pride that it was well filled without costing me one denarius." He pressed too hard upon the swelled paunch so that its song came suddenly forth in an explosive belch. "That is why I say that we must make him king. He will feed us."

He rubbed his stomach tenderly. "I have not had such a feast in months. I say make him king, and then we can live a life of ease. He will feed us. I care not how he does it. He may call down manna from heaven as God did for our father Moses in the ancient days, or he may take the money of the rich men in Israel and with it buy bread for us. It is the same to me so long as he feeds me. I say let us make this rabbi king in Israel, and then we shall feast the remainder of our days!"

So the beauty and significance of this important strange day at Bethsaida was lost to many hundreds in the clamor to make

174

Jesus king over this ancient and fabled land, and when the voices became insistent, the rabbi slipped away from the throng and in the darkening evening shadows disappeared in the hills that came down upon the Jordan valley. "Go back to Capernaum in the ship," he said to Simon and the others. "When I am ready, I will join you."

He was tired and sorely disappointed and sick of heart that the people had so misunderstood his purpose and his mission. All the long day he had labored with them and taught them and lent his strength and great faith to the ailing among them, and now the many had failed utterly to perceive the great things that had been in his heart for them.

So Jesus climbed into the hills, and he lay upon his back with his head upon a rounded small stone for his pillow, and he wrapped his coarse, brown, Galilean homespun robe about him against the cool of the darkening evening. He lay quietly thus, his long legs stretched, his arms inert upon the ground, so that the warming blood could move unhampered through his tired frame. And he prayed to his Father. Sometimes the prayer came forth from his mouth to break the silence about him, sometimes it formed into pleading, intense words that echoed among the rocks and the trees. But more often it remained unsaid in his heart, for Jesus lived close to his Father, and his very thoughts found their way straight to his own great heart.

"Oh, my Father," he cried out after a while, "open the minds of these your children to think and understand and their hearts to feel. Let them know that they are your children, made of your hand, fashioned in your image. Make them worthy of their heritage as children of the heavenly Father. Break the bonds that bind them to things of earth, that keep their thoughts upon the material, that cause them to fritter and fret away their days upon the little and the meaningless; free them, oh, Father, to let their thoughts dwell upon the things that are true and good and beautiful. Cause them to discover the divine purpose in their lives and give them strength of will to act upon it. Make them to know and appreciate that they are children of the king, and to live in accordance with that knowledge."

Jesus lay still now, and the darkness covered him softly, and the stars pricked the mantle of darkness and strengthened their small lights against the power of the night. He lay inert and relaxed, and he listened to the night sounds about him; the hoarse croakings of frogs in the sluggish small waters that seeped slowly into the Jordan, the tiny raspings of insects in the grass about him, the sudden treble note of a night bird, the raucous hoarse barking of a hound in some distant farmyard down in the valley, the low, mournful foreboding howl of a wolf high in the hills.

He lay quiet, and the tiredness went slowly out of him, and a new strength flowed down his arms and along his legs. *Give me faith, oh, Father*, he prayed, though no sound came from his lips, *give me courage, give me strength. Keep my loins girded, Father, and my feet in the path. Show me the way, my Father, and give me the wisdom and the patience and the courage to point the way to these my brothers.*

Jesus lay upon the earth now warming with the coming summer, and he lay still, and he listened. Motionless he lay, his head upon the small round rock, his eyes searching among the stars, his arms thrust out, listening.

Soundless, it came to him. As soundless as the movement of the small violets pushing their slender stems upward around the rim of the stone upon which his head lay, it came. Out of the warming earth. Down from the cold stars. Forth from the boulders and the trees and the venturing brave flowers. The voice came to him, and it grew within him, and it swelled to fill him and encompass him.

Always the voice had been with him, since the earliest days of his remembered childhood. Always the flame had burned deep within him, and the earth and every common thing had been clothed in the celestial light of which later the poets would sing. Always with him there was the vague remembrance of another far world from which he had come, the assurance that as he journeyed from it he was likewise traveling toward it, the conviction that though the world be clothed in the light of common day, for him there would always remain that visionary gleam, for him there would forever be a splendor in the grass, a glory in the flower.

Sometimes, in moments of extreme exhaustion, in days of disappointment, in times of more distress, the voice had stilled to

176

the smallest stirring of a whisper, the flame had dwindled to the feeblest flicker. But in such moments Jesus had turned aside to be still and listen, had paused to close his eyes and see; and always the whisper had grown and increased and swelled into mighty volume, and the flicker had burned and blazed and flamed into great effulgence.

So now as the stillness soothed him and the darkness mantled him, he lay still and listened, and he closed his eyes against even the little light of the stars and looked. And the voice was in his ears, and the light was in his closed eyes, and the voice and the flame grew and increased, and the voice swelled into a majestic mighty symphony of stirring, uplifting sound. And the flame— the flame blazed into a tremendous great radiance of warming, revealing light.

Jesus knew far and beyond all the powers of doubt and darkness to deny that he was one with the Father. Joy possessed his heart, and a new strength took hold upon him. He kicked his legs free of the robe, jumped to his feet, pulled the robe high above his ankles and tightened the rope belt to hold it out of reach of the grass and brambles. Then he started down the hillside toward Bethsaida and the little sea beyond.

And now that the mighty strength of his Father had been renewed within him, his swelling heart could not contain his happiness. It overflowed into a song, an old song of Israel his mother had taught him back in Nazareth, a Galilean song he had sung many a day working with timbers in the carpenter shop of Joseph his father. So singing and whistling, he walked with great strides down the hill, and as he walked he thought of his friends in their little boat headed through the dark waters toward Capernaum.

Thinking of Simon and the Sons of Thunder and dark-browed Judas and understanding Nathanael and Thomas who must always be shown, and the others, Jesus was reminded of his immediate task and the thought gave speed to his feet. Work to be accomplished in the face of the gathering storm, obstacles to be overridden, victory to be achieved, the glorious mission to be performed. *What a boon of the Father*, thought Jesus as he strode through the darkness, *that there is always the solace of work— the promise and hope of victory.*

It is good to lie still and relax and listen for the voice, to close one's eyes and search for the flame. Yes, it is good to be quiet and listen for the still, soft voice.

But Jesus also knew it was good to be busy and vigilant and stirring. For above all the bustle and stir and whirring of work the voice of God can be heard if one has ears to hear. He knew anyone who wished to could hear the voice of the Father in the swish of the oars and the creaking of the ship, in the clacking of the loom, in the flailing of the wheat upon the threshing floors. For the Father does not wish his children to be indolent. He has given them work to do.

And I have my mission, Jesus thought. *I must show the way to the Father. The straight, happy way if men would but have it so. The way of love to the Father of love. That is my mission; for that I was sent into the world, for so has the Father told me.*

And I will be the lightbearer and show the way. Through all darkness and all hell I will hold the torch high and bright and steady against all evil and unto all eternity. I have youth and health and strength and yet a sufficient time. And more than these I have, for I am one with the Father; I am the Son of the Father and am sent of him to interpret him to my brothers. That is my mission. That is my work to do. By all the powers of the Father, through his love working in me, I will do it!

So walking swiftly he passed through little Bethsaida and at length came down to the seaside. The ship had gone now and the throng had started back toward Capernaum. Simon and the others were perhaps a mile and a half across the black waters. But what of that?

He took off his sandals and his brown coarse robe, bundled them into a small pack, and with his rope belt fastened it securely upon his back at the base of his neck. And with a swift glance at the stars to fix in mind the course, he stepped into the cold waters, walked boldly forward. The stinging night's chill of the waters, the darkness, the distance to the little boat pushing slowly forward through the night, all these challenged him. He cast another quick look toward the heavens. The great dome of the sky was alive with countless shimmering bright stars, but over to his left the dark smudge of a rising heavy cloud was curtaining off their light. Soon

178

a storm would be blowing across the sea; soon the waves would be beating upon the little ship out there, and his friends would be lost in the storm and afraid.

He looked over his shoulder to the shore a few paces behind him, peered again across the still curling small waves striking at his legs. And the stars, the rocky hillside, the rippling waters he saw as his Father's and symbols of his love . . . *And I abide in his love. Soon the storm will whip the waters and scourge the trees and the rocks and deluge the warm earth, but I will remain safe in his loving protection.*

Across the little sea under the increasing blackness of the night lay Capernaum. Struggling toward Capernaum in their small ship were his brothers to be soothed and made unafraid of the storm, to be strengthened against the greater storm.

Jesus continued to cross the blackness of the sea. With purposeful strides he walked forward into the blackness of the night.

26

So before the sun had arisen behind him out of the little sea and while the storm still raged about them, Jesus had rejoined Simon and the Zebedees and the others in the ship. And while it was still morning they came to land on the Gennesaret plain outside Capernaum.

The news of the return of the rabbi who had fed the great throng the day before at Bethsaida ran through the city and up and down the crescent-shaped western coast, and almost before Jesus and his friends had finished their morning meal of bread and fish broiled over the coals, another multitude was swarming about the tall Galilean. Soon the throng increased, as another small craft from Bethsaida landed bearing those lagging behind who had taken ship when they had discovered that Jesus had left during the night. From Capernaum and from smaller settlements along the coast, from hamlets hidden back in the hills, from farms and vineyards climbing the sides of the hills they came—sick and blind and lame, deaf and paralytic and possessed of torturing spirits that intermittently seized them and wracked them and left them spent and drained almost of hope.

All day he labored with them, laid his strong, soothing, warm hands upon them and smiled and spoke encouragingly and comfortingly, and whenever he had the opportunity he taught them of the Father's desire to give unto all his children the perfect healing of the spirit. He urged them to think much of the Father and his love for them and his desire that they abide always behind the shield of his love.

When the long accomplishing day was done, tired but happy in the knowledge that he had worked well, Jesus walked back into Capernaum and sought retirement and rest in Simon's house. But still the people pressed about him and sought of him the answer to innumerable questions that disturbed them, and so he went again to the synagogue and stood up before them to teach them of God's ways. And he saw immediately that many of the congregation before him had been in the throng at Bethsaida and also by the seaside that same day on the Gennesaret Plain. And when he saw them, he knew at once what message he should bring from God's word. He would talk to them of things they could understand.

So he would talk of bread. Who among them was not familiar with bread? Who did not understand that in order to live one must eat?

"At Bethsaida you ate of the loaves and the fishes," he said. "You came away with your stomachs burdened. But many of you who ate got no lesson from that feast, but only the sustenance of the wheaten cakes and the fish. And now you come to me, not to hear of the outpourings of the Father's love for his children, but only to eat again, to fill your stomachs and lie down gorged, like the wolf that has glutted himself upon the unwary sheep.

"You are interested in the material rather than the spiritual," Jesus declared. "You put your reliance upon the things of the earth. But I say to you that these things are not the first things of life. You come to me because you think that I may give you these things, because you did eat of the bread and the fishes and were filled.

"But I urge you not to labor for the meat and bread that perish, not to seek the material things that are of themselves of small importance. Labor rather for that meat which endures, which is not eaten today and is gone tomorrow but abides and continues; seek rather the first things, the things of the spirit that are sent you of the Father, the everlasting bread and meat that I shall reveal to you, for I have been sent of the Father to proclaim these things to you, to work his works."

"But, rabbi," a man near him interrupted, either because he was honestly in doubt or because he wished to heckle Jesus, "what must we do if we are to work the works of God?"

"This is the work of God," the rabbi replied, "that you believe in him whom God has sent, that you follow along the way he has sought to show you."

"What sign can you show us, rabbi," another man interposed, "that will make us see that you have been sent of God, that you work the will of God?" He turned upon his thin legs, to let the people see him. "Our fathers, as the Scriptures record, ate manna in the desert. Does not our father Moses record that God opened the doors of heaven and rained down manna upon them, and gave them to eat of the wheat of heaven, and man ate angels' food, and he sent them meat to the full?"

Jesus stood erect before the people, and he seemed to rise in stature before them. "Truly, I say to you," he began, "Moses gave that manna of which you speak to the children of Israel wandering in the wilderness; but that is not the bread from heaven of which I speak. The Father gives the true bread from heaven, for the bread of God is that which comes down from heaven to give life to the world."

"Rabbi," said a squat swarthy Jew directly in front of him, "give us this bread of which you speak and evermore renew it for us that we may always be filled, and never hunger for the lack of it."

"I am the bread of life," answered Jesus. "He that comes to me shall never hunger; and he that believes on me shall never thirst. All that the Father gives me shall come to me, and him who comes I will in no way drive away. For I came down from heaven, I was sent of the Father, not to do my own will but the will of the Father who sent me. And it is the great desire of the Father, and his will, that no one should be lost, but that all should be raised up to a new life. This is the will of the Father: that every one that sees the Son and believes on him may have everlasting life; and I will raise him up at the last day."

In the back of the synagogue a murmur began to grow into a growl. "This man speaks blasphemy," said one, "when he says that he is the bread of heaven."

"Yes, you are right," said another. "Is not this man Jesus, the son of Joseph and Mary of Nazareth, whom all of us have known? Did he not work with his father in the carpenter shop? How is it then that he says he came down from heaven?"

"Murmur not among yourselves," said the rabbi, when the rumble of their mutterings came to him. "No man can come unto me except the Father who sent me draw him; and I will raise him up at the last day. It is written in the prophets that they shall all be taught of God. Every man, therefore, who has heard and has learned of the Father will come to me. Not that any man has seen the Father, save he who is of God; he has seen the Father." He raised his hand to give emphasis to the words he was about to say. "Truly," he declared, "I say unto you that he who believes on me has everlasting life. I am that bread of life. Your fathers ate manna in the wilderness, and now they are dead. But this is the bread that comes down from heaven, sent for man to eat of it and not die. I am the living bread that came down from heaven; if any man eat of this bread, he shall live forever." Then he said another strange thing. "And the bread that I will give is my flesh, which I will give for the life of the world."

Jesus paused, and there was a hubbub again among the Jews about the hall of the synagogue. "How can this man give us of his flesh to eat?" said one tall, lean fellow with a hawk nose. "Does he think that we would eat the flesh of a man? And if we did, does he believe we should never need to eat again? I do not comprehend this strange talk. The rabbi seems possessed of an evil spirit."

The rabbi heard him. "Indeed," he went on, "truly I say unto you, except you eat of the flesh of the Son of Man, and drink of his blood, you have no life in you. But whoever eats my flesh and drinks my blood has eternal life, and I will raise him up at the last day. For my flesh is meat indeed and my blood is drink indeed. He who eats my flesh and drinks my blood abides in me and I in him. We are in fellowship and communion. This is that bread that comes down from heaven. It is not as the manna that your fathers ate and yet are dead, for he who eats this bread shall live forever."

Even some of the rabbi's followers appeared greatly puzzled at his words, and seemed not to comprehend their meaning. "What can he mean?" one asked of another. "These are strange, difficult words. Who can understand them?" Jesus turned to face the man who had spoken. "Does this offend you?" he asked. "What if you were to see the Son of Man ascending where he was before? It is the spirit that gives life; the flesh is of no avail. The words that I have spoken to you are spirit and life. Life is of the spirit rather than of the flesh. Man is a spiritual being. It is through the spirit that we are children of the Father, that we come down from him."

But many among them were lacking in understanding of his words, and others were thinking of their material possessions, their houses and their lands and their many servants, and they put their faith in the hard cold substances of earth; and others were only perverse and stubborn and cared not to learn of the ways of the spirit but were more interested in trapping the rabbi into uttering an offense against the ancient laws. So many of them began to leave the hall, and even some among his followers silently stole out.

At length he paused in his discourse and turned to the twelve men grouped near the front and said, half in challenge and half in sadness, "Will you also go away?"

For a moment they were all silent. John sat without moving, his solemn eyes gazing intently into the face of the rabbi. Nathanael, deep in thought, seemed not to have heard. John's brother James was looking straight ahead, his eyes fixed in an unseeing stare.

Then Simon spoke. "Master," said Simon, "if we leave you, to whom shall we go?" The words had come forth boldly, impetuously. But then Simon spoke more calmly. "You have the words of eternal life. And we believe and are sure that you are that Christ, our promised Messiah, the Son of the living God."

The rabbi's eyes ran along the line of seats on which sat the twelve men. "Have I not chosen you twelve—" he paused, and a look of sadness crossed his face "—and yet one of you is a devil?"

Simon, venturing to look toward the man upon whom the rabbi's gaze had paused for a fleeting moment, saw that Judas of Kiriot sat slumped in his chair, his dark face bent forward so that his eyes were on the floor, his gnarled hands clutching the leather money-bag snuggled against his stomach.

27

Several days after Jesus had made his discourse in the synagogue at Capernaum on the bread of life, Simon came with a basket of fish to the home of Centurion Gaius Sempronius Cercinna.

"We had a good catch, centurion," said Simon. "The warming weather must have fetched them from their shelter under the rocks. I thought maybe you'd like some good fresh ones."

"That I would, Simon," Gaius assured him. "There's nothing more tantalizing to the appetite than fish freshly caught out of the lake and cooked quickly in a pot of deep fat and garnished with greens. And how are the rabbi and the exuberant Sons of Thunder? I haven't seen much of any of you lately."

"We are all very well, sir," rejoined Simon. "But that was one of the reasons I came to see you, as well as to bring the fish. We are taking another trip, and I wanted to let you know."

"Again, Simon? Where to this time? Seems that the rabbi would hardly be rested from the journey he has just finished."

"Well, sir, I think he's planning to go up towards Phoenicia, through upper Galilee into the section around Tyre and maybe as far as Sidon. I don't know just how far we'll journey this time, but when the master sets his feet on the road he usually moves fast and far. He likes to see the country and talk with the people."

"He must be a good traveler. Does he never seem to tire?"

"Oh yes, centurion. He gets tired, but a night's sleep fixes him for another hard day. He's tough as a Lebanon cedar, and he can cross these mountain ranges and swim streams in the valleys day after day until he wearies the rest of us. But this time I think he plans to take it more leisurely. It's a sort of retirement. He wants to get out of the press of this crowded section of Galilee."

"But why, Simon? I always thought the rabbi wanted to be around people. He seems to have a great affection for them."

"That's right, centurion," Simon agreed. "He does. But here

of late he has been sorely distressed at the attitude of the people. They are determined, it seems, to make him king. Particularly since that day at Bethsaida they have seemed to look upon him as the potential leader of a revolution against the authority of Rome. They figure that he would be able to lead a successful revolt, that he'd use his great powers to call down destruction upon the Roman invaders." He paused. "Pardon me, centurion, but that's how we all look upon the Romans, even though some of the Romans, like you, are our friends."

Gaius nodded. "I understand. Go ahead."

"Some of them think he'd feed them every day, he'd call down manna from heaven as did our ancient father Moses when the Israelites were starving in the wilderness." He stopped, his forehead furrowed in thought. "You see, sir, they don't understand him. Some actually cannot follow his thoughts and others don't even try to. That worries him. They seem not to be interested in the truths he teaches, but only in the material things he gives them. Do you see what I mean?"

"Yes, I think so, Simon."

"He isn't interested particularly in material things"—the scowl vanished and his big round face lighted into a boyish grin— "although sometimes after he has had a long swim in the lake or helped us fish all day I have seen him put away a bountiful mess of fish." He sobered again. "The master is always talking of one thing and the crowd is thinking of another, it seems," Simon went on. "He isn't interested, I think, in things like orders and factions among people, or even things as big as governments. I don't believe that he would ever want to head a government. Do you see what I mean, centurion?"

"Yes, I think so. And I suspect you're right."

"I think the master is interested in the man rather than the group. I believe he feels that if a man is right in his heart, that will make men in groups right. I am clumsy with words, centurion. The master can say things! But not me. I am awkward, and I can't seem to make people understand things that I feel, that I myself understand well enough. In fact, sometimes I still have a feeling that maybe after all we should make him our king. And yet—"

"Simon, I don't think the rabbi wants to be king in Palestine. I

186

don't think he'd even want to be emperor of Rome. I don't think he feels that political leadership is his mission."

"You're right, centurion. You can say things better than I can." He paused. "I think the master is planning to go up into the country around Tyre in order to get away from the crowds and let this agitation to make him king die down. All the Jews hereabouts are talking about it, and I hear the reports have even gone down into Judea. I know that crowd at the Temple has heard it, because they miss few things that the people are saying. It can't be very pleasing to Caiaphas or old Annas." He picked up the basket, which a servant had emptied. "Well, centurion, I suppose I must be going. There are many things to be seen to before we leave."

"By the way, Simon," Gaius said, "you remember my friend Marcus Calpunius Lupinus, the wealthy manufacturer at Tyre?"

Simon nodded.

"Should you get to Tyre, I would like for you to go to see him. I haven't heard a word from him since we parted near Jericho on the return from Machaerus. He was carrying a large amount of money, several chests of it, in fact—"

"That's a dangerous country, around Jericho," Simon observed. "The road up from Jericho to Jerusalem is beset by robbers who lie in wait for travelers."

"Marcus was going to Jerusalem. I warned him to take care. I don't suppose anything has happened to him. Perhaps he has been unusually busy and has neglected to send me a message lately. But if it is of little trouble to you to look him up for me, I'd be greatly obliged."

"If we get near Tyre," said Simon, "I'll be sure to do it, centurion. And it's probable that the master will journey that way, certainly into the borders of Phoenicia."

28

Perhaps the best way to get to Tyre, Marcus reflected, *would be to retrace my steps to the Jericho road and down into the Valley of the Jordan.* As he lay upon his stomach on the south side of a protecting boulder and let the sunshine of late spring soothe his weary frame, he did a few calculations. *From the head of the Dead Sea to the lower end of the Sea of Galilee,* he estimated, *the distance as a bird would fly it would be only sixty-five or seventy miles. That would be about half way.* He could follow the Jordan Valley until he reached the Plain of Esdraelon south of Little Hermon. Then he could travel northwestward, cross the River Kishon, and follow along its course north of the stream until he came to the Mediterranean just above Mount Carmel. From there the walking would be straight north along the level seacoast to the River Belus. *There I might find some of my men loading the sand for the glassworks.*

Of course, he further reflected, the Jordan was a meandering stream, and it was crossed by many other smaller streams that wound their way sluggishly into its channel. These he would have to cross—the Brook Cherith, the Farah farther up, and many others—and the actual walking might be more than a hundred miles before he reached the turning-off place. The distance to Tyre from there could easily be another hundred miles, maybe farther, considering the twistings and turnings of the way, the uphill and downhill walking through the Lebanon foothills.

Vengeance would be sweet, thought Marcus, when he finally arrived in Tyre and confronted Tullus. Vengeance would be sweet when he faced that faithful servant whom Tullus had sent to betray him to old Bar Abbas. He lay in the sun and tasted vengeance, rolled it upon his tongue, held it between his lips. *Yes, it will be a great day when I get back to Tyre, recover my money and the control of my business, when I employ able physicians from Ath-*

ens and Alexandria and recover my health. I shall rid myself of those horrid spots, loosen the joints of these stiffening fingers on my left hand.

He had made slow progress since that afternoon he had come upon Bar Abbas on the road that led up from Jericho to Jerusalem. He had walked many a hard mile from the cave near the trail, but even now he was perhaps only a few miles across the mountains from it. The trails had been rough and steep and he had been weak. Perhaps it was the shock of discovering his plight, perhaps the lack of food and the poor quality of the little he had eaten. Sometimes he had even paused to wait while others more weak than he had struggled to keep up with the pitiful procession. And often they had been forced to scream, "Unclean! Unclean!" at an approaching caravan and fall back into the rocks to let it pass. Perhaps more than anything else it was the fact that they were going nowhere, that there was nowhere for them to go.

Yet he had struggled toward Tyre. And he would get there. *Yes, by all the immortals! I shall get back to the glassworks and the weaving sheds and the home on the bluff above the harbor. I shall reestablish myself, and physicians will restore my lost health. And vengeance will be sweet in my mouth.*

And he thought of the girl. Often he had wondered what had become of Naamah. Had she learned that he had given her as a pretty plaything to old Herod? Had she known all along and had been toying with him, leading him along toward a terrible vengeance? *Perhaps that was it. Perhaps she had discovered the truth. She is a clever girl. She had learned the truth and deliberately had set out to have her vengeance upon him.*

No, he said to himself, *I cannot believe that of Naamah. She was not capable of that. She would never have been able to conceal such a scheme behind her smiling, sweet face. No, not Naamah.*

He was glad they had taken her away before they had discovered those spots, the hairless eyebrows, had scurried away from him into the rocks, screaming that he was a leper. Perhaps even now she didn't know, had not yet learned. He hoped she hadn't. For when he got back to Tyre, recovered his fortune, employed the

189

physicians. . . . Well, if he ever saw her again she might never know to what depths he had sunk.

If he ever saw her again—yes, he would. After he had been healed, he would find her. She had been good to him. He would find her. They would start life over together. *Yes, it makes no difference. No, whatever she has done, whatever she will have done . . . that will make no difference.*

He turned over to lie on his back, to let the sun soak into his chest, to let the blood flow freely along his leg. If he lay upon it long or stayed long in one position, it grew numb, as though the muscles had gone to sleep. Perhaps it was just tired from weakness and lack of proper food. Perhaps soon it would be all right, and he could start the long walk back to Tyre.

Marcus lay in the sun and let the warmth seep through his thinning body. The sun felt good upon his chest and his stomach and his legs and his arms. He lay still and tried to feel it sinking deep into the dead spots on his arm and burning into the leg that seemed every day now to be growing a bit less sensitive, a bit less helpful in walking. He thought of the many miles along the meandering Jordan, through the green lush valley, upward to the place where the Plain of Esdraelon came down to the river, across the plain that ran through the Lebanon range, up past the Little Belus and his sand pits, up to Tyre.

Yes, I'll get there, I'll get back my property, I'll have money, I'll employ physicians, I'll find Naamah. A fleeting quick shadow shaded his closed eyes, and looking up he saw that a heavy cloud was crossing the sun.

29

Spring had come and gone and now the still hot sands of summer lay heavily upon the ancient land. Along the banks of the little Sea of Galilee birds took shelter from the sun in the branches of the tall mustard trees or rode the swaying slender stems of the paper-reeds pushing up from the marshlands.

In countless tangled thickets and well-tended gardens the pomegranates had dropped their gorgeous crimson blossoms, and soon the orange, round fruit thrusting out from the lancet-like dark green leaves would be ready for the eating. Berries on ancient gnarled olives were ripening fast now, and upon a thousand steep hillsides the vineyards were purpling with grapes for the wine presses. The white flowers of the juniper had fallen off, but the thick green leaves remained to give shade and protection, and upon the hills and in the protected warm valleys the scarlet Martagons—those lilies so loved by the rabbi of Nazareth—flaunted glories unequaled by the most brazen of the courtesans in the long-ago court of King Solomon.

Late summer is peculiarly a season for calm thought, a period of pause and reflection, a time when the days drift slowly toward the darkness of night, when the weeks relax gradually into the chill of winter.

Jesus loved the summertime. As a child, when there had been respite from his toil in the shop of his father, Joseph, he had gone into the woods near Joseph's cottage to gather small fragrant plants for Mary, his mother, to listen to the birds or lie tense and unmoving behind a log or a stone watching the timid scampering of some tiny hedgehog or even the venturing of a frightened small deer. The woods had been his place to drink in the soft sounds and the good sweet earth smells, and even to swim and dive screeching and yelling with the other boys of the neighborhood in the pond they had built in a bend of the small stream.

Now as he had grown older and become more meditative, as the weight of his work pressed upon him, he seemed to love the summer even more. Spring was a time of sharp challenge, a season that brought with it a renewed urge to greater accomplishment. Fall, too, warned him that there was work that must be done against the coming winter's balancing of accounts. Spring and fall were seasons for action, for work, for effort, for achieving, for extending oneself. And Jesus was a man of action.

But to gird himself for his great task, to temper his spirit and shape his mind to his course, he needed moments of repose and reflection, for out of them he gained strength of body and soul to move unflaggingly to his goal.

So now that summer had returned to Galilee and in the deep woods the lost rain crow raised his mournful lament and in the swamps of evenings the frogs set up their raucous croakings, the rabbi had come back from another strenuous mission of good works to an earned time of rest and meditation. Upon the air stirring up from the valley of the Jordan, now luxuriant in its dark summer growth, he seemed to catch the whispered promises of peace, of surcease from heavy toil, of calm, uninterrupted fellowship with the Father.

In the late spring Jesus had set out with Simon, the Zebedees, and the others of his little band into Phoenicia. He had wished to escape the rising clamor of the unthinking multitudes to set him up as king in all Israel, as the earthly ruler of the scattered lost tribes of the ancient faith now enslaved under the haughty hand of imperial Rome. He had journeyed near Tyre and had gone northward toward Sidon, healing and teaching as he went. Then he had turned east again and crossed the mountains to descend once more into the Jordan Valley just north of the small Lake Merom some fifteen miles above the Sea of Galilee. Here he had crossed the Jordan and had gone through Gaulanitis directly east of the Sea of Galilee to the region of Decapolis in the southeast. Many works of healing he had performed in Decapolis, where the crowds had continued to follow upon his every footstep, and he had been spent and weary before taking ship again to cross the lake northwestward to land at Dalmanutha.

Now Jesus was home again, back upon the western coast of

this small sheet of water that already held so many memories of happy days spent with his friends upon it, of nights of storm or starlit calm, of long, lazy days of easy fishing, of harried days of fighting squalls that had come up fast and unwarned to break upon the little ships.

Only a few miles up the coast, either by walking the road that went up from Tiberias or sailing along the coast, and he would be back in Capernaum, back with his friends at Simon's house. There awaited the long, quiet summer in Galilee, the weeks that would give him renewed strength for the mission.

And he would need strength. For already to Jesus the hard bitter shape of his mission was becoming clearer and ever clearer. Yes, he would need the strength of a summer's meditation with the Father. He would need about his strong, willing shoulders the sustaining, sure strength of his Father's arm.

But even this boon the carping Pharisees were to deny him. For almost by the time Simon and the Sons of Thunder had tied up the ship and had gone ashore to prepare the meal, the word had run like a flame in the tall, dry grass up the coast and into Tiberias and even to Capernaum; and the Pharisees and the leaders in the synagogues and the purveyors of a cold and dead religion came swarming again upon the tired rabbi from Galilee.

"Rabbi," said the leader of the Pharisees who had come out to try him, "we know you do wondrous works of magic, for the report of these works has gone up and down our land. We hear that you claim to perform these works through the power of God; we hear even that you claim to be the Son of the Most High. Now there are many amongst us who know you to be the son of Joseph, the carpenter of Nazareth, and Mary, his wife, nor can we understand how one from Nazareth could be God's Messiah."

"Now, rabbi," the man went on, as shaggy-bearded solemn heads wagged their approval, "in the olden days God gave his servants signs by which he expressed approval of their works. We read that God manifested himself to our father Moses in the burning bush; we read likewise how fire came down from heaven and consumed the sacrifice being offered upon the altar by the prophet Elijah; we read again that when the beautiful Temple of King Solomon was dedicated the holy fire from heaven consumed the sacrifice.

"Oh, rabbi, we are men who seek to know the will of God and to understand his ways, and though we are wise men and scholars and not men of earth, nor are we publicans and sinners who know not the laws and choose not to keep them, yet we are not wise enough to understand your words and how that they proceed from God.

"So, rabbi, to show us that your words are true, that you come from God and were sent of him to lead us in his ways and along his paths, call fire down from heaven that it may be a sign unto us that you have been sent of the Most High to instruct us in his precepts."

Jesus perceived that the man and those with him sought not in humility and out of earnest hearts to know either the ways of God or whether he himself had been sent of the Father. He saw that they sought only to entrap him, to make of him a mockery before the people. And he was not willing to honor their requests that came forth from mean and shriveled hearts. He was not capable of praying of the Father power to perform tricks of magic for the entertainment of a perverse and hypocritical group whose hearts yet remained untouched by the goodness and graciousness of God.

Tall and straight he stood before them and calmly he eyed them, and when he spoke it was with authority. "Why does this generation seek a sign? Have you not lived in the knowledge of the Father, have you not all these years read His word and had His ways taught unto you? Why must you have a sign, a work of wonder, to disclose to you what is true and what is false?" His dark eyes were blazing now, and he seemed to tower above those haughty little bodies. "No sign shall be given to this generation." His words had the timbre of finality. And turning, he walked slowly toward the little ship anchored in the shallows near the shore.

Soon they pulled up anchor, and the ship pushed out to deep water and turned northward to sail toward Capernaum. In Galilee, his native small land of valleys and high hills and swift summer streams now rushing their burdens toward the Jordan or the great Mediterranean, there would be no slow, easy summer of rest and meditation and strength renewed. Wearily, Jesus slumped down upon a folded heavy tarpaulin in the stern and watched the silent Galilean shore slip away.

30

They sailed up the coast and anchored at Capernaum. The Zebedees wished to take their father aboard so that he might bring the ship back from Bethsaida, and Simon wished to see the Roman centurion and report what he had learned on his visit to Tyre.

"I left the master in the borders of Phoenicia and went into Tyre," he told Gaius, when he found him at the officers' quarters in the garrison post, "and there I learned distressing news."

"Concerning Marcus?" Gaius' face clouded.

"Yes, centurion." Simon hesitated. "I will not keep you long in the dark. Your friend at Tyre is missing. He no longer operates the weaving plant and the glassworks. After much inquiry I found a servant who told me that the plants there were now being operated by the man who had been serving as your friend's principal overseer—"

"A fellow called Tullus?"

"That was the name. He said that this Tullus had for some years operated the business under the general supervision of your friend and that he had become thoroughly familiar with conducting it; so when your friend was found to have developed leprosy—"

"Leprosy! Marcus a leper! I can't believe—"

"This man said that the overseer had sent an embittered servant with your friend on the visit to the tetrarch Herod at Machaerus. This servant betrayed him to a band of robbers as he was going along the Jericho road to Jerusalem, and as these robbers were stripping him of his clothing they discovered that he was a leper and fled."

"And what became of Marcus, pray?" Gaius' expression was grave.

"I asked him the same question. He said it was not known, but that since he had leprosy there would be no likelihood of his reappearing at Tyre. And that, of course, centurion, is true. A leper is a dead man walking."

"Yes, that's all too true, Simon," Gaius agreed. "If Marcus really does have leprosy—" He screwed his face into a scowl. "I remember once that he said something about having spent some time years ago in a cave in which lepers had lived—I wonder—" He paused, considered. "Well," he said, after a moment, "that's bad news indeed, Simon. There's only one thing for me to do. I'll get in touch with Tribune Lucius Mallius at Caesarea, and perhaps Pontius Pilate himself, and we'll start a search for Marcus."

So Simon took his leave of the centurion Gaius and went back to his house to say farewell yet another time, for he knew that his friend the tall young rabbi was planning to leave Galilee again, and this time he thought that the journey might be to some far point, for in Galilee it seemed that between the shoving, jostling, sensation-seeking crowds and the sneering, critical Pharisees and scribes the master could find no peace.

They set their course across the lake, and on the morrow they landed near Bethsaida at the northern end near where the Jordan entered. And when the report was given that the rabbi of Galilee had landed, the crowds of lame and blind and those possessed of spirits that tortured them began to follow the small procession into Bethsaida and with pitiful cries to call upon the rabbi to heal them.

One of these who cried with loudest voice was a blind man led by his brother. This man came to join them as they were leaving Bethsaida going northward up the Jordan Valley. And as Jesus talked with the motley group of unfortunates and comforted them and healed them of their sufferings, those about the blind man urged the rabbi to heal him. So he took the man by the hand and walked with him, helping him to avoid the rough places in the road, and he talked with him of the Father's love and how it was possible even though one be blind to see with complete clarity how the Father loves his children of earth. And as he walked the blind man's faith increased, the rabbi's little group could tell by the manner of his talk, and after they had walked for some small distance, Jesus stopped, and stooping down, he lifted up on his palm a small bit of the red dust of the road. Then he spat into his hand and with the forefinger of the other hand worked the dust and spittle into a pasté, and this he rubbed upon the closed unseeing eyes of the poor man.

The rabbi talked gently with the man, and he asked him after a while what he could see. And the poor fellow, his hands held out before him as if for protection against walking into some obstruction, opened his sightless eyes, and the rabbi, steadfastly looking upon him, prayed to the Father that the Father give the man faith.

"Do you see anything, my brother?" Jesus asked, after a while.

"Yes, master, praised be the Father, I see men as trees walking."

The rabbi continued to talk with him and soothe and comfort and encourage him, and after they had gone some further distance, he stopped again, and this time he put his warm strong fingers upon the fellow's eyes. And it seemed that the scales fell completely now from the man's eyes and he shouted that he could see again clearly, and each man before him stood sharply outlined.

Later, when one of the rabbi's followers observed that he knew not that dust of the road mixed with spittle had potency to restore eyesight, the rabbi mildly reproved his friend.

"When a brother's faith is weak," said he, "one should nourish it. The clay and the spittle of themselves have no ability save to strengthen the struggling weak faith of our brother. Despise not to labor to strengthen the faith of even the weakest and humblest among those whom you serve."

The rabbi cautioned the blind man whose sight had been restored and those others whom he had aided against spreading the news that he had come again to that section, and he and his band, now coming to be widely known as the twelve, continued their journey afoot up the Jordan Valley past Lake Merom some fifteen miles until they came to Caesarea Philippi in the very shadow of lofty, snow-mantled Mount Hermon.

Here he found the solitude he had been asking, the opportunity for closer communion with his Father, for a more intimate fellowship with his apostles. Here, on this uplifted eastern plateau at the foot of the mountain range they called the Lebanon toward the Sun-Rising, Jesus could draw strength of body and soul from nature, the handiwork of his Father, unspoiled by the polluting of man. For he loved the mountains, and his soul seemed to soar as his climbing feet pushing higher into the hills brought wider expanses into his view. The love of the hills was in his Nazarene blood; many of his most pleasurable experiences had come to him while he had journeyed through the upland country, many of the greatest utterances that would be recorded of him were said while he stood upon some rounded hilltop looking upon a multitude of earnest, questioning faces.

The summer days were long now, and the hours moved slowly as Jesus rested from the journeyings of the winter and the spring, the many missions of healing and teaching, the struggles with the squalls on the Sea of Galilee, and the myriad comings and goings of a busy, accomplished life. Sometimes he lay upon his back and drew soothing comfort out of the warm earth, and sometimes he swam with Simon and the Zebedees and others of the twelve in some small pond of sparkling cold water. On occasion he took a lunch of fishes and wheat cakes and climbed high up the slope of majestic Hermon.

But always now, in the midst of whatever else he might be doing, he was thinking of the mission and of the Father's will for him. Oftentimes he was momentarily cast down in spirit as he realized the failure of the people to understand his purpose in the world—why he had been sent, what so earnestly he had been trying to teach them. Sometimes for a fleeting second he felt that even the Father, busy about his great duties, had turned from him, had left him to accomplish his task alone. In such moments he had gone in conscious, striving prayer to his Father, and always he had been renewed in spirit and had come from his communion with the Father emboldened and eager to go steadfastly forward.

It was after such a communion one day that Jesus was talking with his friends. The noon meal was finished, and they lay upon the grass in the shadow of a tree. They were talking of their work, recalling past experiences in Galilee, up in the borders of Phoenicia, down in Decapolis and Peraea, discussing the reactions of the people everywhere to the work of the rabbi.

Suddenly Jesus sat up, his countenance serious, questioning. "You are out among the people, passing in and out through the crowds," he said. "You hear what the people are saying. I ask you, who do the people say that I am?"

Quickly Simon spoke up. "Some think that you are John the Baptizer whom old Herod beheaded," he said. "They think that the prophet has returned to life in you."

"There are others," John ventured, "who believe you to be Elijah, the ancient prophet of Israel returned to life. Some say you are one of the other great prophets—"

"Jeremiah, for instance," said Nathanael. "Or Moses the lawgiver. And others of the prophets of olden days."

"Yes," Simon added, "and we hear reports that Herod himself is greatly afraid of you, that he believes you are John the Baptizer returned to life to have vengeance upon him."

Jesus smiled. Then quickly his deep eyes swept the little circle. "But who do you say that I am?"

For a moment there was dead silence, and the eyes of the rabbi's followers were upon the grass. Then Simon spoke, and his tone was bold and assured. "Master, you are the Christ, the long-promised Messiah sent to save us, to lead us back to the Father; you are the Son of the living God!"

The face of the rabbi lighted instantly with a smile of great tenderness. "Thank God for you, Simon bar Jonah," he said. "Your mind has not reasoned this from any material facts you have got hold upon. Rather, your warm heart has told you; the Father in heaven has revealed it to you."

The rabbi laid his hand upon Simon's shoulder, "You are solid, Simon; you are a rock. Hereafter I am going to call you Peter, which means a stone, a rock. And, upon you and those like you, and your faith and strength and love, I will build my following, and all the powers of death will not be able to prevail against them!"

They sat silent now and almost fearful to look upon his face, for it seemed to them that it shone with a heavenly joy. But in a moment the smile was gone, and he was serious again.

"I will need your love and your prayers, my brothers," he

said, after a while. "Soon I shall be tested severely; the powers of death will be loosed against me. I must soon go to Jerusalem, and there I shall face my destiny." He was silent, and though his eyes were lifted to the high white cap of Mount Hermon, they seemed to be looking beyond it. "But the Father will give me strength to go forward steadfastly, to point to the end of the way upon which countless multitudes unto endless ages must travel back to the Father." He seemed to be oblivious of the others.

John, who was sitting on the other side of the rabbi from Simon, spoke softly, reflectively. "The way—the way back to the Father. Master, that is beautiful. You are the Word that reveals the way; you are the Light that makes clear the way . . . You are the Word and the Light." He closed his eyes, leaned against the rabbi's shoulder. "The Way—it makes me see visions, images—angels and men and animals, strange creatures of sky and earth and water." Then John looked up quickly into the radiant face of the rabbi, and he saw tears filling the rabbi's eyes.

"My beloved cousin," Jesus said. His eyes swept the circle of the earnest eyes watching his. "How I love you all, my brothers!" He turned again to John. "Peter is a rock. Peter is the practical man. But you, my cousin, are the dreamer, the poet; you see visions. The world must have the practical man, but it must also have the dreamer. The Father has great need of both."

Nathanael, who had been saying nothing, lifted a gnarled brown hand to tug at his spiked beard. "And you, master," he said simply, "are both."

The rabbi replied nothing, but his smile said more than many words.

On another occasion Jesus spoke of the bitterness of the Pharisees and scribes and the Temple leaders at Jerusalem. They were determined to destroy him and his influence, he declared, for his way, the way he proclaimed as the Father's way, was not the way of the leadership among the Jews, and soon they would grown bold enough to challenge him.

"I must go up to Jerusalem," he said, and his countenance was sad, "and there I must suffer indignities and sorrow and pain, and be put to death. But fear not, my friends, for I shall rise from death within three days."

When he had ceased speaking Simon began to protest. "But master, that must never be. Killed at Jerusalem! Never! Far from it, master. We will never allow such a thing."

Jesus turned his eyes upon Simon. "You do not understand, Peter," said he. "Do you not realize Satan is using you? He would tempt me through you. His words are an offense."

Then he spoke to the group. "If any man will be my follower," said he, "let him deny himself, and take up his cross, and follow me. Let him go all the way, even to death if need be, for in holding to his life he will lose it, and in losing it in my cause he will find it. For what is life but the soul, and what shall it profit a man if he gains everything but loses his soul?"

Such was the talk he made to them while they rested at Caesarea Philippi as the summer days moved onward.

Perhaps it was a week after he had reproved Simon when he took the three, Simon and the Zebedee brothers, and they went high up the slope of Mount Hermon, and as they walked Jesus talked with them. Often before in the many months now that they had been so much with him, the tall rabbi in the Galilee homespun robe had talked. But never, it seemed to them, had he talked with such a warmth, with such an intimacy, and yet with such authority, as he had talked in this day.

He talked much of his mission, and of how he had been sent of the Father to show the way of truth and goodness to the men of the earth, his brothers, and as he talked he seemed to gather strength and vibrancy and power, and a glory sat upon his very countenance until he was transfigured before them. And to his three companions, his three most intimate friends, it seemed that he was not only their friend and brother and leader, but also the ancient lawgiver Moses arisen to give them a new law, the all-powerful, the all-embracing law of love. And likewise he appeared to them not only to be their beloved Jesus and the great Moses of the ancient Scriptures who brought down the tables of the law, but also the thundering, powerful prophet of ancient times, the great Elijah himself. Brought together through space and across time, the three seemed to stand here before them and converse upon this most majestic of Palestine's mountains.

And from out of the mountains they thought they heard a

voice, at once a whispering, small voice and a commanding, loud voice, and they fancied that the voice was the voice of the Father giving his approval to the words of his Son.

". . . my beloved Son, in whom I am well pleased. Hear him . . ."

So touched were they by the power and the majesty that they cast their eyes to the ground.

Then Jesus put his hand upon the shoulder of Simon, the rough, kindly Simon, and upon the visionary, dreaming, warm-hearted John, and then upon the elder Zebedee, James, the third of the trio of the inner companions. When the three raised their eyes and looked again upon Jesus, he smiled, and he was again only the beloved master.

So they went back down the mountain, and they returned to the others, and Jesus knew that for him now the slow, quiet, easy days of summer were fast coming to their end. He knew that he must return to Capernaum, and shortly after that he must go to Jerusalem. For now he knew, beyond all the powers of evil or the love of his brothers to deny, that the course of his destiny pointed straight toward that ancient proud city. Jesus knew that he must go to Jerusalem.

In Jerusalem he would become the immutable and eternal symbol of God's love for man. In Jerusalem he would become for all time and to all generations the uplifted finger pointing the way.

31

Gaius did some quiet investigating at Tyre before he went to see Tullus. He talked with certain businessmen of the city and several of the shop foremen and workers at the dyeing and weaving plants, and the information he obtained agreed very closely with the story Simon had related.

Then he visited Marcus's estate. Tullus at first seemed reluctant to talk of the disappearance of the wealthy son of Senator Marcus Calpurnius Lupinus. He intimated that Marcus had gone on a long business trip and that he was expecting him back in Tyre soon with large orders for the plants. As Gaius prodded him, however, it was evident that Tullus did not wish to talk of Marcus, and during their short conversation the overseer made clear that his operation of the business during the absence of the senator's son was proceeding satisfactorily.

The reluctance of the former overseer, now owner of the glass business, to talk about Marcus confirmed the centurion's suspicions. *Tullus conveniently takes over the business he had run in his master's absence following Marcus's untimely disappearance. Was it only the servant who betrayed his master, or had the overseer also devised this treachery?*

Gaius did not confront Tullus with the story of his ingenious conspiracy to have Marcus waylaid by robbers on the Jericho road in the knowledge that his loathsome illness would be discovered and that he would be abandoned, miles from home and friends, to the hopeless fate of a leper. He did not want Tullus to know how much he knew; he did not wish to excite the overseer's suspicions. For one thing, he would be in better position to search for his friend if Tullus had no knowledge of it; and again, he did not know the relationship of Tullus and Sejanus. The wily prefect might even have been a party to the conspiracy to get rid of the senator's son.

So he thanked Tullus and told him to remember him to Marcus when he returned to Tyre.

From Tyre he caught the first ship sailing southward along the coast. At Caesarea he would report to the tribune Lucius Mallius what he found out. Perhaps the two of them would go to Pontius Pilate. It was a situation that would have to be handled with great care. Pilate, of course, would do nothing that might in any manner tend to jeopardize his standing with Sejanus. And Lucius would be reluctant to do anything that might offend the procurator.

Perhaps the approach would be to appeal to Pilate to send a detachment of Roman soldiers to apprehend old Bar Abbas and bring him to trial for his robberies, which could easily be shown to constitute rebellion against the Roman authority. And with Bar Abbas and members of his band arrested, it might be possible to learn something of the fate of Marcus. Bar Abbas would certainly be crucified, but he might talk before he died. Or some member of his band, bribed with the promise of escape from the cross, might be willing to betray his robber chieftain and reveal what had happened to Marcus.

Gaius was determined to find his friend.

32

At the top of the slope the rabbi Jesus stopped. Then he turned and for a long moment looked back toward Capernaum and the blue Sea of Galilee beyond. Simon, who had been walking beside him, thought he saw upon the rabbi's face a fleeting shadow, perhaps a moment's outward manifestation of an inner sadness or a sudden sharp apprehension. But quickly it was gone, and his bronzed face was wreathed now in a warm smile. "Simon," he pointed. "See, away over there. I believe I can almost pick out the rooftop of your house. And look, is not that the garrison of our friend the Roman centurion? And there in that little cove are the ships. There's where you joined me, my friend. And look at that blue jewel of the sea. On it we have had some stirring days and nights." He swept his arm before him. "It's all beautiful, and I love it. I am reluctant, Simon, to leave."

"But, Master, you have left it many times before. You talk now as if you do not expect to come again to Capernaum and these shores."

The rabbi's face was sad again, and a little sigh came up from deep within him. "Have I not told you, Simon, that we go to Jerusalem? And there many enemies await us. There my mission must be performed."

"But, Master, you have the power—"

Jesus interrupted him. "Have I not warned you against tempting me to flaunt the will of my Father? It is his will that I must proclaim the way even unto Jerusalem." Quickly he turned his back upon Capernaum and the little sea. "Let us be going," he said.

They went down the slope and walked southward through the level country, and by nightfall they were nearing the small valley that ran between the slope upon which Nazareth sat and Mount Tabor to the east. The next day they crossed the River Kishon and walked onward toward the south through the flat lands of the Plain of Esdraelon. And on the next afternoon they passed Mount Gilboa on their left, and crossing from Galilee into the borders of Samaria they came to a village where they had planned to spend the night.

But the people of the village, recognizing the group as Jews who were on their way to Jerusalem to attend the in-gatherings of the Feast of the Tabernacles, were unwilling to give them food and shelter. Instead they suggested very emphatically that it would be best for the rabbi and his followers to proceed onward before the darkness came down upon them.

The hostility of the Samaritans made the quick-tempered Zebedee brothers violently angry. "Master," said John, "these Samaritans, who are not even true members of our Jewish faith, have treated us shamefully. They have not even shown us the reverence that the heathen man of the east customarily shows for his guest. They have spat in our faces, ordered us to leave their borders, refused even to sell us bread against our mounting hunger. Master, they should be taught a lesson. You should call down fire from heaven to consume them, even as our great prophet Elijah called down fire to consume the sacrifice and the wood and even the stones of the altar."

But Jesus rebuked the hot-blooded brothers. "You are forgetting yourselves," he said to them. "You are letting the baseness of the flesh overcome the goodness of the spirit. You are forgetting that you are children of the Father. The Son of Man is not come to destroy men's lives, but to save them."

So they walked on, and when they came to another village they spent the night there. And the next morning they continued southward through the hill country of Samaria and Judea, over mountain and valley and stream, and after several days of traveling they set their course to the east and, crossing above the northern walls of ancient Jerusalem, came at length to the village of Bethany.

Once at Bethany, Jesus laid aside the dust and cares and fatigue of travel. For here lived three of his devoted friends, Lazarus and his two sisters, Mary and Martha. Jesus had known them a long time, and whenever he came up to Jerusalem he lodged with

206

them in their whitewashed cottage here across the Brook Kedron from the great Temple that sat upon the eastern wall of the capital.

Lazarus was a slender, frail fellow. He tended a few small patches just beyond the crown of the Mount of Olives and sold vegetables and fruits at the market in Jerusalem. Martha and Mary kept the house and sometimes earned a few coins working at menial tasks for wealthy families in the great houses on Zion Hill in the fashionable quarter of Jerusalem. But when the rabbi came to visit them Mary forgot her household duties to stay near Jesus and listen to his marvelous stories, for she was completely fascinated by the tall preacher from down in Galilee. And one day Martha, left to prepare the meals and clean the house, was so exasperated with her sister that she complained to the rabbi.

"Rabbi," she said, "Mary has left me to do all the work, while she sits here and listens to your talk with my brother. Should she not share the duties of the household with me, for there is much to do in seeing that the house is conducted in an orderly and proper manner?"

Jesus patted Martha on the shoulder. "You work too hard, Martha," said he. "You are so heavily burdened with small cares. You do so many things that are not necessary to be done. You lose yourself in an excess of small things and thereby miss the more important things. Mary, on the other hand, is interested in the larger things of life and does not fret over the lesser things. I would not take away from her that sense of value. Rather, my sister, I wish that you should not worry over trifling things that cause you so much bother and toil."

So the rabbi, who had come to Jerusalem now that the summer was past and the day was at hand for the Feast of the Tabernacles, the great fall ceremonial week among the Jews, lodged again with Lazarus and Mary and Martha and walked the little way from Bethany, which sat upon the eastern slope of the Mount of Olives about a mile from the summit, to the great Temple built by King Herod on the bluff overlooking the ravine-like valley of the Brook Kedron.

Bethany sat too upon the road that led up from Jericho and along this road came throngs pushing into Jerusalem for the week of the great feast, and sometimes Jesus walked unrecognized with travelers going from many sections along the Jordan Valley up to the Temple. He crossed the rounded summit of the Mount of Olives and then came down the ancient, winding road that led through the Garden of Gethsemane, a small grove of gnarled olives in which they had set up an olive press. Often he stopped here in the garden and rested, especially on evenings when he had turned from the city and its dust and heat and surging multitudes to seek again the peace and calm of the house in Bethany.

Here in the garden there was quietness, and birds twittered in the thick branches of the olives, and sometimes a frightened small animal would dart across a sun-dappled open space to safety in his burrow beneath a stone or in the trunk of a twisted tree. Here there was a chance to think and consider and commune with the Father. Here in the quiet garden and up there in the house beyond the crest of the mount he could attune his ears to the still, small, strengthening voice of his Father, and he could put his own strong, bronzed hand into the omnipotent, great sustaining hand of God.

So Jesus stopped often in the Garden of Gethsemane as he walked from Bethany to the Temple or from the Temple when the day was done back to the shelter of his friends' little home. The garden was the nearest approach he could find here in the bustle and confusion and bickering and trafficking of Jerusalem to the unspoiled natural beauty of his native Galilee.

Here he could consider his mission, here he could establish his feet firmly upon the path. For now the news was getting abroad that the strange, powerful mystic from Galilee, the man of signs and wonders, who had come to attend the Feast of the Tabernacles, was even now preaching and healing from the porches of the great white Temple itself. And as the news went forth, the crowds that surged about him grew, and the anger and the jealousy and the fury of the rulers of the Temple—the high priest Joseph Caiaphas and the former high priest Annas, father-in-law of Caiaphas, and the Pharisees and the scribes and the Sadducees, swelled into a cold determination to rid themselves forever of this strange rabbi from down in Galilee. As guardians of the ritual and creed and theology of a dead religion, along with those pagan purveyors of ornamentation—the vendors who traded in sheep, doves, and cattle even in the Court of the Gentiles of the Temple itself—the religious leaders looked to find and silence this bold Galilean.

These things Jesus knew, and another thing he knew, that soon he must choose his course unalterably and forever.

33

The high priest Joseph Caiaphas settled his long purple mantle about his thin shoulders, leaned forward on the raised center bench in the semicircular line of benches at the southern end of the Chamber of Hewn Stones in the great Temple, and waggled a bony finger.

"Why have you not fetched him here to us?" A dark scowl sat heavily upon his lean, ascetic face. "Did you forget your orders?"

"No, my lord High Priest." The captain of the guard paled. "I have forgot no orders. But no man spoke like this man."

Anger flushed the thin, sparsely bearded cheeks of Caiaphas. And when he spoke it was with a snarl. "So you too have joined those who make haste to follow this young upstart from down in Galilee, this braggart rebel who would overthrow the religion of our fathers, this blasphemer who sets himself up as the holy one of God, as the—the—" he paused. "I will not speak the sacred name," he said.

"Perhaps, my lord High Priest, you have misinterpreted what I have just spoken," the captain of the Temple guards hastened to explain. "It would have been most inopportune to have seized him and dragged him here before the very eyes of the multitude that hold him in such high regard. For great crowds follow upon his heels, swarm about him to catch his every utterance, listen with deep reverence to every word that falls from his lips. Were we to seize him this way, the people would witness the deed, my lord High Priest, and would scrutinize sharply our conduct—"

"The captain of the guard has shown praiseworthy discretion," declared the rabbi Nicodemus. "The rabbi from Galilee is a marked man indeed. I know of myself that the captain's words are true. It would be most indiscreet to arrest him before the people and bring him here—"

"The rabbi Nicodemus, I judge, would counsel that nothing

be done in the light of day—" Caiaphas turned to face the black-robed Nicodemus with a malevolent, thin smile that pulled at the corners of his bloodless lips "—since, if reports coming to us be worthy, our brother is visiting by nights this blaspheming Galilean, is seeking to learn more of this rebel's teachings against the law of our fathers—"

"My lord High Priest, we are forgetting the present duty," interjected another of the Sanhedrin members. "It is not, as I understand it, to castigate one another. It is to find an acceptable manner of bringing this Galilean before us, of disposing of him and his damnable preaching. It is true that he has many followers. Did I not with my own eyes see them surging about him in the porches of the Temple? Did not their countenances betray a strange and fanatical devotion to him? Did I not even hear him speaking?"

Caiaphas turned to face the man who had addressed him. There was a sharp, evil brightness in his small black eyes, a sneer in his voice as he spoke. "Did even you, rabbi of the Pharisees, incline your ears to his words? Did even you, wise in the law of our fathers, swallow them even as do these ignorant boors of Jerusalem, these men of earth of Galilee and Judea?" He smiled coldly. "What were his so powerful words? What did he say?"

"I heard but little," the Pharisee replied. "But his words have great force and power. He speaks with a magnetism of manner and voice, and his words are chosen for effectiveness. I distinctly remember these words, and you will be struck by their power. I understand it is one of his favorite discourses, often repeated. I heard it just yesterday as he stood at the Beautiful Gate. 'I am the bread of life,' he declared, 'I am the living bread which comes down from heaven, and if any man eats of this bread, he shall live forever, and the bread that I will give him is my flesh, which I will give for the life of the world. He that eats my flesh and drinks my blood—'"

"Blasphemy!" shouted the High Priest. "I care not to hear more—"

"Let our brother proceed, my lord High Priest," said Nicodemus. "We should know what the Galilean tells the people."

"Our rabbi Nicodemus would hear more of the Nazarene," the High Priest said shrilly. "Proceed, rabbi."

211

"The Galilean spoke at length of himself as the bread of immortal life," said the Pharisee. "'He that eats my flesh and drinks my blood dwells in me,' he declared. 'Your fathers ate manna and they are dead, but he that eats of this bread shall live forever,' he repeated with emphasis—"

"What did the fellow mean?" Caiaphas asked quickly. "Does he mean that his flesh is actually to be eaten and his blood drunk? Is he mad? What can he mean?"

The rabbi Nicodemus cleared his throat. "The Galilean, as I understand him, uses many figures of speech," he said. "He is a teacher. He uses stories to illustrate his teachings. And he frequently employs a bold figure of speech to emphasize some moral he wishes to drive home to his hearers. I think in this instance he did not mean that his followers were actually to eat his flesh and drink his blood. He has another expression that he likewise frequently employs. He speaks of his followers being 'one' with him and 'one' with 'the Father.' By that he means, I understand, that they are in accord, in understanding, in communion with him and with God. That, I think, may help explain—"

"The rabbi Nicodemus should be well qualified to explain to us the words of the Galilean," observed Caiaphas. He turned to the Pharisee who had been reporting the words of the rabbi who had come up from Galilee to attend the Feast of the Tabernacles. "But proceed, rabbi."

"I report these utterances not in support of them, my lord High Priest, as you must know, but in order that we may better understand him. In this same discourse he spoke of himself likewise as water—'living water,' he termed it. 'If any man thirst,' said he, 'let him come unto me, and drink. He that believes on me, as the Scripture says, out of his belly shall flow rivers of living water.'"

"He knows the Scriptures, truly," said another Temple leader who sat on the other side of the High Priest from Nicodemus. "It is plain the man is no fool. Those words are in the sacred writings."

"All the more reason he is a blasphemer," said Caiaphas. "Were he a mad prophet he would be less guilty. But he deliberately imputes to himself heavenly powers, declares himself to be—" he hesitated, assumed a pious dignity "—yes, I will name the holy name, he ascribes to himself the Messiahship."

"But does our law judge any man before it hears him?" Nicodemus asked. "Does not our law, on the other hand, require that a man be heard—"

"Are you also from Galilee?" another of the Temple leaders spoke up, sarcastically. "Search the Scriptures, Nicodemus. Look carefully. You know that out of Galilee no prophet will arise."

Caiaphas tugged at the short beard at his pointed chin. "We must devise a plan to defeat the Galilean, and do so without causing an undue stir among the people now that the city is filled with those who have come to the week of the Feast." Suddenly his black eyes settled upon a squat, round-faced old man with a long, carefully curled and oiled gray beard about whose shoulders was the purple mantle of authority. "My lord High Priest Annas," said Caiaphas quickly, "in your wisdom gained after long years of service and much study can you not suggest such a plan?"

Old Annas leaned forward on his bench. "My lord High Priest," he replied to his son-in-law, "I have been sitting here enjoying the discussions. I am an old man, and the cares of guiding the people in the ancient worship of our fathers have been heavy upon my shoulders, now lightened at the release of that burden. I do not wish to undertake more." He coughed, and his round fat face reddened. "But if experience brings wisdom, it cautions one always to use judgment, and it is my judgment that you should use this Galilean to defeat himself. In that way the people who support him cannot hold you responsible for his downfall. He will have entangled himself in his own net."

"The wisdom of a sage," observed a Sadducee member of the Sanhedrin seated beyond Nicodemus. "But what—" he turned to face old Annas "—does my lord the former High Priest propose?"

Annas smiled, and his old eyes danced above the darkened bags of flesh at the sides of his great beaked nose. "I think my plan shall not fail. It has a woman at the center."

"A woman? Ah, indeed," Caiaphas faced the former high priest. His sharp eyes, too, were beaming now, and his thin lips had relaxed into a grin. "Where the downfall of a man is sought a woman is always a proper instrument. It was even so with our first parents. But what, my lord High Priest, is your plan?"

Annas stoked the curls of his beard. "They say the Galilean cannot be tempted with women. They say his personal life is exemplary. But even so, I believe that a woman can be used to entrap him." He paused, as the others leaned forward to hear the better, and his beady black eyes danced in their cavernous folds of fatty flesh. "This is my plan! We shall instruct the captain of the guard to find a comely woman, and we shall employ a man and give him a piece of silver, or two pieces, or whatever pieces are required—"

"One piece should be sufficient," observed a Pharisee seated next to Annas, and the dignitaries of Israel smiled along the polished benches.

"—and we shall have sufficient witnesses employed to testify to the act of adultery. Then we shall have this woman brought before the Galilean as he sits in the porches of the Temple, and before the multitudes we shall have him informed that she has been taken in adultery, and then we shall have put to him the question of what should be done with her."

The hard, sharp face of Caiaphas softened and a smile of understanding lifted the corners of his thin lips. "Go on, my lord High Priest," he said. "Your plan appears to have much promise."

Old Annas looked along the line of benches. "And if he answers that she must be stoned to death in accordance with the laws of our fathers, then the people, seeing that he is a man of hard heart, that his vaunted love for the lost and the suffering has its limitations, will desert him, and he will condemn himself before them. But, on the other hand, if he says that she must be forgiven for her sinning, then out of his own mouth he will have convicted himself of advocating disobedience to the sacred laws of our fathers, and he will be revealed before the people an inciter to rebellion against the law and a disturber of the peace of Israel."

Heads wagged along the benches that lined the southern wall of the Chamber of Hewn Stones. "It is indeed a clever scheme," said a Sadducee near the left end of the semicircle of seats. "Either way the Galilean's answer will convict him. He cannot escape."

Suddenly Nicodemus sat erect. "I do not like it," said he. "It is entrapment. Does not the law forbid that a man be led into evil paths? If the Galilean is an evildoer of his own volition, if he is an inciter against the laws of Israel, then let him so show himself to be, but do not set a trap for him as you would entrap a fox."

"If he is fox enough," observed the man seated beside Nicodemus, "he will avoid the trap."

"This trap he cannot avoid," observed old Annas.

"I do not like the scheme," Nicodemus declared again. "I oppose any such procedure. I cast my vote against it."

"The rabbi Nicodemus would be expected to oppose any measure that might be designed to rid Israel of this Galilean blasphemer," said Joseph Caiaphas. "Nevertheless, I believe it a proper measure to be followed. The sacred laws of Israel must be upheld. This Galilean upstart and all his preaching and all his influence and hold upon the people must be smitten from Israel!" He looked right and left along the semicircle of the benches. "Is it not so, my brothers in Israel?"

And to the right and to the left of the High Priest solemn beards, sparse and thin, long and luxuriant, straight and curled, unscented and oiled, waggled their agreement.

34

The week of the Feast of the Tabernacles was drawing near its end, and the rabbi from down in Galilee was tired. He had spent much time upon the porches of the Temple instructing the crowds in the ways of his Father. He had labored diligently and patiently in his consuming desire to show them the true meaning of the ancient laws of Israel, to inspire them to take up a new life, to see with enthusiasm those things that are true and good.

This morning he had arisen early, before the household at Bethany was astir, and had climbed the rise to the summit of the Mount of Olives and descended its slope to the pleasant retreat of Gethsemane.

He sat down upon the bent trunk of an old olive tree and pulled his robe about his shoulders against the early chill of this October morning, for fall was in the air and its cool, sweet breath fanned his bronzed face. Here he could be quiet and think. Here he could draw sustenance from the air of early morning, the smells of earth and dew upon it, of leaves and grass and oil freshly pressed, the morning chatter of the birds, the distant mellowed sounds of a great city stirring to another day's life. Here he could reassemble into a pattern the scattered patches of his life. Here he could commune with his Father.

The world was failing to understand him. Often he felt utterly alone. His followers loved him, Simon and the Zebedees and the others, perhaps even poor Judas of Kiriot; but they were children, they were frail supports upon which to lean, their hearts yearned to follow in the straight course, but their flesh was weak.

And where many failed to understand, were quick to fall by the wayside, to leave the Way, others were openly hostile, determined to destroy him, to obliterate the way along which lay the journey to the Father's house. In Jerusalem during these last days the Pharisees and Sadducees and scribes, these carping men of little hearts, these whited sepulchers filled with the bones of dead men, had disputed with him and sneered at him and sought upon every occasion to confuse and hinder him, and he knew some there were among those who were plotting actually to destroy him.

Yet ahead lay his mission, ahead lay that destiny he must face and accomplish. Respites such as this in the garden at the foot of the slope of the Mount of Olives, moments with the Father, gave him renewed strength. If he could but keep his own hand, this strong hand tanned by the Galilean sun, firmly clutched in the great, strong, abiding hand of the Father—

He would. Yes, with the help of his Father, he would. He would move resolutely forward, proclaiming the way, showing the way, leading along the way. He would be true to the mission for which he had been sent. He would speak his lines, act his part, play out the great drama to the end. And the rest would be with the Father.

So inspired and renewed in spirit, Jesus walked again from the grove of ancient olives, crossed the Brook Kedron, and mounted the precipitous slope that led through the hovels and hunger and degradation of Jerusalem's lower city to the great white Temple high upon the eastern ramparts. Up there he had work to do.

And having arrived there, with a throng of poor and sick and heavy of heart at his heels, he took his seat on the steps that led up from the Court of the Gentiles to the Beautiful Gate, which gave admission to the Court of Women. Ten feet above the Court of the Women and through the Gate of Nicanor was the narrow Court of Israel, and in its center and lifted three feet above it rested the Court of the Priests. Here sat the structure called by the Jews the House of God.

At the front of this upraised court stood the Great Altar of Burnt Offering. This altar was made of rough stone whitewashed, and it stood fifteen feet high. The ascent to the altar was from the south side, and in the southwestern corner a drain that ran beneath the great Temple to the Brook Kedron far down in the ravine provided for disposing of the surplus blood from the slain beasts after the altar had been sprinkled.

Thus when Jesus turned to look through the opening of the

great shining golden portal called the Beautiful Gate, he could see the priests far across the Court of the Women past the Gate of Nicanor upon the Great Altar performing the tasks of their offices.

But the rabbi of Galilee was more concerned with the multitude before him than the priests in their robes of office at his back. People—the plain people of Galilee, the ordinary people of Judea, the poor and forsaken people of the crowded, dark, ill-smelling tenements of the lower city here in Jerusalem— people everywhere were at once his concern and his promise. People were the soil into which he dropped the seeds of his gospel, his inspiring message of good news. There was always the chance that the seed would fall into fertile soil.

So calmly now Jesus sat upon the steps and talked, and men and women and even children listened wide-eyed and intent. Many of them were disposed to go on a Sabbath day into the Temple and some had even heard Caiaphas the high priest, and before him Annas, expound the ancient law of Moses. Caiaphas and the scribes and the Pharisees spoke in a forbidding, stern, cold tone of a vengeful God, a stern and implacable God demanding adherence to a strict and formal code.

But this young man from the lake country of Galilee, this young man of pleasant face, of strong, robust frame and sandy reddish hair burned by the summer sun, was speaking in a different manner. He was expounding to them the law of Moses and the need of obedience to that law, but he was speaking also of another law, a law that seemed to complement and even transcend this stern Mosaic law. He was telling them also of a God different from the kind the priests in the Temple and the synagogues had been expounding. He was describing to them a kind, forgiving Father who looked with compassion and sorrow upon His errant children, who sought to lead them forth from their misery into the serene light of his smiling face. This young man was speaking much of the compelling power and authority of love.

About him this morning sat also a group of the sanctimonious elders of Israel, the professional holy men of the Temple group, and with much searching of the Scriptures they were seeking to involve this young man in the higher spheres of theology with the purpose of leading him into challenging some portion of the law of Moses.

But the small people who pressed about the tall Galilean had no kindly feeling for the cold and righteous-appearing elders who for them made the religion of the fathers a heavy burden upon their backs. These people knew little of the formal religious pattern of the priests and had they understood it they would have had small opportunity or means with which to fulfill its requirements. They understood little of theology. Nor cared they a fig about it. They were intent upon the words, the vibrant, hopeful words of the Galilean. Watching this Jesus of Galilee, hearing his talk, seeing the quick flash of his smile, the sad, gentle play of his thoughts across his countenance, they were warmed and lifted up.

"I am the light of the world," he was saying. "He that follows me shall not walk in darkness, but shall have the light of life." And looking into his face, they were confident that it was so. And they were inspired and the heavy darkness of their hearts was lightened.

But the scribes and Pharisees and the Sadducees among them were intent upon their own cleverness, and so they failed to comprehend the beauty of the young rabbi's words. "You bear record of yourself," one of them interrupted him to declare. "But your record is not true."

The people watching expected to see him flame with a righteous wrath. But he was calm and smiling and serene. "Though I bear record of myself, my record is true," he answered, and though his tone was kind, it was likewise emphatic. "For I know where I came from and where I am going; but you cannot tell where I came from and where I am going. You judge after the flesh; I judge no man. And yet if I judge, my judgment is true; for I am not alone, but I and the Father that sent me." He was still smiling.

"It also is written in your law that the testimony of two men is true, the evidence of two witnesses establishes a fact." He paused, and the people marveled, those who were familiar with this section of the ancient laws, at the Galilean's knowledge of the Scriptures. "I am one that bears witness of myself, and the Father who sent me bears witness. He is the other witness. That makes two. That establishes the truth of the declaration."

"Where is your father to bear witness for you?" the Pharisee demanded. "Is not he the carpenter in Galilee, long dead?"

"You neither know me nor my Father," Jesus replied, calmly. "If you knew me you would know my Father also."

But now beyond the group and two hundred feet directly in front of the steps upon which he sat Jesus saw a commotion down at the Gate of Shushan that gave admittance to the Court of the Gentiles from the Valley of Jehosophat. There was a quick turning of heads, and the throng gave way, and through the narrow lane thus opened there came pushing up to the place where Jesus sat a group of burly fellows shoving before them a woman breathing heavily. The woman, now in front of the rabbi, raised defiant eyes as she straightened her robe that had been disarrayed in the tumult.

For a short moment there was no sound save the woman's hard breathing. Then one of the men who had helped drag her before Jesus, a man whom the rabbi recognized as a Pharisee despite his unprepossessing appearance, stepped forward. "Master," he said, "this married woman was taken in adultery—" he straightened himself, squared his shoulders proudly as if to emphasize his own piety "—in the very act."

He waited an instant, but Jesus, eyeing him calmly, said nothing.

"Now Moses in the law," said the Pharisee, "commanded that such should be stoned." He paused, raised his voice that the throng might hear. "But what do you say?"

There was a whispering among the people. "That, plainly, is the law of our father Moses," a man some paces back from the steps said under his breath to his neighbor, "but I would be loath to see the poor soul so cruelly done to her death."

"The hussy! Look at her reddened lips. Doubtless she has caused many a man to desert his wife and children." The old woman with the soiled, unkempt hair and the missing front teeth fairly hissed her condemnation. "Stoning is too good for her."

The man who had first spoken turned to her. "But it seems not to be the way of the young rabbi yonder," he said. "He seems to be kinder of heart. And yet the law—"

"Let the law be upheld!" The woman's haggard eyes were

ablaze. "Let her be stoned! Then she'll no longer flaunt her brazen self before our men for filthy coins, the harlot!"

But few had heard the words of the man or the woman. For now all eyes were upon Jesus and the woman who stood before him. Without having uttered a word the rabbi bent over and apparently oblivious of the woman, the critical Pharisees and scribes, or the crowd before him, began to make marks with his forefinger in the dust upon the stone at his feet. Slowly, deliberately, even idly, his finger traced out letters or symbols in the dust, though those about him understood not what he was writing.

The woman, now breathing more easily, stood before him, the trace of a sneer upon her reddened lips. Perhaps it concealed more of fright than contempt, some reasoned. Or it may be that she would tempt him with her beauty, others thought. Doubtless she has had her choice of men, has been adored by brusque, domineering Roman soldiers, sought after by the elders of Israel, for her beauty was striking, even after the encounter with these rough fellows who have brought her here. Perhaps even she too was mocking him, sneering at his entrapment by these Pharisees, at his having been made a mockery before his followers, these who fairly worship him. "What shall the rabbi say?" one man whispered to his neighbor. "What answer is there that can be made?"

The rabbi is a good man, a clever man, the people were thinking, *a man of strength even though of great compassion. But can he match wits with these calculating scribes, these hypocritical Pharisees, these cynical, sneering Sadducees? Must he not be made out a man of weak words, of ineffective speech, before these men who understand him* not, *who wish only to see him done to his death?*

Still Jesus said not a word, but with his eyes upon the stone at his feet he continued to trace unknown strange symbols in the dust. And the people watched him, intently, their eyes fixed upon him, their ears eager to catch any words he may say.

"Master, perhaps you did not hear me." The Pharisee stood smiling, confident, before Jesus. "This woman has been taken in the very act of adultery. The law of Moses commands that she be taken forth and stoned to death. But what do you say? What is your law?" He crossed his arms, smiled upon the bowed form of the Galilean writing with brown forefinger upon the dust at his feet.

Now Jesus raised himself, looked straight into the eyes of the confident questioner. The crowd strained forward. The scribes and Pharisees and the Sadducees among them cupped their palms to their eager ears.

"You have spoken aright," Jesus answered. "The law of our father Moses is as you have defined it." He raised his voice slightly. "But you wish to know what is my interpretation of the law." His flashing brown eyes swept the multitude, looked upon the woman standing there with a cold disdain upon her countenance, regarded calmly the merciless hard faces of these rulers of Jerusalem. And then, quickly, he spoke. "My law in this case is this: Let him that is without sin among you cast the first stone at this woman." Smilingly now, his eyes swept the half circle of those watching him. Then he bent down again and once more began to write in the dust.

After a while the man from Galilee raised his head.

The woman stood before him, and back a little way from her those who had been listening to him, the people from the lower city and from the countryside who had come to Jerusalem for the Feast of the Tabernacles. But the scribes and Pharisees, the critical and intellectual Sadducees, had silently departed.

Jesus spoke to the woman. "Where are those who were accusing you? Has no man remained to condemn you?"

She stood silent. Slowly tears ran down her cheeks, and through eyes cleansed with tears she seemed for the first time to see the warmth of his smile.

"No man, sir." She dropped her eyes, and a tremor ran along her body.

Jesus saw it. He stood up quickly, walked over to the woman, looked smilingly into her agitated, tearful face. "Neither do I condemn you."

Now her lips trembled and her blue eyes were shining. "Sir, I was not always thus. In Dacia, where my father was slain and I was taken as a slave, my name was unsullied. But in Rome, and in Galilee, to which I was brought—"

"You have lived in Galilee?"

She nodded. "In the household of a powerful but evil man, and I went with him to—"

Jesus held up his hand. "That is past now," said he. "Look to the future, with its new promise."

"Sir," she said, and Jesus looking deep into her eyes saw that she had been touched, "you seem to understand, to—to—oh, sir—I—" And now she stopped, and tears welled in her eyes and ran unrestrained down her cheeks.

He stood smiling before her, and when the tumult of her emotion had subsided, he spoke again:

"The past is dead and buried," said he. "Henceforth, a new world calls you. The past is gone, buried in your contrition; the future beckons." He paused. "You shall have a new place from whence you came, a new place in Galilee, for Galilee I love. But let it be Magdala and not Tiberias"—his utterance of the name of Galilee's capital had startled her—"and henceforth let your name be—" Jesus paused, and his tanned face was strangely lighted— "the most beautiful of all names, let it be the name of my little Galilean mother—Mary."

She was smiling at him through tears. "Oh, sir, I—I—"

"Go, and sin no more. Go in peace, Mary—Mary of Magdala."

35

When the week of the Feast of the Tabernacles had ended, the rabbi went back across the Mount of Olives to the home of Lazarus and his sisters, and there he spent most of the time during the remaining weeks of the fall.

Occasionally he would return to the Temple and teach the crowds that thronged about him, but sometimes for days he would not go into Jerusalem, for he sought not unduly to inflame the leaders of Judaism against him. His hour, he felt, had not come; his mission was not yet accomplished. So he stayed with Lazarus and Mary and Martha, helping with the small tasks of the household, or tramping the fields and woods and along the quiet small streams, talking with his disciples, seeking to strengthen them against the day when he would no longer be with them.

So the fall days passed, and winter came down upon Judea, and soon it was time again for the holding of the Feast of Dedication, and once more great crowds of devout worshipers from all sections of Judea and down in Galilee and over in Peraea surged into the ancient city. All the inns and hostelries were filled, and Jewish homes made place for visiting relatives, and it was a period of great happiness in celebration of the cleansing of the Temple after its long-ago defilement by pagan hands.

Jesus came, too, to worship at the feast and to join his brothers in their prayers and sacrifices to God, for although he felt at all times a peculiar intimacy with his Father, he delighted likewise to join in his public worship.

But the Temple leaders—Caiaphas and old Annas and their supporters—remained obsessed with their evil designs against the teacher from Galilee, remained bent upon maintaining their own leadership and authority by destroying his influence, or better still, by destroying him. They posted their agents about the

Temple area with instructions to seek to bring him into disrepute with the admiring multitudes.

So this morning, only a moment after he had entered through the Gate of Shushan and was walking along Solomon's Porch, the covered corridor that ran a thousand feet beside the eastern wall of the Temple high above the Valley of Jehosophat, they accosted him. But as was their custom, they came smiling and fawning, their hypocrisy written plainly upon their smug countenances.

"Oh, master," said one, a fat Pharisee, "how much longer must we have doubts? If you are indeed the Christ, the Messiah sent of God, tell us plainly. We would no longer be in suspense about it."

"I told you, but you did not believe," Jesus answered them. "The works that I have done in my Father's name, have they not borne witness? But you have not believed because you have not been of a mind with me, you have not been my sheep. My sheep, those who understand me and are in sympathy with me and with my mission, understand; they know my voice like the sheep knows the voice of the shepherd, and they follow me. They understand what I say to them, and I point out to them the way to eternal life; I give to them a life that they shall never lose, for no man shall ever be able to separate them from me, to take them away from me. My Father has given them to me, has made them to understand me and discern the way I point out to them, and my Father is greater than all; certainly no man shall ever be able to snatch them out of my Father's hand, and my Father and I are one and the same."

"Blasphemy!" shouted the fat Pharisee. "You hear how this Nazarene makes himself equal with God. It is an offense for which he makes himself worthy of death! Does not the ancient law provide that such a one shall be stoned?"

Already several in the mob had run out through the Gate of Shushan to pick up small stones at the top of the rocky precipice that fell away into the Valley of Jehosophat, and now they came racing back with the stones to menace the rabbi.

But he stood among them unafraid and smiling. "Long have I lived among you," he said, "and I have never done any of you harm. Only good works have I done. And now for which of these good works are you taking up these stones to hurl at me?"

"It is not for the good works you have done among us," answered another man, a Sadducee, "but because you utter blasphemy against the Holy Name. You make yourself equal with God."

But the rabbi continued to smile, and he was composed. "But does not the ancient law say in one place, 'You are gods,' and if he unto whom the word of God came called them gods, and the Scriptures cannot be broken, can you say of him whom the Father has sanctified and sent into the world, 'You utter blasphemy, because you say that you are the Son of God'? Let this be your test for me: If I do not the works of God my Father, believe me not to be his son; but if I do his works, even though you do not believe in me, you can believe in what I do; in that way you can believe and know that the Father is in me and I am in the Father."

But neither his demeanor toward them nor his argument was able to convince them, because they had come up to the Temple with their minds closed against him, and so he left them and, gathering his little group about him, journeyed far from the neighborhood of Jerusalem toward his beloved Galilee.

At Bethabara on the Jordan, in the small neck of land that joined Galilee and Peraea and separated them from Judea and Decapolis, he paused and prepared to make a new journey through Peraea. Here at Bethabara, three years ago almost to the day, he had been baptized by John, the thundering prophet of the wilderness. And now John had been dead almost a year, murdered at Machaerus by Herod. Here John had preached and baptized, here Jesus had begun his ministry. Already the accomplishing days of the brave John were ended. And in his heart Jesus knew that the short, busy days of his own ministry were swiftly running to their end.

36

Pontius Pilate's fat round face was livid with anger. "I'll put an end to this business! It's a challenge to the authority of Rome!" He turned to confront Lucius Mallius Galba. "Tribune," he commanded, "I want you to see personally to the carrying out of this mission. I'll dally no longer with these brazen revolutionaries."

Lucius saluted. "Yes, sir," he said. "What are the procurator's orders?"

"Take all the men from the Caesarean garrison you may think necessary—two centuries if you wish—and another from the Antonia at Jerusalem—I'll give you the necessary written authority—and go over to Jericho, which should serve admirably as a base of operations. From there you can fan out into the hills. But be sure to take enough men so that there will be no danger of being ambushed by any of those robber bands. They lurk in the hills and sally forth quickly upon unwary travelers, and should you get your men separated into small detachments they might dare to attack some of them. I want them caught— particularly Bar Abbas and his cutthroats—but I don't want any of my men hurt." Pilate paused a moment. Then he spoke again. "Tribune, I hope we find Senator Lupinus's son. It's a shame that a wealthy Roman citizen has such little assurance of safety in traveling in Judea."

A scowl darkened his face. "I can see how the senator and the prefect Sejanus, the emperor even, would find it difficult to understand how such conditions could be permitted almost within the shadow of Jerusalem's walls. It is difficult for anyone who has not lived out here to understand these Jews. Even the criminals among them prefer to perpetrate their crimes among the Romans." His face brightened. "But I believe you will be able to catch that wily Bar Abbas, and when you do, you'll make the knave talk, eh, tribune?"

Lucius grinned. "Yes, sir, I believe I shall know how to get

227

the necessary information from him. And after we have finished questioning him?"

"Take him to Jerusalem—the Antonia dungeon—and the cross. The cross for every one of these revolutionaries you capture. We must put an end to this flaunting of our authority in Palestine."

"Very well, sir." Lucius saluted. "Are there any further orders?"

"No, I believe not. I want you to prosecute this mission with diligence. But take all necessary precautions. I don't want Roman soldiers killed chasing Jewish revolutionaries. That would be hard to explain in Rome."

The procurator was thoughtful for a moment. Then he turned to face Gaius, who had been standing at attention and a pace behind the tribune.

"Centurion," Pilate said, and his expression showed his concern, "you will aid Tribune Lucius. You are familiar with the country and with the ways of these robbers. And Marcus is your friend." He paused, spoke again, as if to himself: "Should Marcus really have leprosy when he is found—if he is found—that would be bad, very bad indeed. I hardly know in that case what could be done. A leper, rich or poor, is an outcast."

His round face brightened again. "But let us hope we will find him, and that he will be all right. But whether we find the senator's son or not, tribune," he declared, "we've got to clean out those vile revolutionaries, and I'm expecting your men to do it!"

37

Jesus at Bethabara was planning a journey down into Peraea and had sent some of his followers ahead to make arrangements when a messenger arrived from Mary and Martha at Bethany with the news that Lazarus was grievously ill.

"His sisters, master, are most anxious for you to come," the messenger said. "They are very much concerned about him."

"The illness of Lazarus is not mortal," the rabbi replied. "But it will be used for the glory of God, that the Son of God might be glorified because of it."

But he did not return with the messenger. Instead he waited two days before announcing to his disciples that he was planning to go back into Judea.

They were alarmed. "Master," said Simon, "do you not recall how the rulers of the Temple sought that day as you walked along Solomon's Porch to have you stoned to death? Is it not dangerous to go there again so soon after they have shown their evil intentions toward you?"

"But I am greatly needed in Bethany," said Jesus. "My friends are in sore distress. And I must go and awake Lazarus from his sleep."

"But if Lazarus is able to sleep, master," said another of his disciples, "it is a good sign; it means that he is mending, and that he shall soon recover from his illness. There is no greater restorer than sleep; it is the finest of medicines."

"You do not understand," Jesus said, simply. "Lazarus is dead." The group about him was silent. "And I am glad for your sakes that I was not there, so that you may have a strengthening of your faith. And though Lazarus is dead, now let us nevertheless go to him."

Thomas, who had been with him that day at the Temple and had seen him narrowly escape stoning, was convinced that the journey to Judea, to Bethany only two miles across the Mount of

Olives from Jerusalem, would mean not only death for the master but also for all of his little band.

"But let us go anyway," he said, with a sorrowful, resigned look upon his countenance, "so that we can die with him."

So they started south again, and they crossed the Valley of the Jordan east of the mountains, and north of Jericho they crossed the first range of the Lebanons and climbed upward toward Bethany, and as they were drawing near to the village they were met by Martha.

She was almost hysterical when she saw Jesus. "Oh, master," she said, between sobs. "If you had been here, if you had only reached us in time, my brother would not have died. But now he's gone—" She leaned her head against his chest as he put his arm about her shoulder comfortingly, and her tired, thin frame shook convulsively. "Master, we miss him so much! We need him, oh, we need him, and now he is gone. Oh, master, if you had only been here." Suddenly she held up her head, looked into his eyes, and a wan smile seemed to tremble upon her haggard face. "But I know that even now whatsoever you will ask of God, God will give it to you."

Jesus patted her lightly upon her trembling shoulder. "Great is your faith, my sister. Worry not; your brother shall rise again."

"I know that he shall rise again," Martha answered, "in the resurrection at the last day."

Jesus said nothing for a moment, but his dark eyes seemed to search her inmost thoughts. Then he spoke: "I am the resurrection and the life. He that believes in me, though he be dead, yet shall he live. And whoever lives and believes in me shall never die. Do you believe this, Martha?"

She smiled. "Yes, master," she said. "I believe that you are the Christ, the Son of God, the Messiah promised of old." When she had said it, she felt better. A great heaviness seemed to have fallen from her shoulders. The world, which for her had become unhinged with the death of her brother, seemed now to be righting itself. Turning, she started back toward Bethany to tell Mary that Jesus was on his way, was even now almost to the gates of the village. And as she walked, her steps grew faster, and soon she was running.

38

While Lucius and his legionnaires were fanning into the hills west of Jericho in search of Bar Abbas, Gaius selected a small detachment from his garrison at Capernaum and journeyed upward along the road from Jericho toward Jerusalem in the hope that he might come upon some news of Marcus.

Because he was a Roman soldier, and unknown in that section, it was difficult for the centurion to obtain information from the inhabitants. Few admitted that they had ever heard of Bar Abbas; they feared that the Roman soldier was seeking to entrap them, to identify them, perhaps, as confederates of the robber-revolutionist.

But one ancient Jew, a tender of a vineyard that ran up the precarious slope of a hill upraised steeply above the Jericho road, was not afraid to talk. "Understand, soldier, that I have no interest in the doings of this Bar Abbas," he prefaced his revelation. "I am a simple cultivator of the grape on these few acres I had of my father, who had them from his father before him. I pay my taxes when the collector comes; I go up to Jerusalem on the feast days in accordance with the worship of my fathers. But I take no interest in the affairs of government; that is for heads younger and wiser than mine."

He cleared his throat. "But this I do know. In the last spring —it was almost a year ago, in fact—this Bar Abbas, so they said, operated along the road in this vicinity. He and his men hid in the rocks and when travelers came along, fell upon them, robbed them, and sometimes beat them severely, especially those of the ruling class or connected with the administration of the government." He paused, shifted his weight upon his gnarled staff. "And as for lepers, there was back about that same time a group of them who lived in a cave near here. I could point out the place, soldier—" he paused again "—but I wouldn't go near it." Gravely he shook his grizzled head. "It's polluted."

"But the lepers," Gaius hesitated to ask, "they are not there now?"

"Oh, no, soldier, they have been gone many months now, and God be praised for it. They were pitiful, indeed, it is true, and sometimes when I had it to spare I put out a crust for them and a skin of wine. But I never went near them, and I never saw them except at a great distance. And now I am greatly relieved that they are gone. If there was a Roman amongst them, I know it not."

So Gaius continued his way up the Jericho road in the hope that he might obtain a definite clue that would enable him to learn the fate of his friend. And when at length he reached the village of Bethany some two miles east of Jerusalem, he paused, for a crowd had gathered at a whitewashed cottage there, and he hoped that someone in the group might be able to give him information that would be of help in locating Marcus.

But the villagers eyed him suspiciously, and when he sought discreetly to question them, one old man who solemnly combed his beard with his extended fingers spoke: "Soldier, we have gathered here to mourn the death of a friend. That is all. We have assembled for no other purpose."

Gaius assured them that he meant them no harm. "I am searching for a friend who was waylaid by one Bar Abbas, a robber chieftain who some months ago with his band preyed upon travelers passing along the Jericho road," he explained. "I was just wondering if anyone here had heard anything that might enable me to locate—"

"We have heard of this Bar Abbas, soldier—" the old man began.

"But we have in no way dealt with him," a Jew standing beside him interrupted.

Gaius saw that they were too suspicious of him to reveal any information even should they have any. They evidently were anxious for him to leave. He was preparing to go when he saw a group of men and women approaching along the road.

"Those people—" he nodded in the direction of the group "—would any of them likely be able to help me?"

"No, soldier," the younger of the two with whom he had spoken hastened to assure him, "they are friends of the dead man,

232

and two of them are his sisters. They are coming to join in the mourning. They know nothing of Bar Abbas or those he may have robbed. They are simple people of our village. They could give you no aid."

By this time the approaching group was within a hundred paces, and a great excitement surged through Gaius when he recognized the tall man as the rabbi from Nazareth and several of the men as members of his group, including Simon and the Zebedee brothers. He tried to speak calmly, but he was afraid his voice would betray his emotion. "The tall man," he said, "the one in the midst of the group, it seems that I have seen him—"

"Not likely, soldier," the ancient bearded one declared. "He's —he's a Jewish rabbi coming to offer his sympathy and mourn with us at the death of this Lazarus, his friend. You would have no reason to know—" The old man stopped, his mouth open, on his countenance an expression of utter amazement, for the man in the brown robe, now but a few steps away, was walking forward to greet the Roman soldier.

"My brother the centurion from Capernaum!" he said. "Peace be with you. And how do things go in Capernaum, and—" there was a sudden warming of a smile on his face—"how is the little Greek boy?"

"With you, likewise, be peace," said Gaius, responding in the Jewish manner to the rabbi's greeting. "The lad has mended completely and is thriving, sir. And things are little changed at Capernaum."

"What brings you into Judea?" the rabbi inquired, still smiling.

"Rabbi, I am seeking my friend the manufacturer at Tyre who was set upon by robbers on the Jericho road some ten months ago and robbed of his money, and since has not been heard from."

"Perhaps these my friends who live in this community and often travel the Jericho road might have information," the rabbi suggested.

"Master," the old Jew with the long beard volunteered, "I have heard reports of this man of whom the Roman soldier speaks, but I was fearful—"

233

"Have no fear of the centurion," said Jesus. "He is among our friends of Capernaum."

"I am greatly sorrowful, master," said the old man, "that I did not know." He turned to Gaius. "I have heard it said that the man of whom you must be speaking was robbed, and when Bar Abbas was having him stripped of his clothes it was discovered that he was a leper and the robbers fled, as well they should have."

"Yes, this much I have likewise heard," said Gaius. "But now I seek to find him."

"The lepers with whom he found shelter have left that community," the old man said. "I heard it said that they moved farther north into the mountains well beyond Jerusalem. I should add, soldier, that the story was that a woman was with him, and the robbers took her with them. I have heard that she was seen later in Jerusalem, and that she was living in sin."

Gaius, who out of the corner of his eyes had been watching the rabbi, saw that he was listening to the old man's story. But he said nothing.

"Yes," Gaius said to the bearded old fellow, "she was his friend. And I thank you for your information."

"I pray the Father that you find him," said Jesus. Once more his face was serious. "There is much sorrow in the world," he said. "I come here upon a mission that brings us much sadness. Our friend Lazarus is dead."

Gaius noticed now that the women had been weeping. Simon and the Zebedees, who had nodded to him as they came up with Jesus and the women, were likewise solemn faced, and they appeared weary from their long journeying. They stood in a small knot about the rabbi, each apparently deep in his own thoughts, as little groups of relatives and friends had stood countless times before in the presence of death. The sobbing of one of the women, a long, low shudder that shook her weary and grief-wracked frame, broke the unnatural silence.

"Oh, my Lord, if you had only been here my brother would not have died."

"Yes, master," said a man in the group, evidently a neighbor of the dead man, "Mary is right. If you had been here, you could have saved him."

"Yes, master, yes, master," said another; and then another, "Oh, master, if only you had been in Bethany but four days ago."

A woman in the fringe of the crowd began to cry, and others bowed their heads, even among the men, and wept.

Gaius was watching the rabbi. The grief, the deep mourning of these simple villagers, these plain people always so close to his heart, was having its effect upon Jesus. And he, too, was a friend of Lazarus. Gaius would not have been surprised had Jesus also wept with them.

But he did not. Instead, he turned to Mary. "Where have you laid him?" he asked quietly.

"Master," one of the men answered, "it is in the sepulcher yonder in the hillside. Come with us, and we will show you."

The little procession—the weeping sisters, the simple, sorrowing men in their Sabbath clothing, their gnarled, toil-toughened hands scrubbed and their beards combed, the weary, mourning rabbi and his solemn disciples about him, and Gaius and his men in the rear—trudged past the white cottage and through the vegetable garden beyond until they came to the cave in the hillside.

In front of the cave, the opening of which had been sealed by a large stone, the group stopped. For a few moments they stood silently facing the tomb. Then Mary began crying softly, and her shoulders shook, and she leaned her head forward against the shoulder of the rabbi. "Oh, master," she said, more to herself than to the rabbi, "if only you had not been so far away. Oh, master, if only you had been with us, Lazarus would not have died. And now he is gone." Her sobbing shook her weary, spent body.

Jesus, his eyes still upon the silent cave in the side of the hill, patted her shoulder comfortingly. And Gaius, watching the rabbi, saw his eyes filling, and tears ran down his cheeks into the points of his beard, and he lowered his head, and the tears streamed unashamed from his eyes.

Jesus wept.

"The master must have loved Lazarus greatly," said one of the Jews standing near Gaius. "See how he weeps for him."

"Yes," the man beside him agreed. "It is a great pity that he did not get to Bethany last week while Lazarus was still alive. He could have kept him from dying, for has he not done many wonderful works, such as opening the eyes of the blind and healing the lame? If he had only come earlier. It is a great pity indeed. How much sorrowing he could have prevented."

But Gaius, although he heard the men talking, was watching the rabbi. Jesus had quickly overcome the surge of emotion that had caused him to weep, and now he was wiping his eyes with the wide sleeve of his robe.

Then he walked toward the cave entrance. "Take away the stone from the mouth," he said, motioning to a little group of the men who stood near him.

One of the sisters of the dead man stepped forward, her eyes streaming. "Master, you must not remove the stone that seals the tomb. He has been dead four days, and by this time the body has begun to decay, and the odor would be offensive."

"Martha, have I not already told you that if you would believe, you would see the power of the Father manifested before you?" The rabbi's tone was mildly reproving, but he was smiling, and he appeared to have regained his composure completely.

Already the men were shoving aside the heavy stone, and as the mouth of the cave stood revealed, the women moved back a few paces from it. But Jesus walked to the cave mouth. For an instant he peered deep into the darkness of the tomb, and then he looked toward the sky and closed his eyes. Now there was silence, save for the quiet weeping of the dead man's sisters. Gaius saw that the Jews had bowed their heads and instinctively he bowed his head too, though out of the corner of his eyes he still watched the rabbi.

As Jesus prayed silently, the centurion had the illusion that the rabbi actually grew in stature there before him; he had not only recovered his usual calm, but a new vigor seemed to have taken possession of him. Strength seemed to be flowing into him. He stood now with his face to the sky, his eyes closed, his shoulders erect, his weight evenly supported on his brown sandaled feet.

Now he was speaking, though his eyes remained closed. He seemed to be oblivious of those around him, he seemed to be in intimate and loving conversation with someone near but unseen. "Father, I thank you that you have heard me," he was saying. Now his tone became lower, more intimate. "I know, Father, that you always hear me; because of these thy people that stand here with me I have spoken that they may believe that you have sent me."

He ceased speaking, opened his eyes. Now he faced the tomb, walked to the very mouth. Gaius and the Roman soldiers with him, the two sisters, and all the Jews about them stood motionless, holding their breaths almost, their eyes upon the rabbi.

For a moment he looked into the darkness of the cave. Then he spoke.

"Lazarus," he said, and his voice was strong and confident, "come forth!"

For a moment not a sound broke the heavy silence. Not a person stirred. Tense, almost fearful, they stood watching the opening in the cave. And then those nearest to the entrance heard it. A muffled sound, a sort of slow shuffling noise, it came from the darkness of the tomb.

The rabbi stood erect, poised, in front of the cave opening, apparently oblivious of the group at his back, including the two sisters, who stood at his left a pace behind him and could look directly into the cave.

Suddenly the high shrill scream of one of the sisters shattered the unnatural silence. And in that same instant the group of Jews about the cave opening surged back a few paces, for groping his tortuous slow way toward the light came one of the most horrible apparitions Gaius had ever seen. Tall and emaciated, he seemed to be a shuffling skeleton dressed in a white robe that had been bandaged tightly about the sparse frame with yard after yard of linen strips. The strips so bound his legs that he could shuffle his bony feet but a few inches at a step, and other strips held his arms pinioned to his sides. But worse, his head was swathed in a linen scarf held in place by other narrow strips, so that his entire face was covered.

Bedlam started. "Praise God!" shouted an old Jew, "Praise God! Wonders have I beheld this day! Praise the great God!"

Others, too, were shouting, and the two sisters fell into each other's arms, weeping now without restraint.

"By the immortals! Was the man really—" But the stern look upon the face of the centurion cut short the legionary's words.

The rabbi appeared not to notice the commotion at his back.

He was watching the shuffling apparition in front of him. And when the swathed figure seemed to be on the point of collapsing, Jesus sprang forward, caught him by the arm, steadied him. "Lazarus, my brother," he said, "I am here. Do you hear? I have come. Be not afraid."

"Master—" The sound was muffled, for it came from beneath the wrappings that sheathed the scarf about his head. "Oh, master." He straightened perceptibly. Jesus saw it. He beckoned to the men who had edged nearer.

"Unbind him," he commanded. "Let him go."

Soon they had stripped the narrow bandages from his legs and arms and had unbound those that held the scarf about his head, and he stood revealed. Timidly his sisters came up to him, and when they saw him smile and hold out his thin arms to them, they clung to him and their emotion overcame them, and they began weeping anew. Now the others, too, began to press around Lazarus and prod him with questions, so that the rabbi, who had been looking on quietly, stepped to his side.

"He is very tired," said Jesus. "He has come a far journey. And we likewise are weary. Let us go now into the house." Already Simon was opening a way for the rabbi, the thin shuffling Lazarus, and the two sisters, and the little procession started back toward the cottage beyond the garden.

It was then that the rabbi noticed Gaius. He strode over to him. "Centurion," said he, "go and find your friend, and when you have found him, bring him to me."

39

Once again the high priest Joseph Caiaphas sat upon the raised center seat in the semicircular line of benches at the end of the Chamber of Hewn Stones in the Temple.

"Leaders in Israel," said he, his black eyes burning as he looked along the line of robed and solemn members of the Sanhedrin, first to the left and then to the right, "we have assembled upon a matter of most extreme urgency. We must take counsel together concerning what must be done to rid Israel of this young rabbi from Galilee." He cleared his long thin throat. "Some months ago we met for the same purpose, and we set a trap for him—" Caiaphas glanced toward his rotund, luxuriantly bearded father-in-law, the former high priest Annas—"but the Galilean cleverly avoided the trap—"

"The high priest will recall that I cautioned against setting a trap for the Nazarene," observed the rabbi Nicodemus. "It is contrary to the laws of the fathers and the dictates of decency for one Jew to seek to entrap another."

"We expect the rabbi Nicodemus to maintain the same high regard, yes, even worship, for the upstart Nazarene that he has always manifested when the fellow's interest conflicted with the interests of Israel," the high priest declared in his most sarcastic manner, "but, fortunately for Israel, the views of the rabbi Nicodemus shall not prevail. For now we can no longer delay disposition of this troublesome case, and I know that this Sanhedrin may be depended upon to espouse the cause of Israel against any of her enemies." He paused, and now his cold, piercing black eyes calmly surveyed the bearded men along the benches. "The influence of this man must be ended; we can suffer it to increase no further, else we shall shortly be calling down upon our heads the wrath of Rome."

"My Lord High Priest," interjected the rabbi Nicodemus, "I

see not how the spiritual teachings of the Nazarene, which have nothing to do with political matters, concern Rome. Rome, I take it, is not interested in the religious views of the Jewish people so long as they continue to fill the hungry coffers of Rome's tax-gatherers."

"The rabbi Nicodemus knows well how the preaching of this Galilean blasphemer might easily provoke Rome to wrath against Israel," the high priest declared. "The rabbi Nicodemus is more interested in this braggart from Nazareth than he is in fulfilling the vows he took when he entered upon his holy office."

Nicodemus colored, but he held his tongue. The high priest, a thin smile curling his bloodless lips, smote the polished table in front of him. "We can no longer delay, men of Israel! We must act, or all the world will be flocking after this blaspheming opportunist. All Jerusalem rings with the report of his revival of that fellow in Bethany who was supposed to have been dead—"

"Supposed to have been dead, you say, my Lord High Priest?" Nicodemus asked, smiling, and in his voice his colleagues along the semicircle of benches were able to detect his effort at ridicule.

"Of course, the fellow was not dead," Caiaphas replied without hesitation. "Everyone who will give calm consideration to the incident the other day over at Bethany can readily see that the fellow was in a trance and was awakened out of it by the cleverness of this Galilean who was quick enough in the first place to realize that the man was not dead but rather in a deep coma."

"Perhaps," observed Nicodemus, smiling pleasantly, "that accounts for the distinctively offensive odor that issued from the cave when they removed the stone that sealed the entrance."

"My Lord High Priest," spoke up another member of the Sanhedrin, quickly, "I myself heard reports that seemed to be entirely reliable that the man at Bethany, one Lazarus, was actually dead, that his body was beginning to return to the dust from which it was created. Certainly those who were there when the Nazarene worked his magic thought the man dead. And the report has spread throughout Jerusalem. I heard it several days ago of my gardener, who had it from a man who said he was a neighbor of this Lazarus. I know not whether the man was dead or in a coma. But I think that we need not concern ourselves with whether the man was dead or whether he was in a trance. The evil is the same either way, for the Nazarene is being credited with having restored a man to life who was dead, and that is the great threat to the security of Israel and the influence of Israel's leaders." He cleared his throat, stroked his short, stubby beard. "Let us say that this Lazarus was really dead and that the Nazarene restored him. Then he must be a companion of the dark forces, a fellow-worker with Satan himself, and he must be destroyed, and quickly!"

"Indeed," agreed Caiaphas, "the brother's logic is sound. In either case he is a worker of evil, a perverter of our laws, a challenge to our influence and authority, a threat to the security of Judaism!" He tapped the table with long skinny forefinger. "There is no time to delay. Either we rid ourselves of him, or all Israel may suffer at the hands of Rome, the usurper."

"And between this Jew who has done nothing but good," said Rabbi Nicodemus, "who has never lifted his hand but to heal and teach and bless, and the proud usurper, you choose Rome." His voice, the look on his face, betrayed his scorn.

But Caiaphas was not willing to let the remark go unchallenged. "It is either the Galilean or we, either this blasphemer or Israel. And think you not that it is expedient for us that one man should die for the people rather than the whole nation perish?"

40

Passing weeks ground down the sharp teeth of the Judean winter, and warming breezes stirred upward out of Egypt and the desert wastes of the wilderness. The drowsing olives upon the gentle slopes and the vineyards that pushed along the hillsides were stirring now with new life. Pears and apricots and pomegranates, oleanders and the small lilies in the valleys and the flowers from a thousand seeds fetched from oriental lands gave new color to the countryside of Judea and Samaria; and demure, gentle violets ventured from beneath the carpet of green spreading now above the dead grasses.

But up here upon the backbone of the Lebanon range along the borders of Samaria and Judea the spring winds were chill, and Gaius, pushing along the precipitous trail at the head of several of his legionnaires, settled his toga more snugly about his shoulders to shield himself against the sharp gusts.

March had come again. The prophet John had been dead a year, and the tetrarch Herod Antipas had observed another birthday anniversary. And for a full twelve months now Marcus had been missing. Nor in all that time had Gaius had any word of the girl Naamah.

Jesus was some miles south at a little place in the mountains called Ephriam. He had come north from Jerusalem with his band to escape the hostile scheming of the Temple leaders, for as Simon had told the centurion one day when he had come upon the big fisherman at a sandalmaker's shop in the settlement, the master's time had not yet come when he should proclaim before these lions of Israel in their very lair the coming of his kingdom.

For weeks now, whenever he could spare a few days from his duties at Capernaum, Gaius had been searching for Marcus. He had started at the place he and Lucius had left Marcus and Naamah that day a year ago when Marcus and the girl had turned westward to take the road up to Jerusalem. He had located the place along the road where Bar Abbas had waylaid the travelers and had even found and examined the cave to which the lepers had taken Marcus. From that point he had searched in a general northwest direction, through the caves and ridges of the eastern range of the Lebanon across the valley to the west to the ascending slopes of the second ridge. Past Ephraim and high into the hills that ran into the borders of Samaria, the centurion explored.

In his searching he had come upon several pitiful colonies of lepers, and boldly, despite their screamed warnings, he had gone among them to inquire of his friend. But he had been unable to find a trace of Marcus and was thinking of abandoning the search, when only yesterday he had come upon a small group of half-starved lepers sunning themselves among the rocks on the south side of a cliff. They were too exhausted to run away when he came up to them, and they ate gluttonously of the food he gave them before he sought to question them.

"Yes, I know him," one old fellow said, when Gaius began describing Marcus. "He's the Roman, the fellow who was once rich, and so was I—a million years ago in Athens." He twisted his gnomelike head to one side, squinted his one good eye at Gaius. "If you value your friend, if you wish to remember him as a man, soldier, I advise you to turn about and seek him no farther. He is not the man he once was. He is not the man he was that day when I fetched him to the cave after Bar Abbas had robbed him and stripped him. He, too, is a dead man walking, a dead fish cast up on the seashore. Soldier, you can do your friend no good. You only endanger yourself. You should not now be here among us dead dogs."

"I am not afraid," said Gaius. "I must see my friend. Where is he now?"

"Soldier, you must have much love for him," said the old man. "I admire you for it. But you will only cause yourself great pain and grief. Do not go farther. You will be unable to aid him, and he will be reminded all the more of his misery. Count him dead, soldier, for soon we shall all be dead, loosed from our bonds that hold us to this living death."

"I must find him," Gaius said. "Tell me the way he went."

The wizened man lifted his shrunken lean arm to point with the stump of a hand along the trail that ran northward. "If you must find him, soldier," he said, "he went that way, and it was but two days ago, or perhaps three. Time means little to us. But he cannot be far." He laughed again, a hollow rattle in his throat that came out through the glaring wide holes in his eaten-away nose. "He still thinks, the poor fool, that he can get to Tyre and recover his riches. There are six of us here. We saw no reason to go farther. Where would we be going? Death is as near us here as it would be in Samaria or even in Galilee. And we could never get there. We are too weak. The four who went were a little stronger, or perhaps they only thought so. But they were hardly creeping. They won't be far, soldier. But I warn you, turn about and go the way you have come. It will be better that you never lay eyes upon him again."

"Remain here, the six of you," said the centurion. "And when I have found him, I shall bring them back here, and I will procure you food and clothing."

"You say this, soldier, and you are a Roman? But though it is strange to the ears of an Athenian, I honor you for it. I, a dead dog, a fish stinking upon the beach, honor you." He laughed again. "And do not fear that we shall run away. Our legs would not permit it, nor do our inclinations any longer urge it."

41

When Gaius found him he was lying stretched in the sun on the south side of a boulder that protected him from the sharp March wind.

Evidently he did not hear Gaius approaching along the trail, for the centurion, who had been walking several paces ahead of his legionnaires, was almost upon him before he stirred. Then he pulled up his legs clumsily and lifted himself heavily into a sitting position. "Get back! Unclean!" he warned, and his voice was husky and strained. He motioned with one hand while he braced himself with the other, and Gaius saw that the fingers were twisted grotesquely. "You must get back quickly. I am a leper. Unclean!"

But Gaius walked boldly up to him. "Marcus! I've been looking everywhere for you! Now, at last, I've found you."

"You must mistake me for someone else," he said, evenly. "And now, please, go away quickly, before you become contaminated. I am unclean. I have leprosy."

Gaius dropped down beside him, put his arm about the thin, drooped shoulders. "I am not afraid of you, Marcus. I knew about it. For months I have been trying to find you. And I expected to find you like this—or worse."

"By the immortals, Gaius, don't touch me!" he said, trying to pull away. "Cannot I do one unselfish thing before I die? Please leave me, Gaius; I don't want you to contaminate yourself with this terrible curse."

"I am not afraid of you, Marcus," the centurion insisted. "I have come to take you back."

"It was good of you to look for me, Gaius. I have often thought of you, and I thought you would try to find me. But now it is too late; nothing can be done for me, and the only thing you will accomplish will be to get this terrible plague yourself. Please leave me, Gaius; I mean it. I am done for, and I would not have you experience what I have endured during the last year." His voice was rasping, harsh. "Please go now, my friend, before you expose yourself, if you haven't done so already."

"I'm not going, Marcus. I have come to help you, if I can. I tell you I am not afraid of you or the leprosy."

Marcus smiled wanly. "But there's nothing you can do, Gaius. I am far gone; the disease has made much progress."

"No, you are mistaken, Marcus. I shall get you back. I know a physician—"

"A physician can do nothing for me, my friend. I had hopes of getting back to Tyre. I had visions of recovering my money and property and employing physicians—" He paused, made a gesture of futility with his twisted, shrunken hands. "But I have given up the idea. There's no use. It's—it's hopeless."

Gaius sat down, straightened out his legs, leaned back against the boulder. "But with your money, Marcus—"

"Yes, I know, I used to say that," Marcus interrupted. "And I thought then that it was true. But it wasn't. And besides, I have no money. My money's all gone, centurion; my health's gone. I—I'm an outcast."

"Marcus, I don't want to be unkind; but you know now that there are things more to be desired than money, don't you?"

"Yes," Marcus answered, "many things. Health, the first thing. And many others. You were right, centurion. In these bitter months I have realized that you were right and I was wrong. But it matters little now. Everything is past. I am even past seeking vengeance upon Tullus. You know that part of the story, don't you?"

"Yes, I heard how he betrayed you."

"Well, little it matters now, Gaius. I haven't even the energy now to hate. Or to love."

"Then you have forgot Naamah?"

"No, Gaius. I have thought of her often, too, almost constantly, in fact. That is one of the things that tortures me most, the realization that I will never see her again. And I had known her only a few days."

"Perhaps you will see her again, Marcus. Did you know that she got safely to Jerusalem?"

"No, I have heard nothing. I have been completely out of

touch with the world of the living, Gaius. I have been dead, a shriveling corpse shuffling among dead bodies. I'm a dead dog, a smelling fish cast upon the seashore—"

"I talked yesterday with your friend the dead dog, the smelly fish cast upon the shore by the waves—"

"That was the Greek." A thin smile lighted the cavernous drawn face. "He has a very effective way of expressing himself. That fellow was once a rich merchant in Athens. You'd never think it, seeing him now, of course." He held up his own hands, examined them with eyes that seemed all the more staring because the lids had lost their lashes. "Nor do I look like a man who a year ago was a wealthy manufacturer." He shrugged his shoulders, and Gaius noticed that one shoulder was higher than the other.

"But, Gaius, speaking of the girl, sometimes I think those days at Machaerus were only a dream, or else the days since have been only a nightmare." His smile emphasized the strained, drawn look.

"It must have been a frightful experience, Marcus," Gaius said, "but now things are going to be better. I'm sure of it."

"No, centurion, it's too late now. There's nothing that can be done. I suppose I've known it for a long time, but I refused to admit it, I suppose. I just couldn't face the facts." He twisted his frame a bit to get the weight off his left hip. "But it makes little difference. There isn't much pain, and the sun is warm upon my back, and soon it will all be over." He settled himself in the new position. "I am sorry that my life has been such a failure. It has counted for nothing, Gaius. I see it now. I have been selfish, grasping, pushing people down in the belief that I was raising myself up. I have been a fool, Gaius. Yes, I see it now very clearly. I sought to make money, and by the immortals, I made it. But what good is it to me now? Even if I had it still, how could it serve me?" He shrugged his shoulders again, but there was no longer the nonchalance of the old days; the gesture was rather one of defeat, surrender. "I have no friends, except a few pitiful shreds of humanity, lepers like myself—and you."

Suddenly his drawn face seemed alive again, and he leaned forward. "Tell me, Gaius," he said, "why is it that you are not afraid of this vile disease? Why do you not shun me like everyone else does who is not also a leper? Is it—" He hesitated. "Is it because of that Jew worker of wonders you used to talk about? Is it because you have been with him much in this last year?"

"Yes, I suppose so, Marcus. But I have not been with him much, though occasionally our paths have crossed. In fact, I saw him not so many days ago, and when I told him I was seeking you, he told me to find you and bring you to him. He is at the moment in the mountains only a few miles south of here."

"And, centurion, you really think he could heal me."

"I know he can do his part toward healing you, Marcus. But I don't know whether you could—or would—do your part toward healing yourself."

Marcus's face revealed his bewilderment. "What do you mean, centurion?"

"I have not yet come to understand this young Jew very well," Gaius replied. "But he must be in communication with some tremendous power. And he seems not to be able to establish contact with it and use it in helping someone else, unless that other person is likewise eager to help and is confident of his ability to provide this mysterious aid, whatever it is. He calls it faith. He requires that those whom he heals have faith in him, as he expressed it. They must believe that he has the power through his Father, as he calls this supreme power, this God of the Jews, to heal them, or he cannot do it. The healing, it seems, must be a mutual working together. And yet, he even raises people from the dead."

"Really, Gaius? Did you see him raise a dead man to life?"

"I saw a man who had been dead four days, so they said, come walking out of the tomb with the burial wrappings still about him." He paused, but Marcus said nothing. "If he could do that," he went on, "he could certainly heal a leper. In fact, it is on record that already he has healed numerous lepers. But they have all shown their faith in his ability to do it."

For a long moment Marcus was silent. "It will surprise you, Gaius," he said, after a while, "considering the tone in which I used to speak of him, but in these long miserable months I have thought often of that young Jew; in fact, I have never been able to put him out of my mind. Sometimes there were moments when I even hoped that he might come my way and do something for me. But those, of course, were but wishful fancies born out of my desperation, for he is a Jew and if he could he would never heal me, a Roman. Nor would I ask him. After what I have said about him, I would not have the audacity to ask him to help me."

He looked up quickly, and Gaius thought he saw in the shrunken twisted face some of the old spirit. "And I still don't believe he could do it. There must be some trick to these supposed cures. After all, that man could have been in a trance and not actually dead. Why, centurion, these things are contrary to the laws of nature."

"Maybe they are, and then again maybe they are not," said Gaius. "And maybe he is able to summon to himself power that actually does circumvent the laws of nature."

Marcus shook his head slowly. "I think not, centurion. And besides, I am not a Jew."

"The slave boy you gave me was not a Jew. Nor am I a Jew, if you wish to argue that he cured the boy for me."

But Marcus continued to shake his head. "That's true. But for me, Gaius, there is no cure. You must go back, leave me." He smiled, but there was bitterness in it. "I am finished. Soon for me it will be all over. I am sorry that it must be this way. I see things differently now. But it's too late. And I fear for you. Go back, centurion, and ask your Jew healer to safeguard you against contracting this vile disease. Already you have spent too much time with me, but I am thankful to you for having come."

"You are wasting words, Marcus," said Gaius. "I am not going to leave you here. Instead, you and the three others are going back with me to the place where the six are waiting. And then I am going down to Ephraim and fetch the rabbi."

42

Once more Jesus had come into the hill country. He loved the highlands. Up here upon this rugged ridge that ran like a crusted and twisting backbone down through Judea from the northern reaches of his native Galilee, he could look westward toward the Great Sea and eastward in the direction of the desolate reaches of Peraea. Up here was rest and relaxation and recreation of the spirit.

The rabbi loved the lowlands too, but the flatlands, the cities in the valleys, even the plateau of Jerusalem, meant people, and people meant heavy toil of hand and continuous alertness of mind, for Jesus loved people and could never resist turning aside to heal them and teach them and comfort them and raise a prayer to his Father for them. People meant squalor and dust and the crowded misery of Jerusalem's lower city, and hunger and emptiness and sickness and ugliness. Likewise, people meant for him opportunity and challenge and hope. For Jesus people—people everywhere, the high and low, the good and bad, the wise and foolish—meant possibility. For him people were the children of the Father, the sons of God, his own beloved brothers.

His warm, sympathizing, understanding heart longed to transform them, to help them break forth from the dark and fleshly prison of squalidness and hunger and failure into a bright, warm, and clean new world. He wanted to set them upon the way, to show them how to be one with himself and his Father.

So in the world of people he was always busy, eager, tense. He had few moments for calm reflection, for quiet meditation, for earnest communion with the Father, for instructing his beloved followers.

But up here in the mountains near Ephraim toward the borders of Samaria there was tranquility. Here he could think upon the remaining days of this mission, for now he was sure that the day of his great adventure was fast arriving; here he could teach Simon and the Sons of Thunder and Thomas and Nathaniel and Levi and the others, perhaps even dark-browed, furtive Judas of Kiriot, how in the days after he had left them they should point out in his stead his way to the Father.

He had come up into the high ridge of the Lebanon when he had learned of the determination of the high priest Joseph Caiaphas and the Temple henchmen to destroy him. For several weeks now he had been in this retired high place, teaching his band, enjoying their companionship, living very close to them and to the Father, meditating upon the developing shape of his future course. Standing upon the high and commanding Lebanon hills, he had figuratively reached higher for the hand of his Father, and serene and confident he had made his decision.

"Soon now the season of the Passover will be upon us," he said one day to those about him. "It is time we were preparing to depart for Jerusalem, for I have determined to journey across into Peraea on the way to attend the Passover feast."

"But, Master," Simon interjected, "did we not avoid Jerusalem because of the violent hostility of the high priest and the Temple despots? And do you propose now to challenge them in their very stronghold?"

"Simon," the rabbi said, and there was a ringing strength in his voice, "will you once again seek to dissuade me from walking steadfastly along the way of my destiny? Would you have me step aside from the way along which my Father leads me?"

Simon's round bearded face was solemn, almost tearful. "Never, master. It is just—it is just that we love you so much!"

Jesus smiled, and the sternness melted in an instant. "I know you do, my brothers," he said simply. "And do not fear for me or for yourselves, for though I must go to Jerusalem and be offered up, I shall rise again and come to you. Have no fear; only trust in the Father, for will not he love and protect his own forever?"

43

In the calm and peace of these uplifted high hills he had sought with all his earnestness to learn the will of his Father for him. With his Father he had lived in warm and close communion. And now he knew. Figuratively, his Father had placed his strong arm about the shoulder of this his adored Son, had drawn him close and whispered in his ear.

Now no longer did Jesus doubt. "My way is toward Jerusalem," he told those of his band who had come up with him into the mountains above the capital city. "Soon the Passover week will be upon us, and we must eat of the Passover in Jerusalem. In Jerusalem I shall be offered up," he said quietly, "and given into the dominion of death. But I shall rise again. Have no fear. This temple shall be thrown down but in three days it shall be restored again. Be not heavy of heart, for I travel the way of my Father, and his way is good. And I, your brother, shall become the symbol of God the Father's great love for his children of earth."

His heart had been heavy and sad, but now it was light again, for God had spoken to him, and he knew that he was traveling the sure road, and he looked almost with eagerness of his great adventure. "We will journey to Jerusalem by way of Peraea," he said, and they started off once again, the tall leader and these bearded lively youths with whom already he had tramped countless dusty miles through this ancient land.

They had gone only a short distance when they encountered the centurion from Capernaum.

"You have found your friend," Jesus said, when he had greeted Gaius.

"I found him, sir, only yesterday, after long searching. That, sir—" He hesitated, but he saw that the dark eyes of the rabbi were smiling upon him. "That is why I have come searching for you."

"He is in distress, centurion?"

"Rabbi, he is a leper." Gaius lowered his eyes. "He is past traveling, sir. I would have fetched him to you, but—" He paused.

"I will go to him," said Jesus.

"But, sir, he is a Roman. He has long led a selfish life. I fear he has little faith. I am afraid—"

"Come, lead us to him."

"Rabbi, it is but a short way from here where we will find him. And there are nine others."

On the outskirts of a tiny village sprawled upon the side of the mountain they rounded a turn in the road that ran between jagged boulders. And suddenly, from behind one of these great stones they heard a commotion, and then the high, hopeless wailing cry of warning, "Unclean! Unclean! Stay back! Come no nearer! Unclean!"

But Jesus strode forward, and behind the boulder he came upon an old man, twisted into grotesque shape, thin and stooped, his face a chalky waste of bloodless flesh over which the deadened skin was drawn hideously. "In the name of God!" said the old man, and the words coming forth from the toothless cavern of his mouth sounded unnaturally low, as though they had been spoken by a man suddenly aroused from death itself, and Gaius, standing just behind the rabbi, thought of that recent day at Bethany when Lazarus had walked forth in his grave clothes.

"In the name of God, get you back! We are lepers—" He raised a skinny, withered arm and pointed to the left, and then Gaius saw the others sunning themselves behind some shrubs and rocks that screened them from the trail. "We are unclean. Leave us quickly. Leave us to die in peace. In God's name—"

"In the name of God we come," said Jesus. "We are not afraid."

"You are not afraid?" The old fellow laughed, and laughing, Gaius thought with a sudden sickening, he was even more horrible. "Well should you be afraid, stranger," he said. "Dally here and you may become one of us—a member of the company of the damned, the legion of lost souls." He paused. "You must go, and quickly," he said. "We would not have anyone suffer as we suffer. We are outcasts, driven forth from the companionship of our families, our friends. Even the priests will have naught to do with us. Go, stranger, before you become contaminated with this vileness."

253

But Jesus stood, arms folded across his chest, and smilingly looked upon the pitiful old fellow. "I am not afraid of you," he said. "I am your brother. In the sight of the Father we are all his children. He invites us all to abide in his love."

"Stranger, you are wrong," said the old man. "No one loves us. We are outcasts. Even God has turned his face from us. We are abandoned by all. And now you would mock us by speaking of love, of the love of God, whose face is toward the great and the strong of the earth, who lives in the great Temple at Jerusalem, who—"

"Praise God, it is the rabbi of Galilee!" A squat, dark fellow had risen to his feet and was pointing toward the Nazarene. "God in heaven! It is the rabbi indeed! Oh, master—" He started to hobble toward Jesus on withered, unsteady legs. "Oh, master, have mercy upon us!"

The fellow's recognition of the rabbi provoked a babbling of raucous, cracked voices. Some of the men clambered slowly to their feet, tottered forward, arms outstretched, pleading in their curiously large eyes, frightful in their white, wasted faces. Some came crawling toward Jesus on hands and knees, too weak apparently to get to their feet.

Only Marcus lay still, his head against a small stone, his legs thrust out grotesquely. Jesus nodded his head toward him. "He is your friend?"

"Yes, rabbi, he is the one for whom I have so long been searching."

The rabbi, smiling upon the pitiful wretches about him, walked quickly over to Marcus, stood looking down upon him.

Gaius was afraid that Marcus in his false pride would turn to confront Jesus with some sneering, caustic remark. But if the Roman had contemplated such a thing, the warm, compelling dark eyes of the tall Jew studying him stayed his tongue.

The centurion wanted to say something, to intercede for Marcus, to explain to the rabbi that in his misery his friend would hardly be responsible for what he might say. But he seemed powerless to speak. He stood motionless and silent, staring at the two men before him.

Nor could Marcus utter a sound. When he had twisted about

on his numb leg to face the man who had spoken to him, he had expected to see a dark-visaged, scowling, squat Jewish rabbi, a piety-professing religionist like the many he had encountered in his journeying through Palestine. But this man, he had seen at the first glance, was different. He was tall and tanned. His cheeks showed ruddy and smooth beneath the sparse stubble that ran down into the spikes of a blonde, reddish beard. He stood erect, evenly upon his coarse sandals, and his shoulders were wide and square.

All this Marcus saw. But it was the eyes of this young man that held him. He had never seen eyes like these. They seemed to be looking through him, weighing him, exploring the darkest corners of his misspent, fruitless years. Yet there was no hostility in them. They seemed to be sending shafts of sunshine into the depths of his crooked, tortured body.

"Sir, I—I am a Roman." Marcus heard himself speaking, objectively, as if he were some other person. "You do not understand; I am not a Jew though these my companions are for the most part Jews."

"It is you who do not understand," said the rabbi, but there was no tone of reproof in his words. "We are all children of the Father. In his sight we are neither Jew nor Roman nor—" he waved his arm in an embracing gesture—"Samaritan."

"But, sir—" Marcus was pulling up his numbed leg, and Jesus saw that he was attempting to get to his feet. Quickly he reached down, caught the twisted left hand of the Roman, raised him up. Marcus was surprised at the man's strength as Jesus lifted him to his feet, at the grip in the hand that for the instant had closed about his own twisted and flaccid hand. The feel of the rabbi's hand seemed to remain about his half-paralyzed one; he fancied that the feeling was being restored, that new blood was beginning to course along the arm, down into the drawn and knotted fingers. "But, sir, I do no understand the way of the gods—your gods—I—I—"

Gaius had been watching intently, and now the vision was blurring, for tears were welling in his eyes and running down the furrows of his cheeks. Furtively, he dabbed at his eyes with a corner of his toga, and he looked beyond the Galilean to Marcus. His

255

friend was standing, erect now, his numbed and shrunken leg forgotten in the dramatic tenseness of this moment, and tears were rolling unrestrained from Marcus's eyes.

I have never seen Marcus weep before, Gaius said to himself.

The centurion's eyes were flowing now, but his heart was leaping, and never had he experienced such a moment, not even when Lazarus had come shuffling and bound from the tomb at Bethany, for Marcus had fallen to his knees, and his shoulders were shaking, and he wept freely and unashamed as the tremors of his sobbing ran along his thin body. "Oh, sir—" he was saying between sobs "—I—I understand so little, but I know that if you would but—I know you could save even a poor wretch like me for a better life—I know—" He ceased speaking, and his eyes were upon the ground at the feet of Jesus, and now about the tall Galilean the other nine, even the squat Greek from Athens, were flailing the ground with their twisted, poor hands, wailing and pleading piteously.

"Oh, master, heal us," a stooped fellow cried in a sharp thin voice that was almost a screech. "Oh, master, heal us of this vileness. Make us men once more. Give us back life, oh, Son of the Most High God!"

Jesus stood above them, tall and towering. And the tears were in his eyes, and a shadow as of infinite sadness swept across his face and darkened it, as a cloud racing across the face of the sun shadows the field of ripened grain beneath it. But only for an instant, for as he lifted his face heavenward silently and closed his eyes, his countenance was lighted anew. When he had ended his brief prayer, he bent down, caught Marcus by the arm. "Rise," he said. "Get upon your feet, and go and show yourselves to the priests that they may know that God has healed you."

He reached down with his other hand to aid a leper at his feet. "Get up," he said firmly. "And be on your way."

"But master, I cannot walk," the man protested. "I have become so weakened." But now, with the aid of the rabbi, he was standing. He ventured a step forward, and another. "I walk," he said, and made another step. Then he shouted. "I can walk. Praise be to God! I can walk! I can walk!"

The other lepers, too, were shouting, screaming their joy as they ventured forth on thin legs that a moment ago had been feeble and twisted. But Marcus, seemingly in a daze, stood a moment before the rabbi, and then turning away, he began walking after the others, down the trail that led toward Ephraim. Gaius, still too emotionally stirred to speak, watched him. Now Marcus was lifting his left arm, flexing the muscles as he shoved it back and forth, faster and faster. As he walked he seemed to take on new life; his shoulders were more erect, his steps less dragging, his movements freer. And now he was running to overtake the others, many of whom had already begun running and leaping down the trail, mad with joy in their new freedom.

But he did not go far. Gaius and the others, still watching, saw him turn and come hurrying back. When he had drawn near, Gaius knew that he had changed, for though thin and haggard Marcus was handling himself with a new ease, a new confidence.

"Sir," he said, when he had come up to Jesus, "I am sorry. In my sudden discovery that I had been healed I forgot to thank you." Tears were filling his eyes again, and now he sank again to his knees. "Oh, I understand so little, but this—this God—your God—yes, and my God—he is real, I know it; I feel it."

The rabbi, his face beaming, lifted Marcus to his feet, put his hand upon his shoulder. "Your feet, my brother, are on the Way." He turned to the little group of his followers who had come with him. "Were there not ten healed, and has not but this one stranger returned to give thanks to God?"

Jesus turned to Gaius. "And now, centurion, you and your friend will be returning to Galilee, will you not?"

"Yes, rabbi, I must be going back to Capernaum, and I shall take Marcus with me. He can rest there awhile—"

There was a sudden faraway look in the rabbi's eyes, and then his quick smile wreathed his face. "Spring in Galilee. The gentle breath of the warming breezes on the hillsides. The grass and the flowers and the cattle grazing. Centurion, I would like to be going back to Galilee with you. But—" Gaius thought he saw the sudden passing of a cloud across the bronzed face—"we must be on our way to Jerusalem for the Passover."

44

Tribune Lucius saluted. "I am happy to report to you, sir, that the revolutionary and highwayman Bar Abbas has been captured. He is now in one of the dungeons of the Tower Antonia at Jerusalem."

"Excellent news, tribune," said Pontius Pilate, his round face beaming. "I am delighted to hear that after all these months he has at last been taken."

"Yes, procurator," Lucius continued. "It is particularly fortunate in view of the reports we had that he was planning an uprising among the Jews during the Passover week. The man seems to have a strong following."

"And these Jews want only half a chance to revolt anyway," observed Pilate. "This Bar Abbas, doubtless, is the sort of fellow to inflame them to action, even though they know at the start that all they'll get for their trouble will be cracked skulls and spilled Jewish blood. But, tribune—" he paused, leaned forward "—what of the son of Senator Marcus Calpurnius? Did the fellow reveal what had become of your friend?"

The tribune shook his head slowly. "I am sorry, procurator, but we got no information from him except that on the day they captured him they discovered Marcus had leprosy and they fled from him back into the hills, leaving him on the road that leads up from Jericho to Jerusalem."

"Did you put the fellow to the torture? Perhaps he did not tell all he knew."

"Yes, procurator, we soon had him screaming with pain and rage. But he told nothing more. In fact, I think he told all he knew. And I am confident he told us the truth. I am afraid that Marcus was indeed a leper, and that in desperation he may have done away with himself, or else he may have been so depressed at his condition that the disease worked the more rapidly upon him so that now he may be wasting away in some dark cave back in the hills."

A scowl clouded the countenance of the procurator. "But he must be found!" He thumped the table with his fist. "Even now the senator and perhaps the prefect Sejanus are doubtless wondering why we have been so long in finding him." The scowl vanished, and a look of bewilderment followed it. "But if we find him, tribune, and he has the leprosy, what can we do? How can we aid him?"

"Sir, I fear we shall never see Marcus again. But at Jerusalem we may hear word of him. Perhaps Centurion Gaius Sempronius, when he comes up from Capernaum, may have something to report. He will be there with a century from the Capernaum garrison, will he not, procurator?"

"Yes, the orders have already been dispatched to him. I shall see that there is no opportunity for an uprising among the Jews on this occasion. I am bringing in legionnaires from the various stations in Judea and am asking for assistance from those in Galilee. I am determined to give the head of legions at Jerusalem whatever aid he may need to prevent the outbreak of any disorders that might lead quickly to real trouble, for with so many Jews gathered at this Passover occasion it would be easy for some intemperate person to inflame their passions. We must be prepared to put down any troublesome situation that might arise." His frown softened almost into a smile. "I'm glad you captured Bar Abbas, tribune, even though you heard nothing new of the senator's son. That will be one less revolutionary to deal with during the Passover week's festival."

"Yes, procurator, with Bar Abbas in the Antonia dungeon, the chances of a concerted uprising at Jerusalem will be considerably less. I don't believe his followers will be able to do much without his leadership."

"I think that's true, tribune," Pontius Pilate agreed. "But nevertheless I want you to go to Jerusalem well prepared for anything that might happen. I don't trust these Jews. They are a stubborn and unruly people. The sooner I can wash my hands of them the better."

259

45

March was running out to its end now, and the first week of April and the great Passover festival at Jerusalem were fast approaching. So for the rabbi from Galilee there was no time left to rest in his beloved hills and commune at length and in private with his Father. For him there was only time to reach Jerusalem for the feast and the destiny that awaited him there in the crowded citadel of ancient Judaism.

Now as he journeyed down from the mountains in the borders of Samaria and crossed the fast greening valley of the Jordan into Peraea, his disciples sensed a deeper seriousness, an even more intense look upon his countenance, an added brightness in his dark eyes. "It is as though the master were looking through an open window upon some great scene that we ourselves are unable to behold," Simon said one day to John. "Could it be that in Jerusalem he will overthrow the Roman conqueror, drive out Pilate and his tax-gatherers and his soldiers, and set up a free kingdom of Israel? Could that be the reason for the far-away look in his eyes, the look of impending great things just ahead?"

"I know not," answered John. "But something of tremendous importance occupies the master's mind. That is plainly to be seen." He leaned closer to big, bearded Simon. "Do you not recall how he said that at Jerusalem he would be offered up? Could it be that—"

"God forbid," said Simon, interrupting. "Has he not power to slay the conqueror, drive him from our ancient land, and strengthen our cities against the invader? Did you not see him bring forth Lazarus from the tomb? Did you not only the other day see him restore the lepers, even the Roman who had been rich and selfish?"

"But has he not said that he came not to slay but to heal, that his kingdom is not of this world but of the heart? How then could he become king over Israel? Answer me that, Simon."

"I know not how to answer, Zebedee," said Simon. "The ways of the master are not yet understandable to me. But if he goes to Jerusalem and there runs afoul of the Romans or the leaders in the Temple, I know what I shall do. I shall defend him to my last breath. I shall die at his side."

"But that may not be his wish, Simon. Is he not a man of peace? I believe he would seek to defeat all his enemies another way."

"Perhaps you are right," said Simon. "My heart tells me that you are right, but my pride makes me wish to see the Roman invader overcome, beaten into the dust, driven from our soil."

As they journeyed southward toward Jerusalem along the old camel trail east of the Jordan that twisted through Peraea, the rabbi talked often with these young men who for the last three years had been so much with him. He talked to them of the way to the Father, of God's great love for his children, of the sorrow in his heart at the straying from the way of even one of these children. "A certain man had two sons," he said to them one day. "And the younger of them said to his father, 'Father, give me the portion of your property that will fall to me.' And the father divided among his children his property. And not many days after he had made the division the younger son gathered his part together and took his journey into a far country, and there he wasted his substance."

The rabbi, in his inimitable way of telling a story to illustrate a spiritual truth, went on with his revelation of how this prodigal son had finally realized his folly and had determined to return to his father as a lowly hired man. But the father had seen him coming a long way off and had rushed out to greet him joyfully, had restored him to his station as a beloved son, and had made a great feast in his honor. And that, said the rabbi, in a feeble way shows how God the Father will welcome back into the security and joy of his house the repentant son who comes seeking his forgiveness in true spirit of humility and repentance.

Jesus talked with great earnestness, and it seemed to his friends that he was attempting to compress into a few short hours the very essence of his gospel, his story of the Father's love, of his own part in pointing out his Father's Way, to draw with quick, bold strokes his pictures of the kingdom. Many of these brief stories, each dramatically emphasizing the core of truth he wished to leave with them, the rabbi told as they walked the roads now dusty with the feet of other pilgrims going to the great feast. Shrewdly, he clothed these abstract truths in the vivid garments of imagined incidents.

As he traveled through Peraea the news that the rabbi of Galilee was journeying to Jerusalem to attend the Passover went ahead of him and great crowds came out to see him. Farmers left their labors of preparing the land for the spring planting, vineyardists stopped pruning their vines, shopkeepers from the villages barred their doors and came out with their families to see the man whose fame had spread throughout Palestine. They brought their small children to see him, and when the children saw him they instinctively ran to him and thronged about him; and when the rabbi's disciples rebuked the parents, fearing that the rabbi would be tired at the tumult of the children and unable because of their shouts to make clear his message to their elders, Jesus gently scolded the disciples. "Don't push the children away," he said. "Let them come up to me and play."

And then his face lighted as he recognized an opportunity for presenting in dramatic fashion a lesson in perfect faith. "Little children are of the very kingdom of God," he said. "They live in true faith. They have utter confidence in the power and the desire of their parents to protect them and care for them. They do not doubt the love and the strength of their parents. So should we have faith in the love and the strength of our Father. In true humility and with the complete faith of the little child we must yield ourselves to the Father and thereby enter his kingdom."

One day as he was nearing Jericho a young man, a handsome youth who wore expensive clothing and had the manners of the well born, came up to Jesus as the band stopped to rest for a few moments. "He is one of the leaders in this section," Simon whispered to the rabbi. "He is very wealthy."

The young man showed much deference in the presence of the rabbi. "Good master," he said, "I have heard much of you and of the message that you bring. It is apparent to me that you have an understanding of the mysteries of life. I have given much study to the teachings of the leaders of our faith, and I am convinced that there is more to living than we ordinary mortals are able to comprehend. I hold with those who believe that we do not cease to live when we end our earthly existence. I feel that man is immortal, that man may inherit an eternal life." He looked full into the dark eyes of the rabbi. "Sir, I am persuaded that you know of these things for which I grope. I am convinced that you can point the way for me. Good master, what shall I do to inherit this eternal life?"

The earnestness, the apparent sincerity of the young man, appealed greatly to the rabbi. "You understand the commandments, my brother," said he, smiling. And he began to enumerate the commandments laid down in the ancient laws of Moses.

"Yes, master," said he. "I understand the commandments and from my youth I have observed them scrupulously. Will that, sir—" he leaned forward, his concern evident in the intensity with which he was speaking—"will that entitle me to this—this eternal life?"

Jesus looked the young man full in the face. "Would you really inherit the kingdom of the Father? Are you willing to do whatever God requires of you in order to dwell with him in his house?"

A look of bewilderment crossed the face of the young man. "I—master—yes, I would inherit this kingdom of which you speak. I—I would know the requirements—" He paused. "I have come to you to learn. I—I—" He hesitated again.

Jesus, looking deep into his eyes, spoke. "You have lived a model life in the eyes of the community. You have obeyed the letter of the commandments. You have attended the worship in the synagogue, you have fulfilled the law's requirements." The young man slowly nodded his head, the puzzled look still on his countenance.

"But there is one fatal defect in your character. This you must remove before you are fit for the kingdom of God. And until you cast it out, you will never have complete happiness." He paused to give greater weight to his words. "My brother, you are selfish. Even now you seek the kingdom for yourself, without a care that your brothers also enter it. All your life you have centered your efforts upon storing up treasures for yourself. They have become a burden upon your back, a millstone about your neck. Until you rid yourself of this burden, you will not be a fit subject for entrance into the kingdom of our Father."

"How, sir—" once more there was eagerness in the eyes of the young man, in the tone of his voice—"how can I be rid of this burden?"

"There is but one way. Cast it from you. Get yourself from under it. Then you will be free; then you will find the true happiness. If you would free yourself of this burden, then go sell your possessions, rid yourself of this earthly accumulation of goods, and give the money to the poor. Become poor yourself in possessions of this earth and you will find that you have gained new wealth, a great wealth of happiness. Do this, my brother, and follow in his way, and you will find that already you have inherited the eternal life you seek."

"But, master—" the young man's confusion was written upon his sorrowful, embarrassed countenance—"I don't see why I—" He abruptly stopped, turned his face away from the searching, dark eyes of the rabbi.

Jesus, too, turned from the young man, and Simon and John, watching him, saw that the master seemed in pain. "How difficult it is for those who have this great burden of riches to cast it away," he said, and his words were almost a sigh. "How difficult it is for them to see that such riches are often but evidences of great poverty. How hard it is for the man rich in this world's good to understand the real riches of the abundant life. Truly, it is easier for a camel to go through the eye of the needle than for a rich man to enter into the kingdom of God!"

He watched for a moment the young man's retreating back. His head bowed in deep contemplation, the man was going away sorrowful. Then Jesus turned to his disciples, who pressed about him. "We must be going," he said quietly, and there was deep sorrow in his voice. "We must be on our way to Jerusalem, where all those things that were written by our ancient prophets concerning the Son of Man shall be accomplished. For in Jerusalem, I shall be delivered into the hands of the Romans, and shall be mocked, and treated shamefully, and spit upon, and scourged, and put to death."

He glanced at the defeated, sad faces of his friends, who seemed not to understand his words, but only knew that they were sad because he was sad. Then his face brightened, and he squared his shoulders. "But sorrow not, my brothers, for these things are the Father's will, and he shall not desert his Son. For on the third day I shall rise again, and be with you!"

46

In the many weeks that Naamah, also known as Mary, had been employed as a domestic servant in one of the great houses on Zion Hill in Jerusalem she had never ceased to think of Marcus, even though it had been a full year since the robber Bar Abbas had seized them that afternoon on the road up from Jericho.

Naamah was living in one small room in the squalid section across the Valley of the Cheesemongers from Zion Hill. Her quarters were a far drop from the sumptuous apartment she had occupied in the palace of Herod Antipas at Tiberias or on the visits to the great gloomy stone palace of the Hasmonaean kings that served as headquarters of the tetrarch when he was in Jerusalem. Often in these last months she had passed the palace set in the angle of the wall not far westward from the frowning Antonia Tower, where the Roman authority in Jerusalem was centered, but always she had walked on rapidly, hardly taking time to lift her eyes to the high barred windows from which not so many months ago she had looked upon the stirring, motley life of this crossroads of the world. As time goes by the sun, that had been only months ago, she knew, but to Naamah, who now measured her days from last fall's stirring experience at the Temple when the smiling, tall rabbi from Galilee had touched her life so dramatically, it was another age.

Often at night in her shabby small room down here in the lower city, near the wall that stood upon the rim of Jerusalem above the Kedron Valley, Naamah would lie silent and still and recall her experience at Machaerus with the rich Roman. It had been an affair, she readily admitted, but it had been different. Unlike the experience with old Herod and the others, it had been touched and lightened, and perhaps cleansed, with love, she told herself as she lay alone and lonesome. Yes, she had been fascinated by the wealthy manufacturer from Tyre, but she had loved him, too. Now in her longing to see him again she knew it.

All these months Naamah had wondered what happened to Marcus. *Perhaps in his rashness, in his boldness to dispute with the robbers, he had been killed by them and his body left among the boulders, perhaps thrown from some precipice down upon inaccessible sharp rocks below. Maybe they had believed him to be a leper*, for she herself had feared that possibility—and the thought brought a sense of actual pain. *Maybe they had left him, injured and dying, to the wolves and the vultures. Perhaps I myself have been contaminated*, and she recalled her discovery of the strange spots and the lost eyebrows that morning at Machaerus after the tetrarch's party.

On the other hand, she had likewise reasoned, *Marcus could be alive and unharmed, and even cured of his strange malady. He could have escaped from Bar Abbas and made his way back to Tyre, his diversion of a few nights at Machaerus with her quickly forgotten in the resumption of his briefly interrupted routine of piling up wealth.*

In the long nights alone Naamah had even considered the possibility that Marcus had owned her and had given her to Herod. Maybe that was why he had gone back to Tyre—if indeed, he had—without having come to Jerusalem in search of her. Maybe he had sought her out at Jerusalem but had been unable to find her. At any rate, she sought to comfort herself, if Marcus had owned her, he had not seen her before he gave her away.

But invariably, regardless of the thoughts her mind conjured up as she lay in the darkness of her small chamber down here in the city's foul-smelling and densely inhabited region of the poor, she came to the same conclusion about Marcus: her heart cried out for him.

But how was she to find him? Who was there to help her?

She knew of but one person, and he was the rabbi from Galilee. But since that day at the Temple she had not seen him. From Jerusalem he had gone back into Galilee, and she had had no way to go in search of him.

In February he had come again to the vicinity of Jerusalem and everywhere they were talking of his having raised from death a poor man at Bethany. She had determined then to ask an afternoon's freedom from her duties and go seek the rabbi at Bethany. But then he had suddenly left again, into the mountains north of Jerusalem, they said, and she had not seen him.

But now Jesus was back at Bethany. All the city was ringing with reports that the mysterious rabbi was coming to the Feast of the Passover, that he had chosen the great feast as the occasion for overthrowing the Roman yoke and establishing once again the glory and power of Israel. He would be king of the Jews, ruler of the ancient land. Along the twisting narrow alleys, overrun with the maimed and the sick and the hungry and frightened hordes, ran the inspiring rumors.

Naamah determined this time to see the rabbi and seek his help in learning of Marcus. She would put away her timidity and go in search of him at Bethany.

Today was the Sabbath of the Jews, and she was free from her duties on Zion Hill. Today she would go to Bethany, for the Passover began on the morrow, and the rabbi might be too busy with his duties to see her. But the Jews were strict in their observance of their Sabbath and she wished to do nothing to offend the rabbi or them. So she lay late in her bed and in early afternoon she arose and bathed and dressed carefully in the best garments she had, and then she anointed her hair after she had wrung it dry, and let it fall about her shoulders in a gorgeous cascade. Afterwards she bound it up with ribbons and a comb she had borne with her when she had left Tiberias that day for Machaerus, and then from a vial on her dressing table she poured two drops of perfume upon her fingertips and dabbed expertly at the lobes of her ears. And having completed her preparations, she threw a light shawl about her shoulders and over her head until it almost covered her face and walked quietly from the chamber.

But hardly had she locked the door and entered the narrow cobblestone street that led into the larger way that ran down to the Dung Gate when she turned back, unlocked the portal, and returned to her room. Going over to a large chest against the wall, she unlocked it with a small key on the ring she pulled from a pocket concealed in the fold of her robe. She searched deep among the clothing and bed linens in the chest, and soon she drew forth a small white jar wrapped in a linen cloth. She looked at the jar a moment, and then she pulled forth the plug. Instantly the room was filled with the fragrance of costly nard.

No, she said to herself, as she replaced the jar in the chest and closed the lid. *It's all that's left from Herod, and in my old age I may need the money it would bring. Nor would he appreciate it.* She started for the door again, and then deliberately she returned to the chest, unlocked it quickly, took out the small vessel, and without even glancing at it thrust it into the pocket of the robe. Then she began the dusty walk toward Bethany, and when the sun had gone down and the Sabbath was ended, she entered the village and inquired where she might find the rabbi of Galilee.

"He has gone to dine at the house of Simon the Leper," one of the villagers told her. "The house is the largest in Bethany—" he pointed along the meandering road—"upon yonder hill. Simon is having a feast for him. Perhaps you know him; he's a Pharisee, and he has money."

Naamah had heard of Simon, for she recalled the man's startling nickname. He was not a leper, she remembered, and she was not sure how he had been given the name. Perhaps he had contracted leprosy years ago and had been cured, maybe by the rabbi himself; perhaps it was because of the peculiar brownish spots she seemed to remember on one side of his face. If she had ever known she had forgot now. Yet the name seemed very familiar. Perhaps, she thought with a mounting embarrassment, he had been one of those who had visited her in the days before she had encountered the rabbi. Suddenly, it all came to her. Yes, she remembered Simon the Leper now. He was the fat Pharisee who on a visit one night had been so demanding of her and yet so poorly inclined toward paying.

Perhaps it would be best not to encounter the rabbi in the house of Simon the Leper. She stopped, was about to turn around and begin the walk back toward Jerusalem. Then she thought of Marcus. *I must find him*, she said to herself. And she went on toward the house of the Pharisee.

When she arrived, the guests were dining upon the lighted terrace. Boldly she went up to the couch upon which the rabbi was reclining, for she had picked him out as she approached. The rabbi was talking with several of his disciples who sat near him, and as his back was to Naamah, he did not notice her entrance. But Simon the Leper did. And evidently he recognized her.

He stood up, pointed a finger at the woman. "How did you get into my house?" he demanded. "By whom were you invited?" His face was flushed, and the spots upon his cheek stood out all the more boldly.

Jesus, turning his head in the direction the Pharisee was pointing, saw Naamah. Instantly his face broke into a warm smile. "Mary," he said, ignoring the Pharisee's scowling, "Mary of Magdala."

For some uncontrollable reason, she knew not why, Naamah began to weep. Then she sank down upon her knees in front of the couch upon which the rabbi sat and she lowered her eyes, and tears fell in torrents, and her shoulders shook with the release of her long repressed emotion. As she wept here at the feet of the Galilean, she saw that her tears had been falling upon his feet. Hesitant at first, almost fearful to touch him, she reached out with her fingers to wipe off the tears, but they only smeared them the more, and then she did a strange thing. Quickly she reached up, unfastened the braids that held her hair bound upon her head, and it tumbled down about the feet of the rabbi. And now she took the hair in her hand, a great mass of it, and using it as a towel, she carefully wiped the tears and the dust from the rabbi's feet.

Simon the Leper, still upon his feet and frowning, shook his finger at the woman. "Get out of this house!" he shouted. "Don't you know that you were not invited? How did you come here? Out with you, I say!"

Jesus held up his hand. Calmly he spoke. "Be not so impatient with her, Simon. She serves me out of a loving heart."

Simon the Leper laughed. The laugh was a mirthless cracking like the sudden stirring of dead bones, and he smiled righteously. "But, rabbi, you evidently do not know that this woman is a woman of the streets, a consorter with sinners, even with publicans and—and Romans."

"Yes, Simon, but you do not know this woman's heart. You do not understand that she comes to me humbly and contritely upon a mission of great love. While you, my host, have not even provided a basin and water and a towel for the washing of my feet, she has bathed them in her tears and wiped them with her hair."

Simon smiled, for now he would test this young rabbi who flouted the holy customs of Israel. "But, rabbi, know you not that the touch of this woman defiles?"

As Simon was speaking, the air was suddenly sweet with an odor that only the costliest nard could produce, and Simon the Leper, looking down at the woman still on her knees at the rabbi's feet, saw that she had crushed in her hands a slim white vessel, and now the rare perfume was running in little trickles over the rabbi's feet and spreading to form small pools upon the stones of the terrace.

"Love never defiles, Simon," said Jesus. "She has acted in love. And though you, my host, have not anointed my head, this woman has anointed my feet with the costliest of nard."

From his place down the table from the rabbi, Judas of Kiriot, his dark face scowling, spoke up. "Master, this woman has crushed this vessel filled with a precious perfume that was worth much money. She could have sold it and placed the money in our treasury for helping the poor. But instead, she has poured it out upon the stones of the terrace so that the very air is strong with its fragrance."

The rabbi leaned forward, so that he might speak directly to his dark-complexioned disciple. "Why scold her, Judas, because out of the goodness of her heart she has done this for me. For the poor you will always have about you, but you will not always have me." He paused, lowered his voice. "In pouring this fragrant nard upon my feet she has anointed me for my burial. In truth I tell you," Jesus went on, "that what Mary has done here tonight, wherever this good news may be proclaimed hereafter in the whole world, shall be related as a testimonial to the goodness in her heart."

And now, as Simon the Leper and dark-browed Judas watched in evident disapproval, Jesus arose from the couch, and bending down, helped Mary to her feet, made a place for her to sit beside him on the couch. "Now," said he, "tell me what is troubling you."

47

The soldier saluted. "The procurator said no answer would be required, sir." He handed the centurion the roll.

Gaius returned the salute. "Then you may go back to Caesarea at once." The soldier saluted again, quickly withdrew.

Gaius unrolled the scroll, scanned the message. "From Pontius Pilate," he said to Marcus. "Orders to bring the Capernaum legionnaires to Jerusalem for the Feast of the Passover. He wants to make certain that there are no disorders." He rolled up the scroll, pulled open the drawer, placed it inside, and pushed the drawer shut. "Marcus," he said, grinning, "you're going with me."

"But I should be getting on to Tyre," Marcus said. "I want to see what the situation is." He shrugged his shoulders. "Not that it would make any difference—my going, I mean."

The centurion laughed. "I'd like to see Tullus when you get there."

"If I ever recover control of the plants in Phoenicia, I can assure you that they won't be run the way I used to run them. I've got some new ideas I want to try out. Very revolutionary, I would have called them but a few months ago."

"I have an idea you see things in a different light now."

"You are right, Gaius. I have been a fool. I thought I was rich. I would have called anybody in my present shape a pauper. But then I was a pauper, as I see it now, and now, without a denarius, I am rich. I was an outcast, almost dead, living in mental torment, a leper—a leper, Gaius, by the immortals—" He stopped. "Excuse me, centurion, it's just a phrase, a byword. I—I forget myself. But a man who has never been a leper will never understand. And now I'm well. I have my health again. Money! Bah! I can always make money. If I don't get my property back, I'll make it some other way. And this time, I'll do it differently. If I could just find—" He paused, and now he was serious again.

"Naamah?"

"Yes, centurion. I can't get her out of my mind. I would like to do what I could to make amends."

"And that's the only reason?"

Marcus laughed. "No,". he said, "you know it isn't."

"She's likely in Jerusalem. That's where you should begin searching. Come along with me and get at it."

"But the city will be thronged with Jews coming up for the celebration."

"And somebody will know about her, you can be sure."

"Poor girl, I hate to think what sort of life she has had to live during this last year—if she's still alive."

"She probably has lived as well as you were living during that time. And now—"

"You mean, Gaius, that—"

"Yes," said the centurion, "he'll be there. Don't all Jews go up to the Passover feast?"

"Do you suppose he would help me find her, and restore her if she's—" He paused.

"I have never heard of his refusing anyone."

Marcus was thoughtful. "I can never repay him," he said, with a puzzled expression. "Gaius, to be absolutely honest, man to man, what do you think of this Jesus? How do you explain him?"

"It seems to me," said the centurion, after he had reflected, "that I should be asking you that question. You were a leper, or had some ailment that passed for leprosy and that had taken away your health. And now you seem completely restored. And more important—certainly more noticeable to me—you have been changed in your attitude. The narrow, mean selfishness, your disregard of the rights of others—pardon me, Marcus, but that's the way you were—all that seems to be gone. And it has happened since your meeting with him." He paused, looked Marcus full in the face. "What do you think of him?"

"I—I—" Marcus hesitated. "Gaius, I don't know. I haven't come to any definite conclusion. There are some things I do know about him, but I can't sum them up. He's not what I thought he was when I used to speak so disparagingly of him. He's no anemic Jewish rabbi. He is completely masculine, but he is a gentle person, and that might lead a casual observer to think that he had little force. That isn't true; he has plenty of courage, I'd wager." He paused. "That's what I saw the other day. But that isn't all. He did something to me. Once he looks straight into your eyes, centurion, he does something to you. And after all, Gaius, I was a leper. And now I am not. You can't get around that."

"No, you can't," the centurion agreed. "That's something you can't explain away. Marcus, tell me one thing—how did you feel? What seemed to be taking place inside of you the other day?"

"I don't know that I can say, Gaius. He seemed to have a soothing effect on me at the beginning. He seemed to set me at ease. And then the idea came to me that he could cure me if he wanted to. And all of a sudden I was positive that in some way he could manage it."

"That's what he calls faith, I suppose," said Gaius.

"I don't know," Marcus said. "All I know is that I was walking down that trail on my crippled leg and the blood seemed to be warming my bent fingers, and then I felt better inside. And since then I have been seeing more clearly every day what a mean-spirited fellow I had been all my life—and wanting to make amends." He had been looking through the window toward the Sea of Galilee. Now he turned quickly, confronted the centurion. "Now tell me, Gaius, what do you think of him?"

"Marcus, I don't know what I think. He's gentle, in the first place. I am confident he came of gentle folk, even though they are poor. They say he's a descendant of King David. He's a fair man. He wants everybody, rich, poor, high and low, to be fairly dealt with. And he's a man who venerates his fellow man. I don't think he's in the least concerned with the state. I think all his thoughts center upon the individual man; I think he feels that if the individual is right, the society is right." The centurion paused, stood looking through the window upon the boats of the fishermen ringing the curve of the shoreline. "But, Marcus, he's more than that. He says he is the Son of God. I don't know just what he means by that. In fact, he says that all men are the sons of God. I believe he means that everybody is capable of being godlike; I don't know. He is a man, it is true; but perhaps he is more than just a very good man, a very great man, with a clean heart and a clear brain—"

"You mean—" Marcus's expression was intense—"that maybe he's really a god walking the earth?"

"Well, how else do you explain him? Where does he get his power? Were you not a leper? Was not Lazarus dead and in the tomb three or four days? Do mortal men, good men at that, go around bringing dead men to life? How do you explain him?"

"It is amazing to contemplate, centurion. It upsets all our Roman notions of the gods, doesn't it? His god—he—Gaius, I'm all mixed up in my thinking. I can't think any of this out. I just have to—to feel it, I suppose. But what I was trying to say was that if I were to try to construct a god I wanted to worship, I don't know any model that would better serve than this man from Galilee. Wouldn't he make a great emperor?"

Gaius laughed. "Marcus, now you are getting to be a good Jew. Many of the Jews want him to be their king. In fact, some think that at the Passover he will proclaim himself king."

"And do you think he will?"

"No, I don't think he is concerned with organizations, political or otherwise. I think all his heart is in the advancement of the individual. But you were saying that the Jewish God upsets the Roman notion of the gods. Well, has not this Jesus very much upset your previous notions of life?"

"Centurion, he has made me see what a contemptible fool I was. And I'd like to do a little to make up for the pain and trouble I have caused. I don't know why. I just know it."

"The rabbi appeals to all types. I believe the most intellectual man in the world would be intrigued by him, and yet the most ignorant, downtrodden slave could approach him, find peace and strength in him. In other words, I don't think one approaches God—or even this rabbi, who seems somehow to me to personify this governing power in the universe—through one's intelligence so much as through one's heart. The rabbi says his God is love, and I believe it."

He stopped. Then he looked Marcus full in the face. "We've been having the wrong notion of love. Love is no weak thing. The poets talk of the tender passion. Love is tender, yes, but love is strong and enduring and overcoming. Listen, Marcus, the rabbi defeated the cold-hearted slave-driver of Tyre, and how did he do it?"

"I see what you mean, centurion."

Gaius pushed back the bench on which he had been sitting, jumped to his feet. "We've really been having an intellectual discussion, eh? But I've got to busy myself with arrangements for getting the legionnaires to Jerusalem. There's probably a hard week ahead."

48

Judas of Kiriot sat on the bench in the anteroom that opened upon the conference chamber of the palace of the high priest Caiaphas, and though a scowl clouded his dark face he was smiling inwardly at his own cleverness.

It's a perfect plan, he reasoned to himself. *It cannot fail. The master may be angry at first, but when he understands it he will be pleased that I took the situation into my own hands. He is a good man, but his very goodness is defeating him. He is too gentle with his enemies. What the master needs is somebody to act for him when the situation is ripe, somebody to spur him to action.*

In Judas's mind, Jesus could have been king of Israel already two days had he been willing to act when the moment was favorable. For when he came riding into Jerusalem on this first day of the week, his short journey down the slope of the Mount of Olives from Bethany, past the little Garden of Gethsemane, across the Brook Kedron, through the very gates of Jerusalem to the portals of the Temple itself had been one long triumphal procession. He was coming into Jerusalem to proclaim himself Israel's great new king, the wildly cheering throngs had understood, and they had thrown flowers and garlands hastily torn from the greening palm trees along the way under the feet of the donkey he was riding. *Never had the master had such an opportunity before,* Judas told himself. The disciple knew that Jerusalem was swarming with pilgrims come to the great Feast of the Passover—Jews from every section of Palestine, from the coast cities on the Great Sea, from the desert lands south of Jerusalem, from across the Jordan in Peraea and Decapolis, bold fellows from Galilee.

It was the perfect moment to strike, Judas reasoned. And Jesus' cheering followers had thought he would assert his leadership of the nation, would drive out the invading Romans, the bold, proud conquerors of the ancient land. When he dismounted and strode into the Temple, they were tense, holding their breaths as it were, for him to call down the very angels of heaven to smite the usurpers.

But there had been no thunder and sudden sharp lightening from the skies, Judas recalled, no flames licking the earth and destroying in quick white heat the hated Antonia Tower and all the Roman legionaries within. Instead he had done nothing more than overturn the tables of the grasping money-changers inside the Temple and lash at them with a small whip of woven cords for desecrating the House of God. And that evening he had returned to Bethany.

This morning Jesus had come to the Temple again. There was still opportunity to proclaim the new kingdom, to establish anew the independence of Israel, for the multitude had not abandoned hope in the inspiring new leader from Galilee. But Jesus had spent the day at the Temple teaching of all things, telling more stories illustrating his doctrines, denouncing the scribes and Pharisees, talking of the love of God, expounding the Way. Doing these things when he should have been acting.

Yes, Judas told himself, *the master needs someone to push him the last inch over the precipice into accomplishment, into victory over all his enemies, into possession of the glories and the riches of the world.*

It is fortunate for the master that he has me in his band, Judas told himself as he sat upon the bench outside the great conference chamber where even now Caiaphas the high priest and old Annas the former high priest and others of the Temple leadership were conferring. *He needs a practical man, someone to see and seize the opportunity. John is no help, for John, though quick of temper, is a dreamer, a poet, an idealist who is always seeing visions. And Simon is too bold, too quick to speak, too willing to talk before he has considered a proposition, too rash. But I lie awake at night thinking when the master and the others of our band are sleeping. I think much and talk little. Out of much thinking I have evolved my plan,* reasoned Judas, *and it cannot fail.*

In the end the master will be pleased, and he will give me the credit for propelling him into the kingship. And I shall be a great man in the nation. I have been treasurer of his little band; doubtless he will make me treasurer of all Israel, and instead of carrying this small leather bag in which a few small coins make their merry jingling, I shall be keeper of the keys to the vaults in the Temple where the great store of gold is kept safe. I shall be a great man in Israel, and respected, and rich, and I—

The door to the conference chamber opened and one of the guards tapped Judas of Kiriot on the shoulder. "The high priest is ready for you," he said.

You might have better manners, Judas said to himself, as he made a mental note of the guard's face against that great day soon to arrive. But outwardly he gave no sign of resentment; instead, he arose quickly and entered the great chamber.

The thin lips of Caiaphas the high priest turned upward at the corners in a mirthless cold smile. "You are one of the band of the Nazarene, are you not?"

"Yes, most worthy High Priest. I carry the bag for his band."

"And you have come to the sensible and patriotic conclusion that it is your duty to surrender this man to the Temple authorities that he may be dealt with properly in order that the whole nation may be preserved from the wrath of the Romans who hold dominion over us?"

"You have said it, most worthy High Priest."

"You have done well; your name will be long remembered in Israel. And now we must decide upon a proper plan, for it is of great importance that he be taken without causing any tumult among the people. The Galilean has many followers. What do you propose?"

"It would not be wise to seize him at the Temple, where he goes to teach and heal by day," replied Judas. "That might be dangerous, even for us his followers, who might become victims of the wrath of the multitude. But always he returns by night to Bethany to lodge at the house of Lazarus and Mary and Martha, and often he pauses in the small garden called Gethsemane at the foot of the Mount of Olives. There he might be overtaken quietly—"

"Admirable!" The evil eyes of Caiaphas surveyed quickly the elders of Israel, that by his design did not today number the rabbi

Nicodemus or the wealthy Joseph of Arimathea. "Is that not, leaders in Israel, the solution of our difficulty?" Solemnly the bearded faces nodded their assent.

The high priest signaled the captain of the guard to approach. "It will be your task to take a sufficient force and arrest the Nazarene," he said sternly. "Go now with this Judas of Kiriot that you may arrange your plans. It is of utmost importance that the Nazarene be taken quietly and without the knowledge of the multitude."

For a few moments the captain of the guard and Judas talked, their dark faces close together, and then the captain of the guard faced the high priest. "We have arranged our plans, most worthy High Priest," he said. "I think they will not fail."

"That is good," said Caiaphas. He faced Judas again. "You have done a good deed this day for Israel, oh, son of Kiriot. And now, with our great thanks, we excuse you."

Judas turned toward the door, paused, faced the high priest again, spoke hesitantly. "But, worthy High Priest, should there not be a reward for one who is willing—"

"Reward?" He frowned, almost imperceptibly, as if in slight pain. "But you shall have your reward in the appreciation of your countrymen, in the knowledge that you have served well your brothers in Israel."

"But for delivering one's master, when it will mean the shedding of his blood—"

Caiaphas smiled, and there was again the old gleam of cunning in his eyes. "Indeed, my brother, you shall be paid in money, in blood money. You shall have the price of blood, the price of a slave accidentally killed. From the Temple treasury you shall be paid thirty pieces of silver!"

49

Earlier in the day Simon and Judas had purchased a small lamb in the sheep market, which they had then taken to the Temple and sacrificed in accordance with the laws of the Jews.

And now preparations for the ceremonial meal had been completed. Many Jews would be eating the Passover this evening, while others would wait until tomorrow, for difference of opinion had arisen concerning the proper day for observing the great anniversary of the ancient deliverance of the Jews from the scourgings of Pharaoh. Some held that the Passover celebration was greater even than the Sabbath and that therefore it was proper to eat the sacred meal on the evening of the sixth day of the week (which was the beginning of the Sabbath, since the Jews considered that the day began with the going down of the sun), because the fourteenth day of the Jewish month of Nizan, the customary day for eating the Passover, this year came on the sixth day of the week.

The other opinion among the Jews was that the Sabbath took precedence over the Passover and that the eating of the Passover on the evening before the sixth day, therefore, would be sinful.

So Jesus, who would outrage the honest views of no man, had decided to celebrate the Passover on the evening of the fifth day and had instructed his followers to go into the city and make arrangements for the observance. A friend who owned a house on Zion Hill, he told them, would permit them to use a room on the upper floor, and here they would be secluded, apart to themselves, away from the noise and reveling of holiday celebrants.

The rabbi had delayed until late in the afternoon his journey into Jerusalem from Bethany. All yesterday and during the morning hours today he had remained at the home of Lazarus, quiet and meditative, absorbed in his own thoughts. And all the while beyond the rounded hill of the Mount of Olives the sons of Israel from every section of Palestine thronged Jerusalem's narrow streets, surged into the porches of the Temple, trafficked in the market-places, disputing with the shopkeepers over the charges for their wares, and even hurled insults, being careful not to make them too pointed, at the Roman soldiers brought into the city to prevent the staging of a demonstration against the stern authority of Rome. Not until two more days had brought the calm of the Jewish Sabbath descending upon Jerusalem would Pontius Pilate be able to relax his vigilance.

Never had the master been more introspective, Simon and the Zebedee brothers told each other; they had remained close to him since the group had come to Bethany for the Passover celebration.

"He has some great weight on his mind," James had said only that morning. "He is sorrowful because the people make this great religious observance an occasion for revelry. He is hurt at the way this generation has fallen upon foolish and evil ways."

"Perhaps," suggested Simon. "But could it not be that he is thoughtful concerning the kingdom he plans to establish? Could it not be that he is busy with plans for the government of the nation when he has driven forth the proud Roman invader and reestablished the throne of his fathers?"

"No, I think it is neither of these," John ventured. "I think the master's heart is heavy with the contemplation of coming trials and sorrows. God forbid it, but has he not told us plainly that great tribulation would overtake him shortly? When we were in the mountains did he not tell us that in Jerusalem he would be offered up, that he would become the scapegoat for the world's transgressions? And now we have come to Jerusalem, and the Romans are everywhere about us, and his enemies at the Temple are determined to rid themselves of him. The master is sad of heart, it is plain to be seen. Is that not a token?"

"God forbid," said James. "But it may be so. The signs do point that way."

"No, God forbid," Simon spoke up quickly. "I could never bear it. I will fight to my last breath to prevent it."

"But Bar Jonah," John interposed, "did not the master say that it was the will of God that he be offered up?"

"He said that, it is true," Simon admitted, "but, nevertheless,

God forbid it. I could never bear it. And do we not all look forward with hope and eagerness to the driving out of the invader? How can that be if he is killed by the Romans or the conniving Temple leaders?" He shook his head sadly. "God forbid. God forbid."

The lamps in the upper room here at Zion Hill had been lighted, and they had taken their places about the board, the rabbi in the center, the twelve ranged about him, John on his right and Simon at his left. The matzoh had been baked, and now the three flat cakes, each covered with a white linen napkin, rested upon a plate directly in front of the master. Near it was the dish holding the roasted shank of lamb and an egg peeled of its shell that had been roasted hard in hot ashes, while a third vessel contained a sufficient portion of horseradish and other bitter herbs. And in still another dish before the rabbi was the charoseth, a sweet mixture of fruits, nuts, and spices of appealing fragrance.

On the board before the twelve likewise were the bowls of water for the ceremonial washing of hands and the vessels and cups for the wine.

And now John, letting his eyes wander from the quiet, almost sad, face of the rabbi to the symbolic food in front of him, was reminded of the stories told him as a child by his father, Zebedee, and his mother, Salome, and others of his devout forebears concerning that ancient time of bondage when God's chosen race were slaves of the Egyptians. The matzoh, he knew, represented the unleavened bread on which the children of Israel had subsisted as they took flight from Egypt, and the three cakes symbolized the three divisions in the nation—the priests, Levites, and Israelites. The shank of the lamb, roasted to a hard blackness, reminded of the sacrifice, and the bitter herbs recalled the bitterness in their mouths and hearts during the days of their slavery, days even now returned once more to Israel.

When the twelve had settled themselves about the board and it was time for the ancient ceremony to be repeated once again, Jesus reached forth his hand and taking one of the flat matzah cakes, after he and his company had washed their hands in the bowls of ceremonial water, broke it, and pointing to the shank of roasted lamb and the hard roasted egg, recited the ancient words: "Lo! This is the bread of affliction, which our forefathers ate in the land of Egypt; let all those who are hungry enter and eat thereof; and all who are in need, come, and celebrate the Passover."

And he unfolded the story of the exodus from the land of the Pharaohs, explaining the significance of each dish, and when it was finished, he pronounced a benediction, and they washed their hands again, and after he had said grace over the cakes of matzah, they began to eat the meal.

The mood of the master had set the tone of the simple observance of Israel's ancient deliverance, and now the twelve men ate quietly of the paschal lamb, and the green herbs, and the mixture of fruits, their eyes for the most part upon their plates. Grizzled Simon on the rabbi's left, his usual exuberance strangely lost, chewed a portion of the hard meat, sipped of his wine. Along the table the bearded young men and the few of the twelve who were entering upon a deeper age seemed separated and lost in their own thoughts. Thoughtful John, solemn and pained to see the master saddened, leaned forward to glance along the board. The dark brow of Judas of Kiriot, he saw, was creased with scowling. But Levi's eyes were upon the master's face.

And now, as they were finishing the paschal meal, Jesus arose quietly and laid aside his robe. Then he poured water into a basin, and having twisted a long towel lightly about his waist, began to wash the tired and dusty feet of his disciples and dry them with the towel. And though they seemed not to understand why he did this, no one offered an objection until he came to Simon.

"Lord, would you wash my feet?" the big fisherman asked, his round bearded face registering his bewilderment.

"What I am doing now you do not understand, Simon," said Jesus, gently. "But later you will understand it."

Simon drew his feet under him. "Lord," he said, "I would never let you wash my feet."

"If you do not let me wash your feet, Simon," the rabbi replied, "you have no part with me in the work I do."

Simon extended his feet to the rabbi kneeling before him. "Oh, master," he said, and there was admiration in his brusque voice, "wash not only my feet, but also my hands and my head and my whole body."

When the rabbi had finished, he put on his robe again, and

sat down with them. "Do you understand what I have been doing?" he asked them. "I have been giving you a lesson in humility and service. You call me your master, and you are right, for I am. Yet I have been washing your feet, a service customarily reserved for a servant. If I, your master, perform this humble task for you, ought you not be willing to wash each other's feet to serve each other, with true humility of the spirit and suffering misguided humanity about you? In that way, my brothers, you serve the Father."

He sat and talked with them as the hour grew late and darkness overspread the city, and he spoke earnestly of the things of man's spirit, as if he would compress into these short and waning minutes the brave and beautiful truths he had been striving so manfully to show unto them.

Soon now, he said, he would be leaving them. Soon now he would be offered as a sacrifice to atone for man's great sinning, as the paschal lamb that morning had been offered as a sacrifice upon the altar in the Temple. But when he saw that though they understood not his words they were deeply sorrowful, he sought to comfort them. The Father, he said, would send a comforter to them, the spirit of truth, that would remain with them always to give them courage and to sustain them in their moments of sorrow and vexation. "Let not your heart be troubled. You believe in God, now believe also in me, for what I tell you is true. In the Father's house there is room for all, and I am going there to prepare for your coming. If it were not true, I would have told you."

Then Thomas spoke up. "But, master, if we do not know where you are going, how can we find our way to you?"

The rabbi leaned forward, looked into the eyes of this disciple whose doubts inevitably found their way to his tongue. "I am the way, Thomas," said he. "I am the truth and the life. There is no other way to come to the Father."

And he talked much of the Father's love, and he told them always to love one another, for love alone was the great strength and the great joy, and as he talked his heart seemed to go out to them, as if he would embrace them all together and at one time within the compass of his strong arms.

"How I love you all," he said to them, at length. "How much love we share for each other. And yet"—and the smile was gone

285

from his face—"I declare that there is one among you who will betray me."

His words were as a lash upon their backs. For a moment not a man among them said a word. Then John, sitting close to the master, caught the eye of Simon on the other side. "Lord," said John, "who is it?" And up and down the board the grave young men, their solemn faces betraying their deep concern, began to question the rabbi: "Lord, is it I? Lord, is it I?"

"The hand of him that betrays me is with my hand upon this table," said Jesus, sadly. "He who betrays me has been sharing with me the meat from the same dish."

Secretively Judas looked toward the rabbi. It was time that he was saying something, he knew, for if he kept his peace he would be suspected. "Master," he asked, "is it I?"

"You have said it," Jesus replied, and there was pain in his voice.

As they sat dazed and in heavy sorrow at his amazing revelation, he reached forth his hand and picked up one of the flat matzoh cakes. "Soon, my brothers," he began, and there was infinite sadness in his voice, and sorrow seemed to be pressing down with a great heaviness upon his shoulders, "I shall be leaving you. But you will not forget me?" It was almost a plea. "In sorrow and trial and in whatever the coming days may bring, remember me, and think often of me. In times of gladness too, recall our happy days together and what I have told you of our Father and his love."

Now he began breaking the flat cakes into small pieces and he handed them along the board. And when he had said a short blessing over the board, he spoke to them. "Take this bread and eat it as a remembrance of me," he said. "It represents my body that shall be broken for you. Hereafter, my brothers, when you eat it, will you think of me?" And as the silent little company ate of the matzoh cake, tears loosed themselves from the rabbi's eyes and ran down his cheeks. But his lips were smiling.

Then he raised the cup of wine in front of his plate, handed it to John. "Drink of this wine, my brothers. It shall represent my blood, shed as an atonement for the sins of the world. As for myself, I shall not drink wine again until that day when I drink it with you in the Father's kingdom." He watched the cup going its silent round. And a smile trembled upon his lips, and his eyes were moist.

As the cup came to him Judas of Kiriot sipped it quickly and passed it on without once glancing toward the rabbi. His eyes were fixed upon the board before him, a scowl upon his dark face. The rabbi sensed the turmoil within him. "What you are going to do, do quickly," he said.

Without a word, Judas arose and left the chamber. John, leaning against Jesus as they reclined on the couch, felt a tremor run along the master's tall frame as the door closed upon Judas of Kiriot. And looking up, he saw upon his face an expression of deep pain.

50

A sickly pale moon rode high among the thickening dark clouds as the rabbi and the eleven who had remained with him came down from the upper room on Mount Zion and made their way slowly through the narrow streets. Lights blazed from many windows though it was nearing midnight, for throughout Jerusalem in countless homes families were observing the great Passover and eating of the Seder.

The night was oppressively warm, and the rabbi and his little group were tired after the week of celebrating and much walking along the cobblestones of the ancient narrow streets, and their hearts were heavy with a foreboding that seemed to hang over them like the threatening clouds that sometimes obscured the moon. They continued the descent toward the eastern wall of Jerusalem wearily and almost in silence.

Soon on weary, slow feet they plodded through the gate in the wall, crossed the Kedron Valley, and began the ascent of the Mount of Olives. At length Jesus spoke. "All of you this night shall be treated with contempt because of me, and all shall fail me, and flee away, as it is written in the ancient word: 'I will smite the shepherd, and the sheep of the flock shall be scattered abroad.'" John, walking beside the rabbi in the darkness, thought he heard him sigh. And then Jesus spoke again. "But do not be fearful, for though I go to be offered up, I will arise, and after I have arisen, I will go ahead of you into Galilee."

Simon had heard the rabbi, though he was walking a pace behind on his left. He stepped up beside Jesus. "Master, though all men may be treated scornfully because of you, yet that shall never offend me, and I will never fail you."

"You think you will not fail me, Simon," Jesus said to him. "And I wish it were so. But I say to you, truly, before the cock crows you will three times deny that you ever knew me."

"No, master," Simon insisted, "though I die with you, I will not deny you."

The others, too, sought to cheer him. "Master," Levi said, "we will be faithful though it bring us death. We will not desert you."

"Yes, master," declared the elder of the Zebedees, "we shall die defending you against any who may seek to harm you."

By this time they had reached the gate that led into the Garden of Gethsemane. "I am very weary," said Jesus, "and my soul is greatly burdened. Let us pause here for a while. Delay here near the gate, and I will go inside and seek the peace of the Father." Wearily the men were dropping to the grass, and soon they would be asleep, for their eyelids were heavy with weariness and sorrow. But Simon and the Zebedees walked with him farther into the garden. At the edge of a small open way between the olive trees, near the place where they had set up the olive press, he paused.

"My soul is heavy with great sorrow," he said to the three, and in the frail light of the moon they saw weariness and sorrow spread over his countenance, and his eyes seemed to have lost their accustomed luster and to have sunk back into the recesses of his skull. "Wait here a while, and watch with me."

"We will watch here, master," said Simon. "I have my short sword beside me. No harm will come to you."

The rabbi walked a few paces farther towards the center of the deserted, still garden and beside the fallen trunk of a gnarled olive tree he fell upon his knees and buried his face upon his arms extended before him along the tree trunk. For a long moment he was silent and only the clenching of his fists until the nails dug into the palms of his hands and the knuckles shone white in the dappled moonlight revealed the emotional stress under which he was laboring. And when he uttered a sound it was the low anguished cry of a child for the strong, protecting arms of its father, the comforting quiet words of its mother: "Oh, Father," he said. "Oh, my Father, come close to me this night. Be with me; show me the way, keep my feet upon the path. Give me courage, Oh, God, for this night and for the morrow. The way is hard and the path is stony and difficult, but keep my feet in the path, my

Father; make me to march steadfast and true. Make me, oh, God, to face my destiny with strong will and clean heart."

His face buried upon his strong brown arms, Jesus listened for the voice of his Father. And he thought of other times when he had prayed with all his force for the divine strength to move resolutely along the way. He recalled those days in the wilderness when he had been tempted to turn aside; when the evil voice had whispered to him to take another course. Many times the evil voice had murmured into his unguarded ear, but always he had sought the power of his Father to turn his back upon the voice.

"Oh, my Father." His lips were framing the words, for the voice was whispering with deep insistence, the voice was dictating his plea. "Father, if it be possible, let this bitter cup pass from me. Oh, God, if it be possible, if it be possible—this bitter, bitter cup!" His head lay upon his outstretched, pleading arms, and a tremor that seemed to come out of the very ground shook him as a great wind shakes a noble tall tree, and sweat poured from his forehead and ran down to merge with the sweat that was welling up along his arms and his palms were moist with the agony of his exquisite torture. He lay upon his arms, and his tall, strong body was wracked in infinite pain, and he cried to his Father, and he fought against the voice whispering from behind, and he clenched his fists and ground them into his ears to shut out the voice.

"Oh, Father," he cried in his pain, "if it be possible, if it be possible—" And now he lifted his head and he turned his face to the sky where a pale yellow moon raced through mottled clouds. "Nevertheless, oh, Father, not as I will it, but as you will for me, let it be done."

He sprang to his feet, and he paced about the quiet secluded garden, and he walked quickly over to the place he had left Simon and the Zebedees, and reaching down, he shook the sleeping Simon. "Is there no help for me this night?" he cried out. "Will no man stand by me in this hour of my great agony of spirit? Will not even these my brothers give me the strength of their presence?" Simon, rubbing his eyes with his great fist, sat up.

"Master, where—what—" He shook his big head to drain the sleep away. "Master, we were so tired." He reached over to shake the sleeping Zebedees. "We did not intend to fall asleep. We meant to watch with you. We—"

"But could you not watch with me but the one hour?" Jesus asked, his voice betraying his pain. "I am sorely tired, Simon. I need your support. But you likewise need for yourselves to watch and pray lest you become victims of temptation. It is a great battle, my brothers, for though the spirit may be strong, the flesh is weak."

Once more he walked to the fallen olive tree and knelt again beside it, and the agony and the immensity of the hour were upon him to overwhelm him.

For long minutes he wrestled with the voice, and he called to his Father to protect him against the voice, and he begged of the Father to walk beside him and keep his feet steadfast in the way. And he turned his face to the cloud-mottled sky and sought to find the face of his Father beyond the wheeling, sick moon.

"This bitter cup," he said, "oh this bitter cup. Father, dash it from before my lips, hurl it from me, oh, my God, if it be your will. But if this cup cannot pass away from my sight forever until I drink it, oh, Father, cause me to drink it with courage and understanding, and with love."

It seemed that the sweat pouring from him, from his face and his arms, from his hairy chest opened now to the cooling breezes that sent the clouds racing across the face of the moon, from his legs beneath his robe—it seemed that the sweat was his very life blood dripping from his distressed, tired body.

So extreme was the agony that he could not stay upon his knees, for his whole powerful though sorely spent frame was in conflict. Once again he got to his feet and paced the opening between the trees, and once again he strode over to the place where he had left his three most intimate friends. As he had found them before, he found them this time. They slept soundly, sprawled upon the grass, their heads pillowed upon their arms. Nor did he awaken them.

For the third time he knelt at the fallen tree and earnestly sought to learn the will of his Father. "Oh, Father," he pleaded, "show me some other way. Remove this terror from my path."

He lay with his head upon his arms outstretched along the trunk of the fallen olive. And the cold sweat of horror and death

291

and the upreared cruel cross burst from the prison of his tortured body, and his frame shook, and in the pit of his stomach he was sick with the shame and the pain of anticipated horrible death. He lay under the torture, and he clenched his fists and his shoulders shook, and the unfeeling moon raced beneath a heavy cloud, and Jesus of Nazareth was lost in darkness and despair. "Oh, Father, oh, God, the cup, the bitter cup . . . oh, my Father . . . But, nevertheless, not as I will it but as you will it, my Father. As you will it . . . as you will it . . . ."

He lay against the tree trunk, inert and spent, and the storm of his great agitation had subsided now, and he lay still. He lay still and listened. And from out of great distances other voices were coming to him now, and he knew them and recognized them as the voices of the vanguard of heaven. They came down to him from the great round cavern of the skies, they came upward out of the warm womb of the fertile earth of the garden, they stole along the center of the dead olive tree. And as they came, the voice behind him moved backward faster and faster and now it was utterly lost in the glad tumult of the voices before him and all about him. Jesus listened, every faculty of his being alert, and in the midst of the chorus he heard the soothing, strong voice of his Father. "My Son, my beloved Son," said the voice, and Jesus felt the strong arm about his shoulders, and instantly the tremors were gone from his shoulders and they were straight and strong and erect . . . "My beloved Son, in whom I am well pleased . . . yet a little while, yet a little further . . . the burden will be heavy, but I will give you strength to bear up beneath every burden. The way will be hard and rough and steep, but you will be given the strength to travel it."

Jesus listened, and his heart grew light and his sorrow began to melt away. And still the voice was speaking. "You were destined for the great task, my Son. In the eternal plan yours was to point the way. . . . Thus far you have led them. But they, my other sons, are still lost. They are unable to find their way to their Father's house. They are lost in sin and sorrow and without you, my beloved Son, they can never find the way. Lead them, lead them on, my Son. Bring them home . . . these trials will be but trivial nothings of a short moment. Quickly they will have passed away, and then through all the eternal ages my sons shall know through you the way to their Father's house. . . . And you, my beloved Son in whom I am well pleased, through all the everlasting days, wherever truth is known, and goodness is honored, and beauty is esteemed, you shall be lifted up. Your name shall be exalted above all the sons of man, above all the angels of heaven!"

With a new, intense, quick joy in his soul, Jesus arose to his feet as the struggling moon fought its way free of the throttling clouds and swam into a great pool of clear sky. He stood now tall and erect, bathed in the light of the free moon, and the twisted old olive trees, the flowers, the fallen tree trunk, the olive press, all stood out stark and still. But the light from the heavens paled and faded away in the glory that lightened his heart.

Calmly, smiling, he walked over to Simon and the Zebedees. He looked down upon the three sleeping forms. "Sleep on now and take your rest." He no longer required their frail support, for about his shoulders he felt the everlasting arms of his Father. His battle was ended. He had sought in great resignation and pain the help of God. And the Father had come down to him in warm and intimate communion. Once more his Father had shown him the path, had pointed out to him the way, had given him the strength to move resolutely forward along it. "Sleep on now, and take your rest." For them, too, the way would be hard. For them the world would have but scorn and anger and hurt and death. But for them the long days would bring honor and glory, for these youthful young men, these sun-tanned men of Galilee, these youthful fishermen of the blue waters of Galilee, these hard-fisted rough youths with understanding hearts—and their sleeping brothers down by the Gethsemane gate—for them uncounted coming multitudes would have but gratitude and praise.

"Sleep on, my brothers, for the day of trial draws near, the very hour is at hand when the Son of Man will be betrayed into the hands of sinners." He looked down upon them, and he prayed a silent prayer to his Father to sustain them and comfort them.

As he stood over them he heard noises on the way that led up the slope of the Mount of Olives along the road that came out across the Kedron Valley from Jerusalem. He listened calmly, though he knew what the noises portended. Now the voices neared the gate to the garden, and now there was a tumult down at the gate. He leaned over and shook Simon. "Get up," he said, "and let us be ready to go. He who is going to betray me is almost here."

Simon, shaking his big head to drive out the sleep from his eyes, clambered to his feet, felt for his dagger in the sheath strapped about his waist. The Zebedees, too, were awake now, and on the alert, for up the little, twisting path from the gate came a straggling mob of men, some of them carrying torches held high. In another instant they had reached the clearing.

At the head of the motley procession, walking beside the captain of the Temple guard, was Judas of Kiriot. Now he saw the rabbi, standing calm and tall, his arms folded across his chest. "Master, master," he said, as he rushed forward, threw his arms about the rabbi and in oriental fashion kissed him upon the cheek.

"Judas—" the rabbi's voice was steady, but in it there was a note of sorrow and pain—"would you betray me with a kiss?"

Judas turned his head away, said nothing. His eyes avoided the rabbi's nor would he look at Simon and the Zebedees. The captain of the guard, too, seemed paralyzed, unable to utter a sound or make a movement toward the tall man in the center of the open space between the trees.

Then Jesus spoke. "Whom do you seek?" he asked.

For an instant no one replied. Then the captain of the guard, his voice betraying his alarm, answered: "One who is called Jesus of Nazareth."

"I am he," the rabbi replied, his arms still folded across his chest.

But no one offered to lay a hand upon him. Instead, the motley mob seemed to be all the more fearful, and those nearest the rabbi pushed back a pace into the ranks of the ones behind. Plainly, they were frightened, as if they expected the skies to open and rain thunderbolts upon their heads.

Jesus, still in voice unperturbed, spoke again: "Whom are you seeking?"

There was another moment of silence. Then the captain of the guard ventured a second reply: "Jesus of Nazareth."

"I have just told you that I am he. If you come seeking me, then let these my friends go their way."

A fellow on the fringe of the crowd behind Jesus made a step forward. But Simon, who had been watching in that direction, saw him. There was a flash of a great hairy arm, and the fellow screamed, jumped back. The rabbi turned quickly. "Put your sword back in the sheath, Simon," he commanded. "Those who take up the sword will perish by the sword. Violence is no solution for violence." His tone changed, for he had spoken almost harshly to Simon. "The cup that my Father has given me to drink, Simon, can't you see that I must drink it?"

Then he walked over to the fellow whom Simon had wounded. In the moonlight the rabbi examined the man's right ear, from which blood ran freely. He reached into the folds of his robe, pulled forth a kerchief, held it firmly against the cut flesh. For an instant he held it there, and then he spoke to the trembling fellow. "It will be all right," he said, soothingly. When he removed the kerchief the blood had stopped flowing.

The rabbi walked over to the captain of the guard, calmly faced the ring of Temple ruffians and other renegades who had come out to seize him. "Why do you come out with swords and clubs as you would to seize a thief?" he asked them. "I have been teaching every day in the Temple, and you didn't raise a hand against me then. No, you did not offer to raise your hand against me in the daytime and in the presence of my friends, but you have chosen a convenient hour, and you come stealthily and in the dark."

And now the eleven—some of them, like Simon and the Zebedees, standing near the rabbi and the others peering out through the thick shrubs of the garden—waited for the skies to split with a deafening mighty roar and heavenly fire to consume these cowardly henchmen of the high priest and his unholy priests.

But no heavenly fire came down upon the heads of this rabble, no thundering voice proclaimed the establishment of the new kingdom of Israel. Only the yellow high moon sped through the clear space in the sky. Nor did anything happen when the captain of the guard, still fearful, stepped forth and quickly knotted a small rope about the rabbi's wrists.

"The high priest ordered that I bring you before him," he said. He caught the dangling end of the rope.

The rabbi did not resist. Instead, with one quick look at Simon and the Zebedee brothers, he turned, began walking away calmly at the side of the captain of the guard, and the others of the Temple mob fell in behind them.

The Zebedees and Simon, Levi, Thomas, Nathaniel, all the rabbi's small band, turned and ran. Terror clutched at them, raced with them through the darkness, grappled with them as they tripped and fell in the tangle of the garden. No flash of righteous lightning split the heavens; even the moon, fleeing with them high above, fell into the heart of a dense, great cloud. And the eleven, separated now and sorely oppressed, stumbled through the night, lost in darkness and doubt.

51

Gaius with his legionnaires and accompanied by Marcus did not reach Jerusalem from Galilee until the sun was setting on the second day of the Passover week. Already the streets were thronged with pilgrims come to celebrate the ancient deliverance.

They went at once to the Antonia Tower, the frowning austere citadel just north of the Temple, where the troops were given their evening meal and housed for the night. As they were tired from the long journey, Gaius and Marcus went to bed early. The next day Gaius was occupied with settling his legionnaires in the positions to which they had been assigned, and since they were late in arriving they had been given one of the less attractive sections to patrol, the crowded, squalid, ill-smelling area of the lower city down near the Dung Gate. Thus Gaius and Marcus had no opportunity until the following morning to seek out the rabbi, and then they went to the Temple, where the centurion was confident they would find him teaching on one of the colonnaded porticoes.

But though they learned that the rabbi had been there on the second and third days of the Jewish week, no one reported having seen him since. Nor did they see him the next day when they went again to the Temple, the very center and heart of Judaism. Since their arrival in Jerusalem they had been scanning countless faces in the surging throngs that swarmed the streets and packed the market places in the thin hope that they might discover Naamah.

They were not certain, of course, that the girl was in Jerusalem. They were not certain that she was even alive. And had they known that she was somewhere here in this ancient city of the Jews, they would have known likewise that the chances of discovering her in these great multitudes of people—Jews, Greeks, Phoenicians, Romans, dark-hued Egyptians, even an occasional blue-eyed, white-skinned slave from Britannia, or Gaul, or Germania—were remote indeed.

But Marcus, now that he was well again and faced life with new assurance, was determined to find Naamah. And if he could find this tall, strange rabbi from Galilee who suddenly had come to mean so much to him, if he could only find him and seek him once more for his aid, Marcus was convinced he would somehow be led to her.

"It is strange that the rabbi seems to have left Jerusalem in the midst of Passover week," Gaius said to Marcus as they were having their evening meal after their fruitless search. "Tomorrow is the last day of the feast, for it is the Sabbath of the Jews and that will end their celebration this year. Many Jews, in fact, will eat the Seder, which is their symbolical Passover meal, tonight. And the Jews invariably eat the Seder in Jerusalem, if they can possibly arrange it. It seems strange that the rabbi would decide to leave Jerusalem before the Seder has been eaten. Of course, though, he may not have left; in fact, he may be eating the Seder this very night somewhere here in Jerusalem."

They were seated at a small table on the great gallery that ran along the side of the Antonia Tower beside the Temple. Without moving their positions, they could look down into the Temple courts. Gaius nodded in that direction. "Perhaps tomorrow the rabbi will be down there, speaking to the crowds that congregate in the Court of the Gentiles. That's the big open court in which the Temple building itself sits," he explained. "On his visits to Jerusalem the rabbi's custom has been to visit the Temple and instruct the throngs there in his unique views of spiritual matters."

But the following day, after Gaius had made his morning inspection of his legionnaires in the Ophel area and had come back with Marcus to the Temple, Jesus was not there, nor had he been in any of the great porches, the centurion was informed.

"There is but one place to go for information about him," Gaius said suddenly. "I don't see why I had not thought of it before. Bethany. That's where he stops when he is in the vicinity of Jerusalem. The home of Lazarus, the man he raised from death, and his sisters. It's the nearest place to a home that the rabbi has in Judea, I suppose. It corresponds to Simon's house at Capernaum, the rabbi's home in Galilee. He'll either be out at Bethany or the people out there will know where he has gone. We'll ride out to Bethany and see if the rabbi is there."

It was past the noon hour, however, before they reached the home of Lazarus, for there were other duties to be attended to by the centurion before he could leave Jerusalem. And Lazarus appeared hesitant about revealing any information of the rabbi's journeyings back and forth between Bethany and Jerusalem during Passover week, until he learned that Gaius was the centurion from Capernaum.

"I am sorry, sir," he said. "I was fearful that you meant the master ill. I did not know that you were our friend the centurion at Capernaum, of whom the master has spoken." He lowered his voice, as if afraid of being overheard. "These are troubled times, centurion. We are afraid for the master. There are so many at Jerusalem who would have harm befall him, who begrudge his power with the people and lie awake at nights plotting his downfall, who would even slay him had they the courage. The leaders at the Temple are jealous of his sway over the people and they despise his teachings; they continually seek ways of bringing him into disrepute with the multitude. And here of recent weeks there has been much talk of his establishment anew of the ancient kingdom. He talked of setting up the kingdom, but he had in mind a kingdom of the spirit, many of us thought, rather than a new government for Israel. But the Temple group seek always to misrepresent him and discredit him, and we are afraid that harm may already have befallen him."

He lowered his voice again, looked over his shoulder. "You see, he did not return here last night, nor has he been seen by any of us since he left Bethany late yesterday to go into Jerusalem with the twelve to eat the Seder. It is strange, and my sisters and I are worried."

"Do you know, Lazarus, where he was to eat the Passover meal?"

"Only that a friend on Zion Hill had permitted him the use of an upper room."

"Perhaps if we return to Jerusalem and inquire in the Zion Hill section we may obtain some information concerning him."

"I hope so, centurion. That is what I told Mary of Magdala when she came this morning seeking him."

"Mary of Magdala?"

"Oh, that, sir, is not her real name. She is a foreign woman, though of Jewish stock, but she lived for a while in Galilee and when she came to the master humble and penitent, he gave her the new name to signify that she was entering upon a new life. Now she is one of his devoted friends."

"The rabbi has great power to attract people of every race and station and condition to him," said Gaius. "This woman, this Mary of Magdala, what was she seeking of the rabbi? Did she say, Lazarus?"

"I did not inquire, sir, and she was here only a short time this morning. She was anxious to get back to Jerusalem and search for him. The master's mother and the mother of the Zebedees, who have been attending the Passover celebration, went with her. But it seems that she was anxious to find the master to urge him to help her find a friend, a man, perhaps her lover."

"The man, Lazarus, did she say anything about him?"

"I paid little attention, centurion. She talked mostly to the women. As I caught it, though, she became separated from him when the caravan in which they were traveling was set upon by robbers—"

"This woman—" Marcus interrupted the thin, emaciated Jew's recital— "how did she look? Was she well? Was she beautiful?"

"Yes, she is a beautiful woman. And very well, she appears to be. You see, she had been living in sin, so I understand, but since the master met her she has been leading a virtuous life, and if she could but find the man—"

"Lazarus," said Gaius, interrupting, "where in Jerusalem would we be likely to find these women?"

"Were I seeking them," said Lazarus, "I would go first to the Temple."

"Thank you," Gaius said. "We shall go there and make search. But should we fail to see them and should this—this woman return to Bethany, tell her, will you, Lazarus, that the centurion from Capernaum and his friend Marcus are anxious to see her and for her to remain here until they come out of Jerusalem. Will you do

300

this, my friend? You see, we are friends of this Mary, and my friend here is the friend whom she seeks. We are sure of it."

The dull eyes of Lazarus were alive with a new interest. "I will, centurion. I will gladly. I will keep her here at my house until you return."

Already the two Romans were mounting their horses, and a minute later they were galloping along the road that led down the slope of the Mount of Olives and across the Kedron Valley of Jerusalem.

52

When Gaius and Marcus returned to headquarters at the Antonia Tower, after having failed to discover either the rabbi or Naamah at the Temple, they found Simon impatiently awaiting the centurion's return.

Never before had Gaius seen the big fisherman so agitated. "I knew no one else to come to for aid," Simon said, his bluff voice weak and his big frame trembling. "I did not even know whether you were in Jerusalem, sir, but I came here seeking you, and then I went down into the Ophel district where they said your legionnaires were stationed. They told me you had been there this morning but had left. So I came back, for I knew no other place to go."

"We rode out to Bethany, Simon, in search of the rabbi, but he was not there—"

"Centurion, it is about him that I come. He is in serious trouble. I have come for help. You remember he helped you and your friend here—oh, centurion, he is in great danger. They may even already have killed him. Oh, sir—" Simon was upon the verge of weeping.

"Here, Simon," Gaius commanded, "calm yourself. What has happened to the rabbi? We will help, if we can."

"I am sorry," Simon said. "But I have been through such a strain in the last many hours. I have had no sleep in two days, but worse, in his great danger I deserted the master and betrayed him, and now—now he may even be dead."

"Dead! It cannot be, Simon. What do you mean?"

"Yes, dead, crucified. It may well be that he is even now dead. If you would aid him, you must hurry, sir!"

"Simon, your distress has muddled your brain. It cannot be that the rabbi is dead. What has he done? Why would he be executed by the Roman authority? Tell us quickly what you know."

"He has done nothing, centurion. But Judas of Kiriot—you

know him, the one with the black beard who carried the money-bag for us—Judas betrayed him to the Temple leaders, and they sent a company into the garden of Gethsemane in the dead of last night. This mob seized him, and we were frightened and ran away—even I, who was always so sure of my courage—and they carried him before old Annas first and then Caiaphas the high priest, and the Sanhedrin gave him a sham trial and condemned him and sentenced him to death—"

"But the Sanhedrin has no right to pronounce a death sentence, Simon."

"That is true, and they knew it. So they sent him to the procurator Pontius Pilate with the recommendation that he be crucified. This I know, sir, for I saw it, though I stayed well back in the crowd, and I even denied that I knew the master." The big fisherman dropped his eyes to the stone pavement of the chamber in the great fortress. "May God forgive me," he said, and his words were almost a cry. "May the good God forgive me his so unworthy servant. I denied I ever knew him! O my God—"

"But, Simon, what did they charge the rabbi with having done? Certainly he had committed no crime against Rome."

"That I know, centurion. And Pontius Pilate knew it too. He tried to avoid the responsibility of trying the master. He told the mob from the high priest's supporters that the master had done nothing deserving death. He even sent him to old Herod Antipas, who had come down to the Passover feast, on the grounds that since the master was from Galilee and Herod was tetrarch over Galilee, it was the duty of Herod to try him. But Herod only ridiculed the master by having him arrayed in the purple robe of authority, which he did to scorn him, and sent him back to Pilate."

"But what was the charge, Simon? Roman courts cannot try men without charges against them."

"The high priest's supporters told Pilate that he had set himself up to be king of the Jews. They tried to prove that he contemplated rebellion against the authority of Rome, but Pilate quickly understood that the master was speaking of a kingdom of the heart and the spirit—which we still find it hard to understand, centurion. So he stood up before the mob and told them that the master had done nothing deserving of death. But he sent him forth into the courtyard of the Praetorium and had him scourged."

"Did Pilate do that?" Anger, swift and deep, flushed the face of Marcus, who had been listening intently.

"He did so, sir," Simon replied. "I saw it from the fringe of the crowd about the master. It made my heart weep. But I could do nothing. And I was fearful, too."

"And then," Gaius persisted, "what happened? Go on."

"He had him brought back, and showed him to the crowd. He likely thought they would be appeased at the sight of the blood the lashing had brought from his back. But it seemed only to make them all the more determined to have his life. They shouted and raved and even threatened to report to Rome that Pilate countenanced rebellion."

"What did Pilate do then, the cowardly knave?" Marcus asked.

"He reminded them that it was the custom of the Passover celebration for the Roman authority to pardon one criminal being held for trial. He thought they would ask that the master be released. But the crowds shouted for the release instead of the robber Bar Abbas."

"What! That highwayman who waylaid me and left me with the lepers?"

"Yes, sir. He's the man they asked him to pardon."

"Then what did he do?" Gaius asked. "Go ahead. And quickly."

"To appease them he ordered that Bar Abbas be released. Then he took a basin of water and washed his hands before the mob. He said he was doing that to show his innocence of the blood of the master. But he is not innocent. No, never!" Simon's round face was blazing with anger. "He is a murderer, he and those scoundrels who rule the Temple."

"But what did Pilate do, Simon?"

"He turned the master over to the soldiers and ordered him crucified. That's when I slipped away and came on the run from the Praetorium in search of you. But that was many hours ago. It was hardly the third hour of the morning. You see, all this was done by night and in early morning so that the friends of the master would not know that it was happening."

"But the Jews, Simon, would they have rebelled against the

high priest and the rulers of the Temple to support the rabbi had they known what was happening?"

"Indeed they would have, centurion. The Jews love him. Count it not against the Jews whatever befalls the master. Count it but against the false leaders of the Jews, and the cowardice of the procurator. But, sir, if you would help—"

"Yes, Simon," Gaius interrupted. "We must be going. I greatly fear we are too late. There'll be a horse for you in the courtyard. Where—where do you think they took him?"

"Golgotha, I heard the mob shouting. The Hill of the Skull. The place outside the walls where they take the poor wretches to be crucified."

Already they were running for the stone stairway that led down to the courtyard of Antonia Tower.

53

In the thickening darkness three crosses upon the summit of Golgotha stood starkly outlined, their inert, impaled burdens strangely white in the unnatural gloom.

"Oh, master, we are too late!" Simon's words were a wail. "Oh, master, master, my poor master." He pointed to the middle cross and beat upon his hairy chest. "Woe is me. Oh, God, have mercy, have mercy!"

In a daze of horror they climbed the slope of the Skull.

"I cannot understand this strange darkness," said Gaius, and his voice was strained and frightened as though he would talk to keep himself from screaming. "It is but the middle of the afternoon, and yet the gloom is deeper than twilight. The sun seems to have receded far away from the earth. It does not have the appearance of an ordinary storm approaching."

"God is withdrawing his face from the earth, as well he should when men stoop to such wickedness," said Simon. "Oh, my master. Oh, master—" They were nearing the crosses now, and Simon, raising his eyes, looked for an instant into the face of the rabbi. Then he fell upon his face in the dirt of this place of foulness and terrible death and wept bitterly, and his great shoulders shook with the agony of his weeping.

"Oh, my master, my poor dear master, who did only good to all men. Oh, master, master, master!" He beat upon the ground with his fists, and he cried piteously, until those about the crosses began to pay heed to his weeping, even a group of Roman soldiers idling near the crosses.

And then Marcus and Gaius in the deep gloom saw a young Jew come over to Simon and bend down over him, and they heard him speak, and Gaius quickly recognized the man as John, the younger of the Zebedees.

"Cease your weeping, Simon," said John. "He has gone to be

with his Father. Get to your feet, and dry your eyes. He loved you to the end."

"Then he is dead, John?" Gaius asked, hesitantly.

John turned quickly to face Gaius. "It is the centurion from our Capernaum," he said, recognizing Gaius. "Yes, sir, the master has died but a moment ago. He died bravely, a prayer of forgiveness upon his lips."

Gaius ventured to glance toward Marcus. He was looking upward, an expression of horror softened with immeasurable sadness upon his countenance, into the peaceful dead face of the tall young rabbi. The centurion, sick in his stomach, raised his eyes to look upon the still figure of the Galilean. Save for a sparse loincloth, the rabbi was naked, and his whole body from his waist to the broad shoulders, now sagging forward limply, was livid with red welts raised by the whips of Pilate's soldiers. A thin trickle of blood ran down his forehead onto the bridge of his nose, and pressed down upon his head almost to his ears was a circle from which the centurion could see thorns protruding. A gash in his side beneath his heart from which blood oozed slowly showed where a soldier's lance had been thrust. His body sagged against the nails that pinioned his outstretched hands to the crosspiece, but a timber that protruded between his legs supported his body and prevented his weight from tearing his hands from the nails that held them.

"Centurion, I cannot understand it," Marcus said. "He had such great powers. He saved so many others, it is strange that he could not save himself."

"Perhaps he could have saved himself, Marcus," Gaius answered, without taking his eyes from the face of the dead rabbi. "Perhaps he has saved himself." He turned to face Marcus, and Marcus saw that tears were welling in his eyes.

A Roman soldier coming near the two stopped abreast of Gaius. "By the immortals! The centurion of Capernaum!" He glanced at Marcus. "And by the great Jupiter, Marcus! And apparently in the best of health. How did you come here, men? Marcus, we have been searching for you all over Judea. We heard that you were a leper. I am glad that it wasn't—"

"I was a leper, in the last stages." Marcus said it calmly, but with cold disdain. "How does it happen, tribune, that you are here?"

"I had the misfortune to be ordered by Pilate to conduct this execution," Tribune Lucius replied. "I did not relish the assignment. But I am an officer of the Roman army, and I must obey the orders of a superior." He shrugged his shoulders. "You must understand that, my friends."

Marcus pointed to the rabbi, sagging forward from the crosspiece that held his tortured nailed hands. "I was a leper," he said, "and he healed me. He restored me to health. And you killed him. You killed the noblest man I have ever known. You, tribune, you—" Marcus leveled an accusing forefinger at the soldier—"killed a god."

Gaius expected the tribune to draw his sword, but instead, Lucius stood immobile a moment, staring into the face of his accuser. "I know it," he said. "I know it. His innocent blood will forever be upon my hands." Gaius saw that his face was furrowed with pain and grief and fear. "This was a noble man. I knew it at the sham proceedings they called a trial before Pilate. I knew it when I ordered the men to scourge him. Yes, and when they nailed him to the cross, I knew it. I saw it in his every word and action as he bore his God to forgive us, his torturers—even me, and I had just won his blood-stained robe with a throw of the dice —I knew it for certain. By all the gods, I am ruined! This man—" he looked up for an instant at the still figure of the rabbi, and then he dropped his eyes to the ground—"this man was truly more than just a man."

A great sigh stirred through him, and turning away, he walked slowly and with downcast eyes toward the little group of Roman soldiers over beyond the three crosses.

"It is a sad ending to our dream of a new kingdom," Simon said, more to himself than to the group about him.

"It could be but the beginning," John observed. "He said he would rise again, and would be with us."

"Yes, I doubt not but that he has already arisen to sit upon the right hand of God. I know his great spirit lives, and it will be with us and walk hand in hand with us. But we will surely miss

308

him in the flesh." Slowly Simon shook his bearded huge head. "I never knew before how much I loved him."

John's youthful bright eyes were shining through the tears that wet them. "It may be that he will return in the flesh. Did he not say so, Simon? We must be of good cheer and look for his return. And now, I must go and see to the needs of his mother. She is my mother now. He—" his shining eyes lifted quickly to the solemn, still figure, and dropped again—"left her in my charge. Now I have two mothers." He inclined his head toward the right. "They are over there, and they are sorely distressed and frightened, and this darkened sun strikes terror into their hearts. And likewise with them Mary, the wife of Cleophas, and that other woman who of late has loved him so devotedly, Mary of Magdala—"

Marcus wheeled to face the younger of the Zebedees. "She is here, this—this Mary of Magdala? You are sure? You have seen her?"

"Yes," John said. He turned, pointed down the slope to the left. "See, yonder they come. She is the one upon whom the mother of the master is leaning. Come, Simon, we must go meet them, and do what we can to comfort and sustain Mary of Nazareth."

Marcus moved away from the foot of the cross and in the half-light of the unnatural strange stillness of the calm, dead air watched the women wearily mounting the slope. Yes, she was Naamah. She was walking slowly, her right arm about the waist of the older woman. And despite her evident great weariness and her deep distress, she was more beautiful, by far, than she was a million years ago at Machaerus. Marcus, from the obscurity of the deep shadows, saw a new beauty upon her tear-stained countenance.

As they neared the cross the mother of the rabbi looked up into his pale worn face and screamed. "My son, oh, my son, my dear son," she cried, and her anguish wrenched the hearts of those about her. "Oh, how I have feared for you, my boy, how I have besought God to protect you, my little one!" She sank to her knees, and Naamah, sitting quickly on the earth beside her, took her graying head upon her lap and gently stroked her forehead.

And after a few minutes she relaxed into gentle quiet weeping, and soon John came to her and, reaching down, put his arms beneath her arms and raised her gently to her feet.

"Weep no more, little mother," he said, and his voice was soothing and gentle, "weep not for him, for he is with his Father. And God will protect him, and he will protect you, and all the earth will honor the mother of our blessed master. Let us go now back to Bethany, for shortly it will be the Sabbath, and you must rest against the trip we shall soon be making to Galilee."

And now with John supporting her on one side and with Salome the mother of the Zebedees on the other side, Mary of Nazareth looked once upon the uplifted dead form of her son, and then silently squaring her frail, tired shoulders, she walked steadfastly down the slope of the Skull.

Then it was that Marcus stepped forth from the shadows. "Naamah!" he said softly. "Oh, Naamah!"

She whirled about to face him. "Marcus, it is you!" For an instant her face was transformed, he saw, and it brought quick joy to his own distressed heart; but in the moment the smile had gone, swept away in a sudden terrible apprehension. "What brings you to this terrible place. Could it be that—"

"No," he said. "I had nothing to do with this—this frightful thing. I am one of his friends. I came here seeking his aid in finding you. But we were too late."

He walked toward her. "You are cured, Marcus. The eyebrows have grown back. The spots—oh, the leprosy is gone!"

"You knew?"

"Yes, I was terribly afraid that—that morning at Machaerus. I had sought his help in finding you. You see, he had—he had shown me a new life."

"I know about it. His friends have told me. He healed me, too. He cured me of this leprosy." He caught her, held her head against his chest. "Oh, I have thought of you so much in the long, hopeless days," he said as he clasped comforting arms about her, "and now upon such a bitter day we find each other."

The tearful Naamah pressed closer to Marcus, but not all her tears were those of sorrow.

54

As Marcus and Gaius were entering the great stone edifice upon Zion Hill built by Herod the Great that now served as the home of the procurator during his stays in Jerusalem, they met the wealthy Joseph of Arimathea coming from Pilate's conference room.

"I have just received permission of the procurator to remove the body of the rabbi of Nazareth and prepare it for burial in the new tomb I had excavated some time ago in a garden near the Hill of the Skull," Joseph revealed to the centurion after they had exchanged greetings and Gaius had introduced Marcus. "I am going now with Rabbi Nicodemus to attend to the burial. Soon it will be sunset, and the Sabbath will be upon us. In accordance with the customs of the Jews, we wish to have the body properly put away before the coming of the Sabbath."

Some of the women, Naamah among them, had remained at the Place of the Skull to view the body of the rabbi after it had been laid away in the tomb. Then they would go out to Bethany to remain over the Sabbath day, and there Marcus had arranged with Naamah to meet her.

Marcus and the centurion entered the adjoining chamber, and when a servant of the procurator signaled that he was ready to receive them, they entered his audience chamber.

Pilate stood behind his desk. His round face, its heaviness emphasized by the closely cropped graying hair, was pale and he appeared agitated and uneasy. The centurion saluted, and Marcus bowed; they spoke to the procurator in a coldly formal manner. When he recognized them, his countenance relaxed into a quick smile. "I am happy to see both of you," he said. "I was not aware that the son of Senator Marcus Calpurnius had been rescued from the cutthroat band of the robber Bar Abbas. We have lost much sleep over you, my friend. Tribune Lucius and the centurion here, as well as other officers and men of our Roman contingents in

Palestine, have sought you over many a mountain trail."

"I am thankful to you and to them, procurator," Marcus replied, eyeing the procurator coldly.

Pilate's eyes shifted uneasily. "We had heard that you were a victim of leprosy," he said, in an apparent effort to be cordially familiar. "I am happy to see that the reports were in error."

"The reports were not in error," Marcus declared, without taking his eyes from the procurator's face. "I was in the dying stages of the disease when I was found by my friend the centurion here and a little while later healed by the Jew whom you sent to the cross today." Marcus paused, but he did not shift his eyes for an instant from the paling face of the procurator. "That is why I come before you today—to protest in the name of a citizen of Rome your betrayal of justice, your failure to do your duty as the procurator of Judea, and your plain display before a host of subject peoples of that one vice that Rome will not countenance, a trembling and cowardly heart!"

Anger flushed the pale round face of Pontius Pilate and for an instant he looked straight into the menacing eyes of Marcus. Then he dropped his eyes to the desk behind which he stood, and the two Romans watching him saw defeat sweep his face and shake his stout frame. "I was trying to serve the interests of Rome as best I could," he said, the resonance gone from his voice. "I was convinced that the Jew had done nothing deserving of death, but the powerful leaders among the Jews were demanding his crucifixion, and they are continually keeping up a tumult with the results that the reports get back to Rome. And I thought that he had no influential friends. I had no idea, of course, that the son of Senator Marcus Calpurnius was among his friends—" He stopped, swallowed.

"And you would administer justice according to the influence of the defendant's friends?" Marcus said it with cold venom. "Perhaps during the long months I was in hiding in the mountains as a leper the principle upon which the administration of Roman justice is based was changed." Marcus paused, but he did not take his eyes from Pilate's face. "Procurator, today you have made a great mistake." Now his tone was calmer, but he was deadly serious. "Never in all the days of your life will you be able to recall this day and right the mistake. You have sought to walk the path of expediency rather than the path of right. This man whom you have slain understood this, and he sought to make the right way clear. The rich and the powerful and the leaders of the Jews and the Greeks and the Romans—the influential everywhere, for a time, perhaps—will bow to the expedient. They will say that the way proclaimed by this young rabbi from Galilee was a good way but an idealistic, impractical, unworkable plan. But they will be wrong. His way is the only practical, workable scheme by which individuals—and he respected the individual, no matter whether he had what you call influence or not—it is the only plan by which individuals and nations will be able to live together in peace and happiness. And you, Pontius Pilate—" he leveled a forefinger at the procurator "—have murdered this man." He turned, strode toward the door, wheeled about to face the strangely silent, pale Roman.

"I came here to thank you for having sent parties in search of me while I was a leper, but also to inform you that hereafter I will urge upon Sejanus—who, I think, being very much like you, will not remain many months longer in his post—and likewise upon the emperor that you be removed from the office of procurator of Judea as being unfit for that assignment, and that you be sent—" he hesitated an instant "—to some far removed and insignificant post, perhaps in a remote province in Gaul, where you will have little opportunity to do further great mischief."

Turning upon his heels, without a further look at Pilate, he strode the length of the chamber, Gaius beside him. At the door he paused, faced about to confront the procurator, still standing, silent and dazed. "Pontius Pilate, would I had the goodness, as he had, to forgive you, as he did. But I cannot. Know you, procurator, that your name, through all the endless ages, will live in infamy! Today you have murdered a god!"

He strode through the door without a backward glance. Behind him stood Pontius Pilate, his mouth half open, his eyes staring, unseeing.

55

Gaius braced his knee against the heavy leather traveling pouch, pulled hard at the thongs and tied them. "Well, that finishes my packing," he said. "Today I'll get all my men together—they're probably wandering all over Jerusalem now that the Passover's ended and they're off duty. Tomorrow we should be ready to start back to Galilee. And I'll be glad to head for Capernaum. But I—" He stopped, his face clouding.

"I know what you're thinking," said Marcus. "I'm thinking the same thing. Listen, Gaius. I've asked you before, and you've asked me. But in the face of what happened yesterday, what do you make of it?"

The centurion shoved the pouch under the edge of the couch, sat down. "I can't get it out of my mind," he said. "It was terrible. Crucifixion, even to a Roman soldier, is dreadful enough. But him. Unfair, cruel, utterly heartless; but to one of his temperament, think of the agony! Scorned, jeered at, mocked, tortured, and then left to die, alone and in agony, misunderstood and unappreciated."

"Yes, I know what you mean, Gaius. I feel the same way you do about it. But what do you make of him? Was he, after all, just a good man with a quick brain and a warm and understanding heart?"

Gaius slumped back into the cushions of the couch. "Maybe so, Marcus. He's dead, isn't he? Would a god die? Would not a god be able to save himself?" His face was grave, pained. "I don't know. He's—he's the greatest mystery I've ever known anything about." He sat up, his eyes intense, inquiring, demanding. "What do you think of him now?"

"I don't know what I think. But I know that I was a leper and now I am not."

The centurion's expression changed, relaxed. "Yes," he said.

"That's something you cannot ignore. And Lazarus was dead. I saw him walk forth alive. But why—why should he allow himself to be killed?"

"Gaius, we are Romans. Unlike you, I have had little contact with the rabbi, and I don't know much about the religious customs of the Jews. But they have just held their great Passover feast. Maybe the rabbi gave himself as a sacrifice in the same manner that a devout Jew offers a lamb upon the altar in the Temple. Perhaps he felt that was the only way to reconcile mankind with this divinity with which he must have held such intimate relationship. I don't know."

Marcus stood up, walked slowly across the room, his eyes upon the floor. Suddenly he wheeled about. "But this I do know: the rabbi had a sound philosophy." He stopped, his face thoughtful. When he spoke again his voice was calm, his tone serious, reflective.

"Centurion," he said, "the world's in a bad way. Everywhere nations—Rome, Greece, Egypt, everywhere you look—are striving for power, building armies that overrun defenseless people, seeking alliances under the guise of strengthening their defenses. We are nominally at peace, we Romans, generally speaking. We may be at our supreme power, I don't know. They may say of us later that the age of Augustus and Tiberius constituted our golden era." He faced Gaius, his face almost pained, and he put out his hand in emphatic gesture. "But we aren't strong, centurion. We are rotten at the center. Morally, we are decadent. Our philosophy is wrong. It won't work. It will lead, I don't know when, but I know it will in time, to disaster."

His expression changed again, softened. "This rabbi's plan, though, if I understand it, will work. Our concept leads invariably to war and ruin. But his idea if carried out would bring all nations and individuals to a peaceful way of life. If the individual man would just maintain a right feeling toward other men and toward this—this divinity the rabbi seemed always to be in communion with, according to what I have always heard of him, Gaius, why wouldn't that solve all this trouble between the races and peoples everywhere?"

"I think it would, Marcus. But still, what do you think of him?"

"I—I don't know. He's a mystery to me. But he seems to have had a command upon some tremendous power—" He broke off suddenly, confronted the centurion. "Listen, wasn't I a leper?"

"This is the way I see it," Gaius said. "We don't know much about him. But we, nevertheless—and we are Romans and not Jews, mind you—feel a peculiar intimacy with him. A mother doesn't know her child. Yet she feels very close to him, so close that she would die for him. We call it love. Perhaps that is the key to everything. The mind cannot fathom the mystery. But love crosses far beyond the limits of our sight. Love bridges the chasm, and we go across upon love." He stopped. His eyes were aflame. "Perhaps that is it. Love is the bridge. The rabbi was a bridge-builder through the great love he had for everybody. Yes, and maybe that is the key to the mystery. We cannot know. But we can love, and there is no limit to the far reaches of our love, there is no limit in distance or in power.

"Listen, Marcus—" the centurion's eyes were bright with a new light—"I have heard the rabbi talk often of his God, his Father, he called him, but I never heard him describe him but in one way. He always said that his God was love. Maybe, Marcus, it is not necessary to wrack one's poor earthbound brain to find the key. Maybe it is necessary but to love. Maybe that is the key to the rabbi."

"I don't know, centurion," Marcus said quietly. "But I know he changed my view of things. And I'm glad. Though I don't have a denarius, I have a better feeling inside of me. And now that I have found Naamah—" He paused. "Centurion, do you suppose she'll go back to Tyre with me, and me a penniless vagabond?"

"If I were you, I'd be getting out to Bethany and having a word with her. Tomorrow we're leaving, you know, and early."

"I already have an engagement with her for this evening," Marcus said, "and I may spend the night out there with your friends, Lazarus and Simon and the Zebedees."

56

Under the calm, unhurried Judean stars they sat upon the small terrace behind the cottage of Lazarus. Once again, as they leaned back upon the couch set against the whitewashed wall, her head was upon his chest and the fragrance of her hair rose about him.

"My precious Naamah," he said. "I have sought you so long, I have wanted you so much. And now that I have found you, don't you see that I can never give you up? Don't you know it?"

"Yes," she said, "and have I not thought of you and longed for you likewise during the hard, cruel nights and the bitter days? But now that he has suffered so much and given his life, is it right that I—"

"Oh, Naamah—" he interrupted her, and his voice was pleading. "You have been through a terrible ordeal. You cannot think clearly. He would not expect you to punish yourself in order to show your love—Naamah, can't you see, my dear?"

"It was terrible," she said, shuddering. "Marcus, you can never understand. Never can I erase that picture from my mind. Oh, the horror, the terror. I saw him die."

"It was only yesterday," he said. "It is so near. You are still terribly shocked. But time will heal the wound, my dear, and I will try to make amends for everything—"

"Your understanding and love has already done that." She reached up, patted the hand upon her shoulder. "I love you so much, Marcus. Like him, you have been gentle and understanding."

"No," said he, "not like him. But I would like to try to be more like him. And he wouldn't want you to punish yourself, dear Naamah."

"No, I know he wouldn't," she replied. "But I wouldn't feel right having so much joy after—after—oh, Marcus—" She clutched his arm until he could feel the nails pushing almost into

317

the flesh. "I—I cannot think clearly. I am puzzled, and hurt, and all I know is that I love you, but press me no more this night, for I am so distressed. Tomorrow, perhaps, after we have shown him our feeble respect, in a week, or a month, perhaps when you come again to Jerusalem—oh, my dear, I love you."

He slept in the little hayloft above the stable behind the whitewashed cottage with Lazarus, Simon, John, and the others of the eleven who had come back to Bethany; and Naamah and the rabbi's mother and Salome and others of his friends among the women slept in the house, where they had prepared the ointments for the anointing of the rabbi's body on the morrow.

And hardly had he fallen asleep, it seemed to him, when a heavy hand was shaking him and he opened his eyes to see the bearded round face of Simon bending over him. "The women have the spices and ointments prepared to take to the garden of Joseph of Arimathea for the anointing of the master's body," said Simon. "We wish to go to Jerusalem while it is yet before the dawn and many people are stirring. And Mary—she of Magdala— wishes that you walk with her on the journey to the tomb."

57

Once again a procession of the rabbi's followers, now dwindled to a pitiful few and bearing a forlorn, fled hope, descended the slope of the Mount of Olives, passed the gate that led into the Garden of Gethsemane, crossed the Brook Kedron, and entered the sleeping city.

They said few words to each other, for they were busy with their own thoughts.

Just a week ago they had come along this same way, and with joy and shouting and singing and light hearts, for the master was riding forth to the Temple to establish the kingdom. Cruelty and oppression and injustice would be overthrown, driven forth forever from Israel with the fleeing Romans. Righteousness would be established for its eternal reign, and the master would sit upon the ancient throne of his father David. This had been the dream but one week ago.

Now they walked in silence and with agonized hearts, each thinking his own thoughts. A group of weary, frightened, forsaken men, defeated with victory at their reach, they walked along the twisting, dusty road into the quiet city.

Six days ago, Judas had walked this way, Simon recalled, as the dark brow of the carrier of the leather pouch came sharply before him. He had walked this way again the night of the Passover feast as he had led the high priest's motley gang in search of the master. But Judas of Kiriot would walk this path no more. His dream of forcing the hand of the master, of leading him to the place where he would have to assert his great power, had failed miserably, had burst like a bubble with the realization that he had sought out of the selfishness of his heart to counter the divine plan. They had found dark-faced Judas, his countenance twisted into an eternal scowl, hanging at the end of a rope . . .

Each had his own thoughts. Once—a great measure of years

ago it must have been, and yet he knew it was not—Marcus, walking ahead with Naamah, recalled, with a sharpness that seemed to make the vision a reality, three young Romans at Tyre had discussed what constituted power. One had said money. Plainly, he had been wrong. He smiled at the thought. The young man who once owned factories and ships and slaves had not a denarius now. Another had put his faith in the triumph of truth and goodness and beauty. Ha! He had been more in error than the first youth. Jesus of Nazareth, the personification of all these virtues, lay dead, overthrown, foully slain, and truth and goodness and beauty had been entombed with him. The other young man? Yes, Tribune Lucius had been right. He had put his faith in the strength of might, in the power of the mailed fist. No, it was not right. But in a solitary tomb in a little garden near to the foul Hill of the Skull Jesus of Nazareth lay dead.

Each thought his thoughts, as they trudged through the thinning darkness of this April morning in ancient Jerusalem. Soon now the sun would burst above the rim of flat-topped houses, above the walls and gates of the city, but there would be no light in their sunless, broken hearts. Soon now the birds would begin their joyful singing, but joy had fled the souls of these weary, beaten, desolate men and women trudging along the cobblestoned narrow streets toward a garden and death.

So after a while they came to the tomb lent by the wealthy Joseph of Arimathea as a shelter for all that remained of this smiling, strange young man, who had led them and loved them these three brave, glorious years.

Naamah and Marcus were walking ahead. In the chill gloom of the early morning, as they came around a sharp bend in the path that led to the tomb's mouth, he felt her shoulders tremble, and then she broke away from his arm and ran the remaining steps.

The tomb's mouth yawned wide in the half-darkness. A large stone that had sealed it had been rolled to one side.

Naamah, Jesus' Mary of Magdala, walked quickly to the entrance, peered inside, her hand over her forehead to shade from her eyes the thin veil of light outside.

"The body is not there," she said. "I can see the grave-clothes folded and lying on the bier where the body was placed the other afternoon." She turned now, wide-eyed, her face drawn into lines of dismay and deep sorrow. "Oh, Marcus," she said, "they have stolen away his poor dead body. Not content to torture him and murder him, they have now carried off the body to dishonor it!" She whirled about, ran down the path toward Simon and John and the others of the rabbi's forlorn band, who were helping the women with their burden of spices and ointments.

Simon and John were the first to reach the tomb. John even ran ahead of the big fisherman, for he was of lighter build and faster. At the tomb's mouth John paused and looked in, trying hard to adjust his eyes to the gloom inside. But Simon ran past him into the cavern.

In a moment he came out. "Mary is right," he said. "The body has been taken away. The linen grave clothes have been folded neatly in one place, and the napkin that was bound about his face lies bundled up a little way apart from the linens." His grizzled broad face was troubled. "It was probably the doings of the Temple leaders. They would even show disrespect to the dead, the knavish hypocrites."

By now the other had approached the tomb's entrance. "There is nothing we can do here now," Simon said, after a moment. "Let us go back into the city and see if we can learn what they have done with the master. And it will be best that you women return to Bethany and wait there until we come and report what we have found."

But Naamah remained. Sobbing, her shoulders shaking with the tumult within her, she leaned against the side of the sepulcher. Nor was Marcus able to comfort her. The tears of her anguish ran freely down her cheeks, and a tremor coursed along her frame, and it seemed that sorrow would consume her.

After a while she stopped and peered again into the empty tomb. And as she looked at the place where the rabbi had been laid when they had released him from the cross, she grew quieter and the sharpness of her grief was blunted, and she seemed to hear inward voices soothing her and inquiring of her grief. She was sure they proceeded from the tomb itself, from the very bier upon which the young rabbi had been lying, and she was sure the voices came not from her heart but rather from the comforting great heart of the Father of whom the tall Galilean had so often spoken in words of deepest devotion and affection.

Turning, she walked away from the tomb a few paces toward the bend in the path where it was lost from sight behind a rounded tall shrub. The voices were still calling to her. *Why do I weep? Why am I sorrowful, and why do I face the future so hopelessly? Perhaps ... perhaps ...* The voices were warming, soothing ... *It may be ... it may be, after all ... but no, no, it cannot be. They have stolen him away—*

The man's back was to her as she rounded the bend in the path where the bush stood. In the gathering light she could see his outline. Perhaps he was the gardener. He might know—

The man turned. He had heard her walking along the gravel of the path, Marcus a little way behind. "Why do you weep?" the man said.

"Sir," she said, ignoring his question, "if you know anything of him, if you had anything to do with removing his body from the tomb, if it was not wanted there and you were asked to carry it away, oh, sir, if you will but tell me where the body is I will have it moved." Now the man was walking toward her. "If you will, sir," she said. "I am so distressed. If you will but help me—"

He was near her now, and the sky was growing lighter as the dawn came fast over the quiet, secluded garden. Then he spoke.

"Mary!" he said. "Mary of Magdala!"

An instant she stood, immovable and staring, as fixed and still as the tomb at her back. Then she screamed, and her voice was high and shrill with joy.

"Master! Oh, master!"

Over the eastern walls of the uplifted ancient city the sun suddenly shot its warming rays and the garden of the new tomb of Joseph of Arimathea was bathed in light. But the light of the sun was not so bright as the light that burst upon her heart.

He was tall and straight and smiling. He greeted Marcus. "Peace be with you," said he, and as his hands moved in the gesture of salutation Marcus caught fleeting sight of a spreading dark bruise about a jagged, torn spot in the palm of each hand.

And now the rabbi, seeing their confusion, spoke again.

"Mary, tell my disciples, and Simon"—he smiled as he named the rugged fisherman—"that I go before them into Galilee." His smile recalled for her that day at the Temple when he had lifted her to her feet and set her upon a new course. "It is spring, and I know it is beautiful there. The mountains, the lakes, the fields, the lilies—" For the shadow of an instant there was a faraway look in the rabbi's dark eyes. Then he faced Naamah, and at the same time his eyes were upon Marcus beside her. "Mary," said he, and his eyes were sharp and smiling, "will you not soon likewise be journeying into Galilee—and perhaps beyond?"

Naamah glanced fleetingly at Marcus. Then she spoke to the rabbi, "Yes, master, to Galilee—and beyond."

Smiling, she looked quickly at the radiant tall Roman beside her. And when she turned to face the rabbi, he was gone, around the bend in the path beyond the tall shrub.

Now she was weeping again. But when Marcus lifted her chin to look into her tearful face, her eyes were shining.

The Christian Epics Series

Ben Hur

Bold Galilean

Quo Vadis

Simon of Cyrene

Soul on Fire

Moody Press, a ministry of the Moody Bible Institute,
is designed for education, evangelization, and edification.
If we may assist you in knowing more about Christ
and the Christian life, please write us without obligation:
Moody Press, c/o MLM, Chicago, Illinois 60610.